Excel

ADVANCED SKILLS

ENGLISH

YEAR 6

AGES 11–12

READING AND COMPREHENSION WORKBOOK

Get the Results You Want!

PASCAL PRESS

Tanya Dalgleish

Reprinted 2016 (twice), 2019, 2020, 2021

Updated in 2023 for the NSW Curriculum and Australian Curriculum Version 9.0 changes

Reprinted 2025

ISBN 978 1 74125 480 8

Pascal Press
PO Box 250
Glebe NSW 2037
www.pascalpress.com.au

Publisher: Vivienne Joannou
Project editor: Mark Dixon
Edited by Michael Wyatt
Proofread by Michele Croucher and Mark Dixon
Reviewed and answers checked by Glenda Walsh
Cover, page design and typesetting by DiZign Pty Ltd
Printed by Vivar Printing/Green Giant Press

CONTENTS

How to use this book

This book is designed to help students improve their reading comprehension skills and become more competent, reflective and critical readers.

It provides a step-by-step method of answering different types of comprehension questions, including those in standardised tests such as NAPLAN. Students are taught the strategies to read effectively.

The book is organised in four sections.

Reading strategies

This section begins with a summary of the way the Step-by-step guide works for each type of comprehension question dealt with in this book. It defines the eight useful reading strategies frequently referred to. Once students have worked through Sections 1 and 2, they can use this guide to answer the mixed questions in Section 3.

Tips

- Make sure each student has ready access to the Step-by-step guide on page 4 as a useful reference when answering comprehension questions.
- Teach or revise the reading strategies of skimming and scanning, as well as ways to improve reading for understanding using the strategies of visualising, connecting, predicting, inferring, monitoring and judging (reading reflectively and critically).
- Have students complete the practice activities.

Types of questions

This section deals with the five question types covered in the book. There is a chapter on each type: fact-finding, inferring, synthesis, language and judgement.

Each chapter begins with a sample reading text and step-by-step guide to reading that text and answering the particular comprehension questions.

There are five to six questions for each text. These are mostly multiple choice but at least one question per text requires a short written answer. In some cases the student will require extra paper.

Tips

- Start with the chapter on fact-finding questions because these are usually the most straightforward questions to answer, depending on the complexity of the text. Judgement questions require higher-order thinking skills so they are dealt with last in the sequence here.
- Read and discuss the sample text at the beginning of the chapter. Point out the text's structure and language features. Discuss the content of the text and its purpose and audience.
- Talk to students about the type of question, how to identify it, what it's asking for and how to answer it. The Step-by-step guide makes clear to students the thought processes involved in reading with understanding.
- Discuss the strategies that competent readers use when reading a written text and answering comprehension questions.
- Discuss the answer explanations. These make it clear to students why their answers are correct or incorrect.
- Have students independently complete the comprehension tasks in each chapter.

3 Bringing it all together

Mixed questions

This section provides 17 reading texts with mixed question types for further practice.

Tips

- Have students complete the comprehension tasks independently in this section.
- Have students check their own answers and compare them with the answer explanations.

4 Answers

This section explains why answers are correct or incorrect. A suitable written answer is supplied for each short-answer question. The multiple-choice and short-answer questions enable the students to self-assess.

Tips

- Assess students' results. Analyse the patterns of correct and incorrect answers in students' results to identify areas of strength and weakness to assist with further development. Use this information to target and revise areas that need further attention.
- Identify the kinds of comprehension questions students are having difficulty with. ESL students often have most difficulty with inferring types of questions and questions which require background knowledge, or which use idioms that native speakers of English grow up using or knowing. English idioms can cause problems for many students, but especially students for whom English is an additional language or dialect (EAL/D). Comprehension questions that depend on these concepts and ideas are specifically taught in the language questions section of this book.

Text overview grid

The Text overview grid on pages 129–134 provides a summary of the types of texts covered in the reading comprehension section of this book. It also offers additional teaching points and suggested ideas for student writing. Writing practice in different forms and genres will consolidate students' understanding of how texts are constructed and help them develop critical literacy.

Types of texts

The texts included in this book are defined according to their purposes: informative, imaginative and persuasive. Extracts from classic texts have been chosen to support the Australian Curriculum English Literature strand. Texts have also been chosen to support General Capabilities (Ethical Behaviour, Intercultural Understanding) and Cross-curricular Priorities (Aboriginal and Torres Strait Islander Histories and Cultures, Sustainability, Asia and Australia's engagement with Asia) of the Australian Curriculum.

READING STRATEGIES

Step-by-step guide

This section provides a summary of the way the **Step-by-step guide** works for each type of comprehension question. On page 5 you will find definitions of the eight useful reading strategies frequently referred to in this book. Once students have worked through Sections 1 and 2 they can use the guide below to help them answer the mixed questions in Section 3.

Reading the text

STEP 1	**Skim** the text to see what it is about and how it is organised.	✪ **Read** the title. Look at the illustrations and other visual elements. Make **predictions** about the subject and purpose of the text.
STEP 2	**Read** the text. **Monitor** your reading to make sure you understand it.	✪ **Visualise** and **connect** with the ideas in the text. **Think** about what you already know about the subject and the type of text. Make **predictions.** Make **inferences**. Reflect on meanings and make **judgements**.

Answering specific types of comprehension questions

STEP 3	**Read** the question. **Think** about what type of question it is. Work out what you need to do to answer it.	✪ For a **fact-finding** question you need to find the part(s) of the text where the answer is stated directly. pp. 28–31 ✪ For a **synthesis** question you need to think about how ideas and information relate to each other in the text. pp. 36–39 ✪ For an **inferring** question you need to read between the lines to work out an answer that is not stated directly in the text. pp. 44–46 ✪ For a **language** question you need to work out the meaning and effects of the language used in the text. pp. 56–59 ✪ For a **judgement** question you need to make judgements about the information and ideas in the text, the writer's purpose and the values and attitudes embedded in the text. pp. 68–71
STEP 4	**Think** about the text. Remember what you have read and **visualised**. **Scan** the text to find the relevant parts. Look for key words or phrases. **Re-read** part or all of the text if necessary. Find answers directly stated in the text. **Infer** meanings or work out the answer using clues and evidence in the text and from your own knowledge. Think critically. Draw conclusions. Make **judgements**.	✪ For a **fact-finding** question, scan the text to find the relevant parts. Look for words or phrases used in the question. Re-read parts of the text or the whole text if necessary, to find the answer. ✪ For a **synthesis** question, scan the text to find the relevant parts. Look for words or phrases used in the question. Re-read parts of the text or the whole text if necessary. Pull together the threads of meaning and draw your own conclusions. ✪ For an **inferring** question, scan the text for the relevant parts. Re-read parts of the text or the whole text if necessary. Use clues in the text to help you work out what is implied to answer the question. ✪ For a **language** question, scan the text for the relevant parts. Re-read parts of the text or the whole text if necessary. Examine how language is used in context. Use your knowledge of language conventions, persuasive devices and figurative language to answer the question. ✪ For a **judgement** question, scan the text for the relevant parts. Re-read parts of the text or the whole text if necessary. Think critically. Make judgements based on evidence in the text and your own knowledge and understanding to answer the question.

Terms used in the Step-by-step guide

Skimming

- Skimming over the text before you start reading tells you a lot about the text and how it is organised.
- Look at the text's structure and features. Skim headings and subheadings. Look at visual elements. Predict the purpose and audience for the text.

Good readers notice all of these things as they skim a text.

pp. 6–7

Visualising

- Visualising (forming mental pictures) as you read helps you maintain focus during reading, connect to the meaning of the text and remember what you are reading about.

Good readers visualise what they are reading about and store these images in their short-term memory.

pp. 8–10

Connecting

- Connecting your own life and experiences with what you are reading helps you make sense of the text. Think: How is this story like my life? What does this remind me of? What do I already know about this subject? Have I seen this kind of text before? Where? What do I recognise about the language of the text and its structures and features?

Good readers connect to ideas in a text as they read. They relate new knowledge to existing knowledge and understanding about texts, themselves and the world.

pp. 10–14

Predicting

- Making predictions about a text before you start reading, as well as while you read, helps you engage with the text. Predict what the text will be about. Predict the purpose and audience for the text. If you come across a word you are unfamiliar with use the context to predict what the word could be and its likely meaning. Predict what will come next in the text.

Good readers continually make predictions about a text and revise their predictions as they read.

pp. 15–17

Inferring

- Making inferences as you read means working out what the writer is suggesting when it is not stated directly in the text.
- Writers often leave it up to the reader to read between the lines of a text. They give enough clues and contextual support for readers to be able to infer the intended meanings. Sometimes writers leave meaning open to the reader's interpretation.

Good readers make inferences as they read, reading between the lines to work out intended meanings in the text.

pp. 17–19

Monitoring

- Monitoring your reading means thinking about the text as you read and making sure it makes sense. When you monitor your understanding of a text you realise very quickly when meaning breaks down. You re-read parts of the text to revise your understandings.

Good readers monitor their reading to maintain meaning as they read. They read on, to confirm or refute predictions and inferences, then re-read and revise understanding when inferences don't make sense. They self-correct.

pp. 20–21

Judging

- Judging means thinking critically as you read. You judge the information and ideas in the text and the ways these are expressed or implied. Making judgements about a text is an important part of being critically literate.

Good readers make judgements about a text, its context and its purpose as they read. Critically literate readers can judge whether a text is reliable, trustworthy, relevant, current, accurate, interesting, entertaining or useful based on their own purposes for reading. Critically literate readers can make judgements about the attitudes and values embedded in texts.

pp. 21–26

Scanning

- Scanning means looking quickly through sections of a text for specific words, phrases or images. Scanning is useful when checking for facts.

Good readers can quickly find what they need in a text without having to read whole texts or sections of text.

pp. 26–27

Reading with understanding

This section provides practice activities for the eight strategies referred to in the **Step-by-step guide** on page 4. These strategies support reading with understanding and answering comprehension questions.

They are:

1. Skimming
2. Visualising
3. Connecting
4. Predicting
5. Inferring
6. Monitoring
7. Judging (reading critically)
8. Scanning.

Effective readers use these strategies simultaneously without even being aware that they are doing so. They make decisions about which strategies to use depending on the text and their purposes for reading.

① Skimming

What is it? **Skimming** is a useful quick 'first glance' strategy to get a general idea of what a text is about and how it is organised, as well as its purpose and audience. Skimming a text's structure and features helps you to make predictions and judgements about the text before you even read any of the text. When you skim a text you can often tell whether it is an informative, imaginative or persuasive text. You notice features such as lists, paragraphs, columns, diagrams and maps. You skim a text to judge whether you want to read it.

How do you do it? When you skim a text your eyes move quickly across and down, or zigzag over the text, stopping briefly at the parts that get your attention such as headings, words in bold or illustrations.

For example, you might:

- skim a novel to get a general idea of the author's style, the chapter titles and what the illustrations tell you, then use this information to make a judgement about whether or not to read the novel
- skim a recipe book for a photo of something that you'd like to eat then read that recipe
- skim a reference book to judge whether it will be useful for a class project.

Have a go!

Skim the texts below. You don't need to read them. Just glance at the shape of each text and how it is organised to identify more about it. Work as quickly as you can. Choose a label from the box for each text.

report newspaper article website narrative

Octane Dance

www.octanedance.com.au

OCTANE DANCE

For 12 to 17-year-olds
Classes to suit all dancers/all fitness levels
whether you aim to perform or want to get fit
or you just want to meet other people who love music and dance.
Beginners welcome. First class free. Mention this page.

hip hop | breaking | popping | urban contemporary | contemporary | jazz | lyrical jazz | tap

Great music
Great venue: main room/smaller dance rooms/lounging area.
Funky urban industrial vibe
A range of teaching styles. Our teachers are professional dancers and performers who have a passion for dance and have been dancing themselves since they were very young.
Guest teachers and choreographers—from around Australia and internationally

Your first class is FREE!

Home | teacher bios | class descriptions | class timetables | fees | what to wear
merchandise SHOP | performance schedules | sign up | venue hire | contact us

White Fang

In advance of the dogs, on wide snowshoes, toiled a man. At the rear of the sled toiled a second man. On the sled, in the box, lay a third man whose toil was over, a man whom the Wild had conquered and beaten down until he would never move nor struggle again. It is not the way of the Wild to like movement. Life is an offence to it, for life is movement; and the Wild aims always to destroy movement. It freezes the water to prevent it running to the sea; it drives the sap out of the trees till they are frozen to their mighty hearts; and most ferociously and terribly of all does the Wild harry and crush into submission man—man who is the most restless of life, ever in revolt against the dictum that all movement must in the end come to the cessation of movement.

But at front and rear, unawed and indomitable, toiled the two men who were not yet dead. Their bodies were covered with fur and soft-tanned leather. Eyelashes and cheeks and lips were so coated with the crystals from their frozen breath that their faces were not discernible. This gave them the seeming of ghostly masques, undertakers in a spectral world at the funeral of some ghost. But under it all they were men, penetrating the land of desolation and mockery and silence, puny adventurers bent on colossal adventure, pitting themselves against the might of a world as remote and alien and pulseless as the abysses of space.

Extract from *White Fang* by Jack London, 1906, Chapter 1

A ....

B ....

THE PERTH TRIBUNE

21 NOVEMBER 1978

The Last Whale

A female sperm whale harpooned yesterday will be the last whale killed by the Australian whaling industry.

Cheynes Beach Whaling Station is Australia's last whaling station. Operating since 1952 it is now being decommissioned. This brings an end to whaling activity that has forced humpback, southern right whales and sperm whales to the brink of extinction in Australian waters.

Improved technology such as the harpoon cannon, the toggle harpoon, deck cannons, faster chase boats and later factory ships and the use of aircraft to spot whale pods increased the efficiency of whaling and led to the rapid depletion of whale stocks. This forced the Australian government to ban all commercial whaling before whales become extinct in Australian waters.

Tangalooma in Queensland was once the largest land-based whaling station in the southern hemisphere. It closed in 1962 after decimating the number of humpbacks off the east coast of Australia from an estimated 15 000 to 500 whales in ten years. Humpbacks have been protected under Australian law since 1963.

The first Greenpeace campaign in Australia saw protestors involved in actions against Cheynes Beach Whaling Company vessels last year, drawing international attention to the industry at that time.

Whaling was one of Australia's first industries. Whale oil was a lucrative export business in the early colonies and used for lighting and candle making. Whale baleen was used for women's corsets. Later the oil was used in cosmetics while whale meat was used for animal food.

The value of the industry varied greatly over the years as the price of whale oil was affected by market influences. The introduction of vegetable oil and the advent of commercial drilling for petroleum oil in USA in the late 1850s reduced the world's reliance on whale oil.

Sixteen thousand sperm whales have been killed in Australia waters since 1952. The final season's catch for the Cheynes Beach station was 698 sperm whales.

Bushfires

Bushfires are disasters that occur each year in Australia and in many other parts of the world. Bushfires kill people and animals, and destroy farmland, natural forest and bushland. They destroy people's homes and other buildings, and threaten towns and cities. Bushfires have a devastating effect on families and communities.

Bushfire risk is assessed using information about wind, humidity, temperature, rainfall and vegetation. In Australia bushfires are categorised as grass fires or forest fires. The worst forest fires usually involve eucalypt trees. Eucalypt leaves are highly flammable so eucalypt forest fires are extremely intense. A eucalypt tree can explode in a ball of fire. The most severe and largest bushfires in the world occur in south-eastern Australia during summer and autumn. The north of Australia experiences bushfires during winter, which is the dry season there.

People can accidentally cause bushfires when they leave campfires or barbecues smouldering or unattended, especially on windy days. People also cause fires when they toss burning cigarettes onto the ground where dry grasses can easily catch fire, or when sparks from power tools ignite fires on hot, dry, windy days.

When bushfires are deliberately lit it is called arson. Arson is a criminal offence and if perpetrators are caught and convicted they face long jail sentences, especially if people have died as a result of their deliberately lit fires.

Scientists predict that climate change will cause fire weather conditions to worsen. The south-east of mainland Australia will become hotter and drier in the future. One report, published by the Bushfire Cooperative Research Centre in 2007, using CSIRO simulations, suggests that fire danger could increase by as much as 15 to 70 per cent by 2050. The report found that climate change is causing average temperatures to rise and the number of extremely high temperature days to increase. Bushfire weather is likely to occur earlier in the season than in the past and to last longer—for example from October through to March. The numbers of professional firefighters required in the future is expected to double by 2030.

C ....

D ....

Answers

A Skim the layout and notice the visual elements and design to judge that *Octane Dance* is a website that advertises dancing.

B Skim the layout and notice that the text is written in paragraphs. Look at the illustration. Judge that it belongs in an imaginative text. *White Fang* is a narrative.

C Skim the layout and notice the columns and headline. Judge that *The Last Whale* is a newspaper article.

D Skim the layout and notice the factual photographs. Judge that *Bushfires* is an informative report.

② Visualising

What is it? **Visualising** means making mental pictures or picturing information in your mind as you read. Visualising helps you engage with a text so you understand it more readily and remember what you've read.

How do you do it? You picture in your mind what is described in the text.

For example you could:

- read a factual description of an animal and visualise what it looks like
- read a recipe and imagine what the final product will look, smell and taste like when it is cooked
- visualise the setting described in a narrative
- visualise a character in a novel based on a description given by the author or another character as narrator.

Have a go!

Read the text. Visualise the person described and answer the question below.

> Oh! But he was a tight-fisted hand at the grindstone … Hard and sharp as flint, from which no steel had ever struck out generous fire; secret, and self-contained, and solitary as an oyster. The cold within him froze his old features, nipped his pointed nose, shrivelled his cheek, stiffened his gait; made his eyes red, his thin lips blue; and spoke out shrewdly in his grating voice. He carried his own low temperature always about with him; he iced his office … and didn't thaw it one degree at Christmas.
>
> Extract from *A Christmas Carol* by Charles Dickens, 1843

A

B

C

D

Which picture best suits the description? Explain your choice.

....

....

Answer **D** is correct. This photograph shows a thin man with sharp features and a stern cold expression. He wears old-fashioned clothing, which fits with the style of language used in the text. His facial expression seems cold or icy. **A** is incorrect as the man in this photograph is not thin with a sharp nose and shrivelled cheeks, and the text does not describe a moustache. **B** is incorrect as this man is wearing a Santa hat. Even with his angry expression you should guess that someone as cold as the man described in the text would not wear a funny hat. Moreover, his modern clothing style does not suit the language of the text. **C** is incorrect as this man is wearing modern clothes. The language used in the text should lead you to visualise an old-fashioned clothing style.

Have a go!

Read the text. Visualise the scene.

> The aliens look like giant spiders. They stand two storeys tall. Their heads have eight eyes in a circle. They have a body with eight legs and an oversized abdomen. Eye-witness reports suggest the aliens seem to have an exoskeleton made of resin, wax or a plastic-like substance. Scientists have yet to determine whether these spiders are an intelligent life form themselves or merely a method of transport and destruction operated by aliens either internally or by remote control.

Sketch or draw what you have visualised.

Share and discuss your sketch with a friend. Compare similarities and differences in the way you each visualised the aliens.

Have a go!

Read the text below. Visualise the scene.

Space craft, each the size of nine football fields hover above the cities spewing out giant gossamer webs. The webs are incredibly strong and resilient. They prevent the military from successfully launching land to air missiles. When missiles are fired they are caught and held in place by the webs.

Sketch or draw what you have visualised.

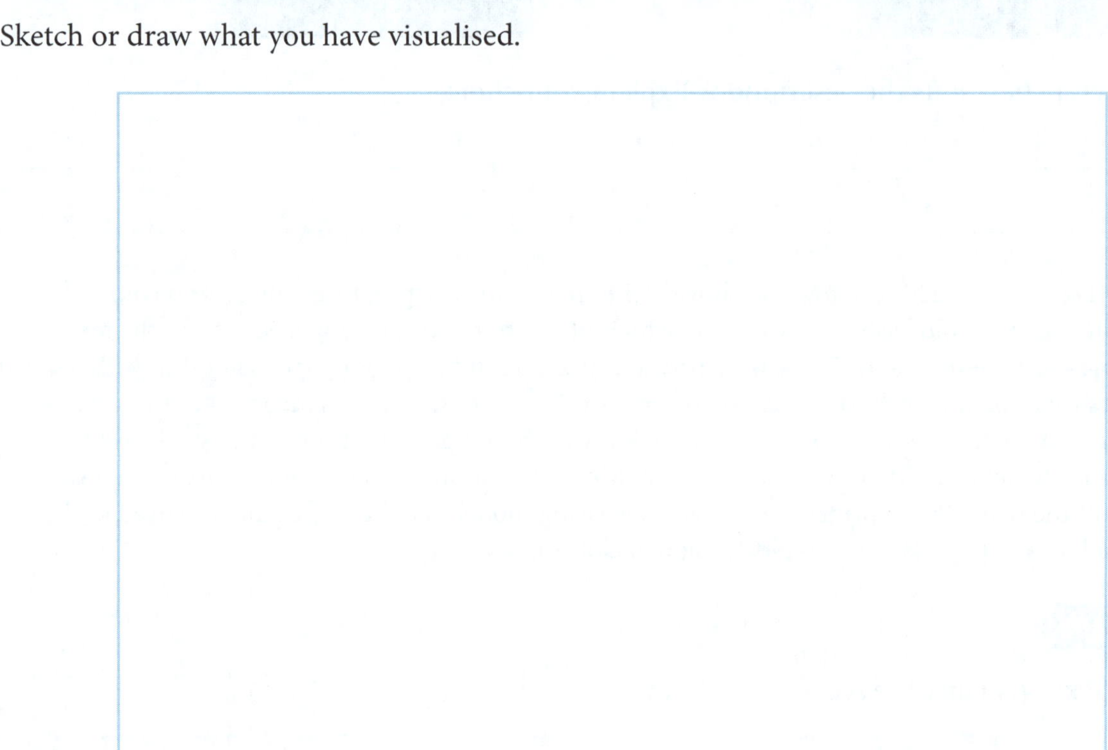

Share and discuss your sketch with a friend. Compare similarities and differences in the way you each visualised the scene described.

③ Connecting

What is it? **Connecting** with a text means relating it to yourself, your life and the world in which you live. It means making connections between things you already know or know about and the new information in the text. Connecting helps you understand and remember what you read. Readers connect to texts in different ways based on their own life experiences.

How do you do it? As you read a text you make connections with your own knowledge and experiences. You connect with a text when you think such things as:

'This reminds me of …'

'I saw something like that …'

'I've read this kind of text before.'

'I already know some things about this subject.'

For example, you might:

- connect with characters in a story because you understand their feelings from experiencing something similar
- connect with the ideas in a newspaper article if you are interested in the topic—a topic of interest will capture your attention and engage your feelings in a way that makes you connect to what is written
- connect your experiences of cooking and your understanding of recipes to your reading of a new recipe.

Have a go!

Read the text. Connect with the text by empathising with characters and their situation. Then answer the questions below.

> My dad is in hospital with lung cancer. He'll have surgery today to remove the cancer. Mum says he'll be fine. "He's tough," she says. "He'll have the surgery and maybe radiation. Then he'll stop smoking and he'll get well again." I am so angry with him. I want to yell, "I told you not to smoke! I told you to give it up." I want to shake him. But I don't. I want to tell him I'm angry. But I don't. I'm frightened. I want everything to be the way it was. I'm scared for Dad. I feel like there's rocks in my stomach. I don't like waiting here.

A Describe the feelings experienced by the narrator.

....

....

B Have you ever experienced any of the same feelings as the narrator? How do your experiences connect to the ideas in the text?

....

....

C Who do you empathise with in the text and how does the author make you do this?

....

....

Compare your answers with the following suggestions:

Answers

A If you connect with the narrator's character and situation you will easily recognise that the narrator feels angry with his or her father for smoking and getting cancer. The narrator is frightened and worried and feels helpless. There is nothing the narrator can do to help his or her dad, only wait.

B Your response to the text will depend on your personal experience of loss or grief or anger and how it is similar to, or different from, the narrator's situation. If you have not experienced watching a loved one in hospital and worrying about them you might try connecting the ideas in the text to a novel you have read or a film or television program you have seen.

C You can judge that the author wants readers to connect with and empathise with the narrator, rather than the dad, because the dad's point of view is not presented.

Have a go!

Visualise the scene described in the following stanzas from the poem *The Fire at Ross's Farm* by Henry Lawson. Use all your senses to connect with the scene. Think about what you see, smell, hear, taste and feel and then answer the questions below.

One Christmas time, when months of drought
Had parched the western creeks,
The bush-fires started in the north
And travelled south for weeks.
At night along the river-side
The scene was grand and strange—
The hill-fires looked like lighted streets
Of cities in the range.

The cattle-tracks between the trees
Were like long dusky aisles,
And on a sudden breeze the fire
Would sweep along for miles;
Like sounds of distant musketry
It crackled through the brakes,
And o'er the flat of silver grass
It hissed like angry snakes.

It leapt across the flowing streams
And raced o'er pastures broad;
It climbed the trees and lit the boughs
And through the scrubs it roared.
The bees fell stifled in the smoke
Or perished in their hives,
And with the stock the kangaroos
Went flying for their lives.

A What can you see?

....

....

....

B What can you smell?

....

C What can you hear?

....

D What can you taste?

....

E What can you feel?

....

Compare your answers with the following suggestions:

Answers

A You should see lines of fire across the hills; giant trees bursting into flames; the wind blowing smoke and flames through the trees and across streams, pushing the flames and carrying the smoke into the sky; animals such as cattle and kangaroos racing to get out of the fire's way; and paddocks of silver grasses now an ocean of flames.

B You should smell burning leaves and trees, soot and perhaps burning animals.

C You should hear the fire crackling, hissing as the grass fires spread, popping, banging and cracking like gun shots, a wild roaring and loud explosions.

D You should taste soot, smoke, dirt and dust.

E You should feel intense singeing, scorching heat and dryness; a dry, raw throat; sore stinging dry red eyes. The hairs on your arms and legs and eyebrows should feel scorched.

How you connect with the ideas in a text depend on your personal experiences. If you have had experiences of bushfire or any fire or you will visualise and imagine the scene differently from others who haven't. Alternatively you might connect to the text because of other texts you have encountered that describe or show bushfires, including news reports.

Elaborating

What is it? Another way to help you connect with a text is to elaborate on it. **Elaborating** means adding extra details not stated directly or implied in the text. A reader's elaborations don't alter the meaning of the text but add fine details that make the text more relevant personally.

How do you do it? As you read think about the meaning of the text and fill in details for yourself.

Have a go!

Read the text. Visualise the scene described. Answer the questions below to elaborate on the text, filling in the details that the writer has not stated directly or inferred in the text. Make sure you add details that don't alter meaning.

I helped Dad unload the groceries from the car. He'd bought all the food for Mum's surprise dinner and all kinds of delicious treats. We didn't plan to do a lot of cooking—it was too hot. And Mum wouldn't want everyone working when they should be enjoying themselves anyway. The cake was in a box. It was Mum's and my favourite kind. Dad and I started laying the food out on the dinner table. I couldn't wait for Mum to get home from work.

What kinds of delicious treats can you see?

....

....

What kind of cake is it? Describe it.

....

....

Answer Your elaborations help you connect to the text. They can't be wrong as long as you haven't changed the meaning of the text. Your elaborations about food treats and special cakes will be different from other people's and based on your own experiences and background.

Have a go!

Read the text and then sketch or write a description of the scene as you visualise it. Elaborate on the text, filling in the details that the writer hasn't stated directly or implied in the text. Make sure you add details that don't alter meaning.

My dad is in hospital with lung cancer. He'll have surgery today to remove the cancer. Mum says he'll be fine. "He's tough," she says. "He'll have the surgery and maybe radiation. Then he'll stop smoking and he'll get well again." I am so angry with him. I want to yell, "I told you not to smoke! I told you to give it up." I want to shake him. But I don't. I want to tell him I'm angry. But I don't. I'm frightened. I want everything to be the way it was. I'm scared for Dad. I feel like there's rocks in my stomach. I don't like waiting here.

....

....

....

Answer The writer hasn't described the scene, so the way you visualise it will depend on your experiences of hospitals though personal involvement or through television or narratives you have read. You will most likely visualise a hospital bed with the dad lying on it. He may be asleep. He may have tubes attached. The narrator could be sitting in a chair beside the bed. Or the narrator could be outside the hospital room, not wanting to go in. The scene you visualised will vary from the way other readers would have visualised it because of the ways you connect to the text and make it personally relevant.

④ Predicting

What is it? **Predicting** means thinking ahead as you read a text and guessing what might come next based on what you understand so far. Predicting makes you an active reader. It helps you connect to the text and remember what it is about.

How do you do it? As you read you use evidence in the text to make predictions. You can change your predictions as you read on and get new evidence.

For example, you can predict:

- the contents of a book by skimming its cover
- the meaning of a word from its context or from reading on and finding out more
- the next word in a text using your knowledge of language patterns
- what an article in a newspaper will be about from the photograph that accompanies it
- what might happen next in a narrative.

You can predict the meaning of an unfamiliar word in a text by thinking about how it's used in the context of the sentence, paragraph or whole text.

You read *The great white shark is an apex predator.*

You predict the meaning of the term *apex predator* using your knowledge of great white sharks and the word *predator*. You might also know that an *apex* is the point at the top of something so you predict that an *apex predator* is at the top of the food chain.

Read on. *It has no natural predator other than the killer whale.*

You can confirm that an *apex predator* is a predator at the top of the food chain. Few animals hunt or eat an apex predator.

Have a go!

Read the text below and answer the questions to make predictions about the text.

> Lying on her stomach on the damp ground Alura willed her heart to stop thumping inside her chest. She tried to breathe quietly. She needed to see if the animal was still blocking her escape.

A Make a prediction about the type of text this is.

....

Answer You are most likely to predict that the text is an adventure narrative. The clues are the setting (*damp ground*) and the fact that the protagonist needs to escape an animal.

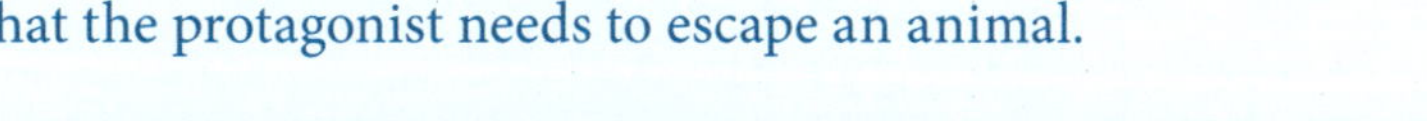

Read on to confirm or refute your prediction.

> She listened for signs that the animal was still feeding beside the path. It had stopped making the snuffling noises. Everything was quiet. Alura sensed that the forest was holding its breath. She slowly raised her head above the log and peered through the foliage into the gloom, looking for any sign of movement. She scanned the path as it wound through the trees. Empty. That didn't make sense. The animal couldn't have vanished. She scanned both sides of the path again. Then she raised her eyes and peered into the trees that lined the path. There! The slightest of movements. She froze. Staring straight at her from where it squatted on the limb of the largest tree was the creature. Its yellow eyes locked onto hers.

B What type of text is it?

....

Answer You should confirm your prediction that this is an adventure narrative, but you might also predict now that it could be an adventure fantasy, based on the creature with yellow eyes and on the unusual name of the protagonist, Alura. When you think of a yellow-eyed animal that can climb trees you might predict a tiger or lion, but the protagonist calls it a creature so you can't be sure what it is at this stage of the story.

C Make a prediction about what might happen next.

....

....

Compare your predictions with a friend's. How were they:

similar? ....

different? ....

Answer You might predict any of the following scenarios:

- that the animal attacks Alura and she overpowers it
- that Alura communicates with the animal in some way and calms or tames it
- that someone or something else joins Alura and they fight the creature together, or the creature, realising it is now outnumbered, skulks away.

You might also have predicted something entirely different. Your predictions will be based on your understanding of the text so far and the possibilities alluded to in the text, as well as your knowledge of texts in the same genre (fantasy or adventure narrative). If you read more of the text you would be able to confirm or refute your predictions.

Have a go!

Use your knowledge of language (grammar and vocabulary) to predict the words that are missing in the following sentences:

A Alura ducked .... the log.

B The creature was a mere twenty metres behind and gaining on her. Alura ran .... through the trees.

C The creature was huge. It had enormous fangs. It looked ....

Answers

A When you read the sentence you can readily predict that the missing word will be a preposition from the start of the prepositional phrase that tells where, for example 'behind', 'below' or 'under'. You can infer the missing word's meaning 'to go under' because of the meaning of the verb *ducked*.

B You can predict that the missing word is an adverb. It tells how Alura ran. You can infer that she would have run 'quickly' or 'swiftly'.

C You can predict that the missing word is an adjective such as 'terrifying' or 'ferocious'. The previous sentences describe the creature's appearance in ways that give readers an image of a frightening-looking creature. Also, the use of short sentences increases the pace of the reading and adds to tension in an adventure text. This matches the idea that Alura is running and a dangerous creature is chasing her and catching up.

5 Inferring

What is it? **Inferring** is when you use all the information in the text to work out what the writer means when information is not stated directly in the text.

How do you do it? You think as you read, reading between the lines to work out what is implied by the writer.

Have a go!

Read the following text, infer meaning and then answer the questions.

> Eddy trudged along the footpath. He did not want to go to soccer practice. He was really annoyed with his mother for making him sign up for soccer in the first place. And today, he'd told her he didn't feel well. But she didn't believe him, as usual.

A Does Eddy enjoy playing soccer?

....

B Why didn't Eddy's mother believe him?

....

Answers

A You should infer that Eddy is resentful about being forced by his mother to play soccer. You should infer that he does not enjoy soccer practice and therefore probably doesn't like playing soccer either.

B You read that she didn't believe him, as usual. You could infer that Eddy regularly says he feels sick to get out of soccer practice or some other activity he doesn't want to do. You could also infer that Eddy's mum is a distrustful or suspicious person and maybe Eddy really is sick this time.

Have a go!

Read the following text, infer meaning and then answer the questions.

> Luca tore along the path. He wanted to get to the soccer field before everyone else. He needed to show the coach he was keen and committed to the team. The position of centre forward for Saturday's match was being assigned today and he really wanted it.

A How does Luca feel about soccer?

....

B How does Luca feel about the coach?

....

Answers

A You can infer that Luca loves playing soccer and practising soccer because of the way he races to get to practice and arrive first.

B You can infer that Luca is respectful of the coach. He intends to prove to the coach that he deserves to be centre forward. You can infer that he is not going to whine, nag or beg for the position of centre forward, but demonstrate by his actions that he deserves the position.

Have a go!

You can often infer how writers feel about a subject from their use of emotive or evaluative language.

Read the text. What can you infer about the writer's attitude towards dogs on the footpath?

....

....

Little penguins have rookeries around the cliffs of Manly harbour, a short walk from where Nana lives. Every time I visit with Nana we go for a walk around the waterfront just along from where the Manly ferries come in. I've never seen a penguin there but signs along the public footpath say 'Look out. Penguins about', so they definitely live in the area. Manly's little penguins are listed as endangered due to habitat loss and because dogs and cats attack them and dogs disturb their nesting sites. There's a 'dog on leash' section of pathway but Nan and I always see dogs off leashes. The dogs go madly rushing around and barking, tripping people and disturbing the penguin rookeries.

Answer The writer feels concern for the penguins and is annoyed and angry about dogs being off-leash on the footpath. Emotive words used in the text in relation to the dogs include *attack … disturb … nesting sites … go madly rushing around and barking, tripping people and disturbing the penguin rookeries*. The writer uses words that convey a negative attitude about the dogs.

Have a go!

Read the text. Visualise the scene and make inferences to answer the question below.

While Tom was eating his supper, and stealing sugar as opportunity offered, Aunt Polly asked him questions that were full of guile, and very deep—for she wanted to trap him into damaging revealments. Said she:

"Tom, it was middling warm in school, warn't it?"

"Yes'm."

"Powerful warm, warn't it?"

"Yes'm."

"Didn't you want to go in a-swimming, Tom?"

A bit of a scare shot through Tom—a touch of uncomfortable suspicion. He searched Aunt Polly's face, but it told him nothing. So he said:

"No'm—well, not very much."

Extract from *The Adventures of Tom Sawyer* by Mark Twain

"… stealing sugar as opportunity offered …"

What does this imply?

....

....

....

Answer You should visualise Tom sitting at the dinner table eating. You can infer that he is sneaking spoonfuls of sugar from a jar or bowl whenever Aunt Polly isn't watching. You can infer that sugar is a special treat and Tom doesn't get to eat it very often. Stealing implies that Aunt would not have been happy if she had caught him.

⑥ Monitoring

What is it? **Monitoring** meaning means noticing as you read when a text doesn't make sense. Monitoring meaning means thinking as you read so that you immediately recognise when meaning breaks down or you lose the thread of the text. Maintaining the thread of the text is part of remembering what you have read. It is important for understanding the text and for connecting meaning across the text.

How do you do it? You think as you read to make sure what you're reading makes sense to you.

- Think as you read.
- Question the text: Does that make sense?
- Self-correct when meaning breaks down, by re-reading previous sentences, sections of the text or the whole text to clarify things you might have misunderstood, misinterpreted or forgotten.
- Adjust your predictions and rethink your inferences if you need to.

Have a go!

Read the text. Visualise the scene and answer the questions below.

> Rocky lifted his head suddenly and growled. Janie looked up from reading her book. Rocky growled again; low and menacing. Janie looked at him. He jumped off the bed and rushed to the bedroom door pushing his nose underneath it. His ears were back, his hackles up. He continued to growl. Janie closed her book.

A Describe the dog you see and explain why you visualise the dog to look like this.

....

....

....

Answer Most likely you will have visualised a large angry guard dog because it has the name Rocky and a low menacing growl and it is acting like a very protective guard dog. But you could have appropriately visualised any kind of dog based on your own experiences of dogs. This is a way you connect your personal life to the ideas in a text. You can continue to visualise your own dog for the rest of the narrative, unless the writer eventually describes the dog for readers.

B Read on. Visualise the scene and monitor your understanding about Rocky.

> Janie went to the door of her room. Rocky was still growling. She opened the door. Rocky scampered through. His little fluffy legs skittered on the timber floors as he raced down the corridor and around the corner towards the kitchen. He was now barking loudly.

Describe the dog you see now.

....

....

....

Answer You should visualise a small fluffy white dog. Monitoring your reading enables you to change the way you visualise aspects of the text whenever the author provides you with additional information.

⑦ Judging

What is it? **Judging** a text means reading critically and evaluating as you read.

How do you do it? Think beyond the words in the text as you read and make judgements about ideas, the writer's purpose and values, and the intended audience for the text.

For example, you can judge:

- an informative text's usefulness or trustworthiness
- a character's behaviour in a narrative
- the context in which a text was created
- the values and attitudes embedded in a text about gender, race, religion, culture, society, sexuality, appearance, age and ability
- the effectiveness of a text in achieving what you judge to be the writer's purpose
- the importance or relevance of ideas in a text
- the effectiveness of the way language is used in a text (emotive and evaluative language, persuasive devices, figurative language)
- whether there are alternative perspectives on the ideas in the text
- whether a text represents a dominant or minority viewpoint.

Have a go!

Read the text and then answer the questions to judge the character's behaviour and motives.

My dad is in hospital with lung cancer. He'll have surgery today to remove the cancer. Mum says he'll be fine. "He's tough," she says. "He'll have the surgery and maybe radiation. Then he'll stop smoking and he'll get well again." I am so angry with him. I want to yell, "I told you not to smoke! I told you to give it up." I want to shake him. But I don't. I want to tell him I'm angry. But I don't. I'm frightened. I want everything to be the way it was. I'm scared for Dad. I feel like there's rocks in my stomach. I don't like waiting here.

What is your opinion of the narrator? Explain.

....

....

Answer Your opinion about the narrator will be based on evidence in the text, the way the author has constructed the character and the language used to help you empathise with the character.

You may judge the narrator to be too angry or judgemental about the father's smoking. You might judge the character to be mean for wanting to yell at the father when he is so ill in hospital. You might judge that in a similar situation you might express grief or you might be more positive like the narrator's Mum. Or, you might judge the character to be realistic in expressing anger and frustration. You might agree that the narrator has a right to be angry with the father.

Have a go!

Read the text. Use evidence in the text to make judgements.

While Tom was eating his supper, and stealing sugar as opportunity offered, Aunt Polly asked him questions that were full of guile, and very deep—for she wanted to trap him into damaging revealments. Said she:

"Tom, it was middling warm in school, warn't it?"

"Yes'm."

"Powerful warm, warn't it?"

"Yes'm."

"Didn't you want to go in a-swimming, Tom?"

A bit of a scare shot through Tom—a touch of uncomfortable suspicion. He searched Aunt Polly's face, but it told him nothing. So he said:

"No'm—well, not very much."

Extract from *The Adventures of Tom Sawyer* by Mark Twain

A When is the story set?

....

....

B What judgements can you make about the relationship between Tom and Aunt Polly?

....

....

Answers

A You can tell that the story is not set in modern-day Australia. You might judge that the story was written some time ago, based on the old-fashioned sounding English used. For example, "*middling warm … warn't it?, "No'm*" ('No Ma'am'). You can also judge by the fact that Tom was *stealing sugar* that sugar was valued as a treat and was perhaps expensive or not easy to come by. This contrasts with modern times where sugar is readily available and most people regard it as inexpensive.

B You can judge that Tom is wary of Aunt Polly. He is worried about getting caught stealing sugar. The author as narrator tells us Aunt Polly's questions are *full of guile*, meaning 'cunning', so we are alerted to expect that Tom is likely to get into trouble for something. The narrator tells us that Tom is suspicious of Aunt's motives for asking him questions (*A bit of a scare shot through Tom—a touch of uncomfortable suspicion.*). He tries to read her facial expression but there's no evidence in her face that she is angry or suspicious about his doings (*He searched Aunt Polly's face*). He answers her questions cautiously, suspecting that she is trying to trick him or trap him into admitting wrong-doing. We can judge that Aunt Polly is likely to outwit Tom.

Have a go!

Read the text. Make judgements to answer the questions.

> Fog everywhere. Fog up the river, where it flows among green aits and meadows; fog down the river, where it rolls defiled among the tiers of shipping and the waterside pollutions of a great (and dirty) city. Fog on the Essex marshes, fog on the Kentish heights. Fog creeping into the cabooses of collier-brigs; fog lying out on the yards and hovering in the rigging of great ships; fog drooping on the gunwales of barges and small boats. Fog in the eyes and throats of ancient Greenwich pensioners, wheezing by the firesides of their wards; fog in the stem and bowl of the afternoon pipe of the wrathful skipper, down in his close cabin; fog cruelly pinching the toes and fingers of his shivering little 'prentice boy on deck. Chance people on the bridges peeping over the parapets into a nether sky of fog, with fog all round them, as if they were up in a balloon and hanging in the misty clouds.
>
> Extract from *Bleak House* by Charles Dickens

A Do you judge this to be an effective description of an English fog? Give two or three reasons for your opinion.

....

....

B What judgements can you make about the setting of the text?

....

....

C What judgement can you make about the skipper?

....

....

Answers

A You should judge the text to be an effective description of an English fog because of the way language is used to help you visualise the fog obliterating everything (*Fog everywhere*). It covers everything, including the river, the meadows, the marshes, the heights, the ships, barges and boats; and it gets inside everything including *people's eyes and throats.*

Verbs are used effectively to describe the actions of the fog: *flows, rolls, creeping, hovering, drooping, pinching.*

Imagery is used effectively. For example, you can visualise the people on the ship decks peering down into a *nether sky* of fog, with fog all round them, as if they were up in a balloon and hanging in the misty clouds.

B Evidence that the setting is not modern day includes terminology such as *ait* (a small island), *collier-brigs, the rigging of great ships, 'prentice boy* and the fact that the skipper smokes a pipe.

C You should judge that the skipper sounds ill-tempered because he is described as *wrathful.* You might also judge him to be big because of the description of him in the close cabin. The narrator directs the reader's empathy towards the shivering little apprentice on the deck (in the cold open outdoors) whose character contrasts with the skipper's.

Have a go!

A writer's choice of words alerts readers to the author's values and attitudes. Read the text and then answer the question.

> Imagine being a wild orca swimming the ocean with your pod, roaming thousands of kilometres each year, free and intelligent and sociable. Now, imagine being captured and kept in a swimming pool and made to swim round and round in tiny circles for decades.

What would the writer think about killer whale and dolphin performances in theme parks?

....

....

Answer You can judge that the writer would have a negative opinion about venues that keep whales in captivity for human entertainment. The writer uses terms such as *free* and *captured* to convey an opinion.

Have a go!

1 A writer's choice of words alerts readers to the writer's values and attitudes about gender, race, religion, culture, society, sexuality, appearance, age and ability. From each pair of expressions below, choose the one that is the more inclusive and unbiased.

A a wheelchair-bound person OR a person using a wheelchair ....

....

B manager OR manageress ....

C compere OR master of ceremonies ....

D air hostess OR flight attendant ....

Answers

A *Person using a wheelchair* is the appropriate term. The term *wheelchair-bound* defines the person in terms of wheelchair dependence, which is negative, instead of recognising that he or she is a person foremost who also happens to be using a wheelchair as a mobility device.

B *Manager* is the appropriate term for males and females in management positions. Historically managers were all men. When females were first appointed to managerial positions they were identified by the term *manageress*. The gender of a manager is not relevant to the role.

C Males and females can be *comperes* of shows or programs. *Master of ceremonies* is an old term. It was used at a time when only men could be comperes of programs. Nowadays men and women have equal right to be comperes. *Compere* is a gender-inclusive term.

D *Flight attendant* is the gender-inclusive term that is used for males and females in the role. *Air hostess* is a derogatory term because it implies that only a woman can do the job. In the past males were called flight attendants while females in the same role were called air hostesses. Male and female flight attendants are part of the cabin crew.

2 Make judgements about the ways language is used to discriminate. What is wrong with each of the following sentences?

A William was carrying on like an old woman. ....

B Harry was acting like a nutter. ....

C Gays have nice clothes. ....

D An Asian family lives next door to us. ....

E We need someone to man the second-hand book stall at the fete. ....

Answers

A This statement is an example of negative labelling. It is derogatory and endorses a stereotype of elderly women. It implies that negative behaviour is the norm for elderly women.

B This statement makes fun of and stereotypes people from a minority group, people who have mental illnesses. Mental illness comprises a broad range of illnesses.

C The term *gay* is normally used to refer to homosexual males. This sentence endorses a stereotype and is inaccurate as a blanket description of all gay men. It also trivialises and demeans a minority group.

D The term *Asian* is often used to refer to people from a broad range of countries, cultures and ethnicities. If you have people living next door to you it would be helpful and polite to enquire about their specific heritage. The people next door might be sixth-generation Australian and identify as Australian. Or they might be sixth-generation Australian and celebrate their Chinese, Filipino or Indonesian heritage.

E This sentence uses the term *man* to mean 'person' but by using a male-gendered term it makes women invisible. The sentence should say 'We need someone to staff/run/manage the second-hand book stall'.

8 Scanning

What is it? **Scanning** is a strategy that helps you find specific information in a text. When you scan a text you look quickly through it for particular words, phrases or images you want to locate. You scan a text when it is not necessary to read or re-read the whole text to find the specific information you need. Scanning is useful for fact checking.

When answering reading comprehension questions it is important to read the whole text before attempting to answer any questions. If you read the question first and try to simply scan the text for answers you are unlikely to answer accurately questions that require inferring, synthesis, language and judgement skills, and you might not find the exact answer required for a fact-finding question.

How do you do it? Look quickly through the text to find the part you need then examine that area more closely. You can scan a page, a paragraph, a list, an index, a menu bar in digital texts, a glossary or a table of contents. You can scan headings and subheadings.

For example, you can scan:

- a text that you have already read to check your memory for the facts
- an alphabetical list for your name
- a list of ingredients in a recipe to look for particular ingredients
- a product catalogue to see if the item you want is available or on special
- an invitation to a function to find out what time it starts
- a group photo for your image
- a map for a place name or icon
- a graph for a particular item.

Have a go!

1 Scan the text for answers to these questions:

A What is palm oil? ....

B Is palm oil used in lipsticks? ....

C Are tigers one of the species endangered because of palm oil plantations? ....

Palm oil is a vegetable oil. It is used in thousands of products including shampoo, ice cream, margarine, chips, biscuits, toothpaste, chocolate, lipstick and candles. It's the most widely used vegetable oil in the entire world because the oil palm tree is quicker and cheaper to grow than other oil-producing plants.

The problem with palm oil is that oil palm trees grow where rainforests grow, so large areas of rainforest in Indonesia and Malaysia have been cleared indiscriminately and the land converted to palm oil plantations. This has led to large-scale habitat loss for endangered species like orang-utans, rhinos, elephants and tigers. It has also meant that some indigenous people have had their land and livelihoods taken from them and sometimes also their homes.

Answers **A** a vegetable oil **B** Yes **C** Yes

2 Scan the text below for answers to the following questions:

A What was the date of the first bombing of Darwin? ....

B How many times was Darwin bombed? ....

C How many people died due to the Darwin bombings? ....

Darwin was bombed on 64 occasions between 19 February 1942 and 12 November 1943. The first attacks involved four Japanese aircraft carriers situated in the Timor Sea. Two hundred and sixty planes were launched from the carriers in two waves. The first wave lasted for around forty minutes and bombed the town, the hospital, the military and civilian airports and the harbour. The second attack lasted an hour and came twenty-five minutes after the first had ended. It focused on the Royal Australian Air Force Base in Parap, a suburb of Darwin. The Japanese planes had been spotted flying over Bathurst Island thirty minutes before the first attack but Darwin RAAF operators presumed these were American planes and so did not sound air raid warnings. As a result of the attacks approximately 250 people died, up to 400 people were wounded, eight ships were sunk and around twenty planes were destroyed.

Answers **A** 19 February 1942 **B** 64 **C** 250

TYPES OF QUESTIONS

Step-by-step guide to **fact-finding** questions

Fact-finding questions involve finding information that is stated directly in the text.

Use this **Step-by-step guide** to help you read the text and **find facts** to answer the questions below. Circle the correct answers or write your answer on the lines.

STEP 1	**Skim** the text to see what it is about and how it is organised.	**Read** the title of the text, *The Law in Australia*. Look at the illustration. Notice that the text is written in paragraphs. Make **predictions** about the subject and purpose of the text.
STEP 2	**Read** the text. **Monitor** your reading to make sure you understand it.	**Visualise** and **connect** with the ideas in the text. **Think** about what you already know about the subject and the type of text, a report. Make **predictions.** Make **inferences**. Reflect on meanings and make **judgements**.

The law in Australia

A law is a rule that all the people have to follow. Laws are made to protect people and ensure that society runs smoothly and that everyone is treated fairly. Most laws in Australia are made by Federal or State Parliament. A proposal before Parliament for a new law or the revision of an existing law is called a 'bill'. Members of Parliament discuss these bills in detail or refer them to special committees for review or recommendations, before voting to approve or reject them. If approved they become an Act of Parliament.

When people think a law needs to be changed, they lobby Members of Parliament (MPs) to act on their behalf. Lobby groups try to persuade MPs to adopt their points of view. Lobby groups have specific interests. Sometimes the interests of lobby groups benefit the majority of people in Australia. Sometimes lobby groups represent minority interests and not the interests of the wider community.

Laws made by judges are called common laws. When a judge is making a decision about a case in a court of law the judge can base the decision on a previous court case or set a 'precedent' that then becomes the new law. Judges need to be able to set precedents because society changes and the legal system has to keep current with the times, with new technologies and with new types of crimes and criminals. Common law allows laws to change as quickly as necessary without having to wait for an Act of Parliament.

Local governments can also pass laws for enforcement within local areas. Local government laws must operate within the boundaries of Federal and State laws. Local laws deal with issues such as housing developments, land use, parking, waste management and noise pollution.

Police and the courts can enforce laws. If people break laws they can be arrested and punished. Punishment can include a fine, community service or a jail sentence.

Question 1 How are most laws in Australia made?

A by an Act of Federal or State Parliament

B when lobby groups make requests

C when police and the courts enforce them

D when Members of Parliament discuss bills

STEP 3	**Read** the question. **Think** about what type of question it is. Work out what you need to do to answer it.	This is a **fact-finding** question. You need to find the part of the text that says how most laws are made.
STEP 4	**Think** about the text. Remember what you have read and **visualised**.	**Scan** the text. The part that tells you the answer is in paragraph one.

A is correct. The answer is stated directly in the text. You read *Most laws in Australia are made by Federal or State Parliament (see lines 4–5).*

Check the other options to confirm why they are incorrect. **B** is incorrect because lobby groups requesting new laws is only one step in the law-making process. **C** is incorrect because the police and courts do not make the laws. The text states that some laws are made by judges as they make decisions in court. **D** is incorrect because Members of Parliament discuss bills for new laws and can vote for or against the bills in Parliament.

Question 2 What are the consequences of breaking the law?

A Lawbreakers deserve to be punished.

B Lawbreakers can be arrested.

C Lawbreakers might have to pay a fine, do community service or go to jail.

D Police and the courts can enforce laws.

STEP 3	**Read** the question. **Think** about what type of question it is. Work out what you need to do to answer it.	This is a **fact-finding** question. You need to find the part of the text that tells about the consequences of breaking the law.
STEP 4	**Think** about the text. Remember what you have read and **visualised**.	**Scan** the text. The part that tells you the answer is in the last paragraph.

C is correct. The answer is stated directly in the text. You read *Punishment can include a fine, community service or a jail sentence (see line 25).*

Check the other options to confirm why they are incorrect. **A** is incorrect because it is a statement of opinion rather than an answer to the question. **B** is incorrect because it is only part of the answer. **D** is incorrect because, even though it is a fact, this answer does not tell you the consequences of breaking the law.

Question 3 What is common law?

A laws that keep up with changing society

B laws that people are commonly expected to obey

C laws that keep up with new types of crime

D laws made by judges to suit changing times

STEP 3	**Read** the question. **Think** about what type of question it is. Work out what you need to do to answer it.	This is a **fact-finding** question. You need to find the part of the text that defines common law.
STEP 4	**Think** about the text. Remember what you have read and **visualised**.	**Scan** the text. The words *common law* are in paragraph three.

D is correct. The answer is stated directly in the text. You read *Laws made by judges are called common laws. When a judge is making a decision about a case in a court of law the judge can base the decision on a previous court case or set a 'precedent' that then becomes the new law (see lines 15–17).*

Check the other options to confirm why they are incorrect. **A** and **C** are incorrect because they say what common law does rather than define what it is. **B** is incorrect because this is not a definition of common law. It is an expectation for all laws.

Step-by-step guide to **fact-finding** questions *continued*

Fact-finding questions involve finding information that is stated directly in the text.

The law in Australia

A law is a rule that all the people have to follow. Laws are made to protect people and ensure that society runs smoothly and that everyone is treated fairly. Most laws in Australia are made by Federal or State Parliament. A proposal before Parliament for a new law or the revision of an existing law is called a 'bill'. Members of Parliament discuss these bills in detail or refer them to special committees for review or recommendations, before voting to approve or reject them. If approved they become an Act of Parliament.

When people think a law needs to be changed, they lobby Members of Parliament (MPs) to act on their behalf. Lobby groups try to persuade MPs to adopt their points of view. Lobby groups have specific interests. Sometimes the interests of lobby groups benefit the majority of people in Australia. Sometimes lobby groups represent minority interests and not the interests of the wider community.

Laws made by judges are called common laws. When a judge is making a decision about a case in a court of law the judge can base the decision on a previous court case or set a 'precedent' that then becomes the new law. Judges need to be able to set precedents because society changes and the legal system has to keep current with the times, with new technologies and with new types of crimes and criminals. Common law allows laws to change as quickly as necessary without having to wait for an Act of Parliament.

Local governments can also pass laws for enforcement within local areas. Local government laws must operate within the boundaries of Federal and State laws. Local laws deal with issues such as housing developments, land use, parking, waste management and noise pollution.

Police and the courts can enforce laws. If people break laws they can be arrested and punished. Punishment can include a fine, community service or a jail sentence.

Question 4 **What is a *bill* in the text?**

A something you get when you buy something or use a service

B a proposal before Parliament to add or change a law

C a proposal discussed by a special committee

D an Act of Parliament

STEP 3 **Read** the question. **Think** about what type of question it is. Work out what you need to do to answer it.

- This is a **fact-finding** question. You need to find the part of the text that tells what a bill is.

STEP 4 **Think** about the text. Remember what you have read and visualised.

- **Scan** the text. The part that describes a bill is in paragraph one.

B is correct. The answer is stated directly in the text. You read *A proposal before Parliament for a new law or the revision of an existing law is called a 'bill' (see lines 5–6).*

Check the other options to confirm why they are incorrect. **A** is incorrect in the context of the text. **C** and **D** are incorrect because they describe what happens on some occasions rather than define what a bill is. A bill might sometimes be discussed by a special committee (**C**) and a bill is sometimes passed as an Act of Parliament (**D**).

Question 5 What does a lobby group do?

A A lobby group talks with Members of Parliament.
B A lobby group changes laws.
C A lobby group passes bills.
D A lobby group promotes a point of view to Members of Parliament.

STEP 3	**Read** the question. **Think** about what type of question it is. Work out what you need to do to answer it.	✪ This is a **fact-finding** question. You need to find the part of the text that tells you the role of lobby groups.
STEP 4	**Think** about the text. Remember what you have read and **visualised**.	✪ **Scan** the text. The part that tells about lobby groups is in paragraph two.

D is correct. The answer is stated directly in the text. You read *When people think a law needs to be changed, they lobby Members of Parliament to act on their behalf (see lines 11–12)*. Lobby groups try to persuade MPs to adopt their points of view.

Check the other options to confirm why they are incorrect. **A** is not the full answer because the function of a lobby group is to persuade Members of Parliament to act on their behalf rather than simply to talk with them. **B** and **C** are incorrect because a lobby group does not change laws or pass bills—it pressures Members of Parliament to do so on behalf of its members.

Question 6 What laws does local government make?

....

....

STEP 3	**Read** the question. **Think** about what type of question it is. Work out what you need to do to answer it.	✪ This is a **fact-finding** question. You need to find the part of the text that tells about laws made by local government.
STEP 4	**Think** about the text. Remember what you have read and **visualised**.	✪ **Scan** the text. The part that tells you the answer is in paragraph four.

You read *Local laws deal with issues such as housing developments, land use, parking, waste management and noise pollution (see lines 22–23)*. Your answer needs to paraphrase or copy this information.

Fact-finding questions

Use the **Step-by-step guide** on pages 28–31 to help you read the text and **find facts** to answer the questions below. Circle the correct answers or write your answer on the lines.

Australia's highest military award

The Victoria Cross for Australia is Australia's highest military award. It is awarded to military personnel who show extreme bravery, heroism or self-sacrifice in the line of duty. It was established in 1991 to replace the original Victoria Cross, now referred to as the Imperial Victoria Cross. The Imperial Victoria Cross dates back to 1856 when Queen Victoria reigned over the United Kingdom and the British Empire. It was an award of the British Crown to honour soldiers from countries in the Commonwealth, whether they were fighting in the military units of their own countries or in units for other Commonwealth nations.

The Imperial Victoria Cross has been awarded to ninety-six Australians:

- six times for action during the Boer War (1899–1902), a war fought in South Africa between the British and the Dutch-Afrikaner settlers, known as Boers
- sixty-four times for action in World War I (1914–1918), a war whose combatants included Britain and Germany; nine of these VCs were awarded for Gallipoli
- twice for the conflict in North Russia (1919)
- twenty times for action in World War II (1939–1945) in campaigns against Italy, Germany and Japan
- four times for the Vietnam War (1962–1972), when Australia (in conjunction with other nations such as the United States) supported South Vietnam against North Vietnam.

The last Australian recipient of the Imperial Victoria Cross was Warrant Officer Keith Payne, for gallantry on 24 May 1969 during the Vietnam War. Payne was awarded the medal for instigating a rescue of more than forty men.

The Victoria Cross for Australia has more recently been awarded for the war in Afghanistan:

- 2009 to Trooper Mark Donaldson
- 2011 to Corporal Benjamin Roberts-Smith
- 2012 to Corporal Daniel Keighran
- 2014 to Corporal Cameron Baird (posthumously).

Note: *posthumously* means 'after death'.

1 What is Australia's highest military honour?

A The Victoria Cross
B The Imperial Victoria Cross
C The Victoria Cross for Australia
D a medal

2 The Victoria Cross was the highest military award for Australian personnel between:

A 1856 and now.
B 1899 and 1972.
C 1856 and 1991.
D 1991 and 2014.

3 Who is entitled to receive a Victoria Cross for Australia?

A Australian soldiers who die in the line of duty
B Australian military personnel
C Commonwealth military personnel who fought for Australia
D Australian army soldiers who are brave

4 What are the origins of the Imperial Victoria Cross?

A It is named after Queen Victoria.
B It was established by Queen Victoria for soldiers of the Commonwealth.
C It was created to honour Australian soldiers who fought for the British Crown.
D It is a British military award for Australian soldiers.

5 The Imperial Victoria Cross was last awarded to an Australian in

A 1991. **B** 1856. **C** 1969. **D** 2014.

6 How do you earn a Victoria Cross for Australia?

....

....

....

Answers and explanations on p. 97

Fact-finding questions

Use the **Step-by-step guide** on pages 28–31 to help you read the text and **find facts** to answer the questions below. Circle the correct answers or write your answer on extra paper.

Consumer glossary

Carbon price

A carbon price is a price paid by businesses for producing carbon emissions. A price on carbon helps to prevent pollution. Businesses can choose whether to change their practices to produce less carbon or to pay the price.

Cruelty free

A cruelty-free product is one that has been produced without testing it on animals or deriving it from animals.

Ethical consumer

An ethical consumer is a person who makes purchasing choices that are sustainable and socially just and that protect human and animal rights.

Fair Trade

Fair Trade labels on products mean that producers or growers have been paid a fair price for their goods. A Fair Trade product is usually one that has been produced in a developing country and sold in a developed country. Fair Trade goods include coffee, tea, cocoa, honey and chocolate.

Forestry Stewardship Council

The Forestry Stewardship Council works to promote responsible management of the world's forests.

Marine Stewardship Council

The Marine Stewardship Council works to promote sustainable fishing practices.

Organic

A Certified Organic label on a food product means that it was produced without the use of synthetic pesticides, herbicides, additives, fertilisers, hormones or processes such as chemical ripening, genetic modification, nanotechnology and irradiation.

Sustainable

Sustainable means 'able to be maintained'. A sustainable product is one that regrows or is renewable and whose use has minimal negative impact on the environment.

Sweatshop free

A sweatshop is a workplace where workers work in poor or unsafe conditions for low wages. Sweatshops mainly exist in developing countries. A 'sweatshop free' label or an 'Ethical Clothing Australia' label means that the item was made by workers whose rights were recognised and who were treated ethically.

1. What does Fair Trade mean?
   - **A** A grower swaps produce such as coffee for tea so there is a fair trade.
   - **B** Workers are treated fairly.
   - **C** People are paid fairly for their produce.
   - **D** People are paid to grow coffee, tea, cocoa, honey and chocolate.

2. What is a carbon price? Choose all that apply.
   - **A** a penalty for releasing carbon into the air
   - **B** a price for polluting
   - **C** when people pay carbon to the government
   - **D** a price to prevent pollution

3. Which statement is true according to the text?
   - **A** Sweatshops are dangerous workplaces.
   - **B** Sweatshops make sweets.
   - **C** Workers sweat in sweatshops.
   - **D** Sweatshops make 'Ethical clothing for Australia'.

4. A sustainable timber industry: what does this mean?
   - **A** Each felled tree is replaced.
   - **B** Felled trees are replaced and the forest ecosystem is maintained.
   - **C** People continue to buy timber furnishings for their homes.
   - **D** Timber industry workers worldwide ensure that only the largest trees are cut down.

5. Which is most likely to be organic?
   - **A** eggs labelled 'farm fresh'
   - **B** farm chickens given growth hormones to help them grow bigger
   - **C** bananas grown without the use of chemicals
   - **D** tinned fruit with artificial preservative added

6. Why is sustainability important? Write your answer on extra paper.

Answers and explanations on pp. 97–98

Fact-finding questions

Use the **Step-by-step guide** on pages 28–31 to help you read the text and **find facts** to answer the questions below. Circle the correct answers or write your answer on the lines.

Asylum seekers

The term *asylum* is defined in the dictionary as 'a place of sanctuary or safety'. Asylum seekers, therefore, are people who leave their own countries because they seek places of safety. Some asylum seekers seek political sanctuary, others seek religious sanctuary. Some are persecuted in their own country because of their race, their social group, their views or their gender. Asylum seekers are at risk in their own countries because the governments of their own countries cannot or will not protect them. All asylum seekers seek freedom to live their lives in safety, free of fear and persecution.

Most asylum seekers seek asylum in neighbouring countries. Some travel further by whatever means are available to them. Asylum seekers apply for refugee status and are labelled refugees once officials can confirm that their claims are genuine.

Australia is a signatory to the Refugee Convention of 1951 and the revisions made to the Convention in 1961. The Refugee Convention is the key international document by which refugees are identified. As a signatory to the Convention, Australia has moral, legal and humanitarian obligations under international law to protect refugees.

Refugees to Australia have often arrived in waves after major events. Refugees from European countries such as Germany and Poland came to Australia after World War II. During the 1970s asylum seekers and refugees arrived from Vietnam as a result of the Vietnam War. Bosnian and Croatian refugees arrived during the 1990s. Since the year 2000 refugees have been arriving from countries in the Middle East such as Iraq and Afghanistan, and African nations such as the Sudan and Somalia. Refugees have made valuable contributions to Australian society.

1. Asylum seekers are people who
   - **A** flee their homes due to war or conflict.
   - **B** want to live in another country.
   - **C** leave their own countries because it is unsafe for them to stay there.
   - **D** arrive in Australia by boat.

2. What is the definition of a refugee?
   - **A** a person who signed the Refugee Convention
   - **B** a person who came to Australia from Germany or Poland after World War II
   - **C** a person whose refugee status has been acknowledged as genuine
   - **D** a person who contributes to Australian society in many ways

3. People become asylum seekers for which of the following reasons? Choose all that apply.
   - **A** They fear for their safety.
   - **B** They have too much freedom.
   - **C** Their own government is not protecting them.
   - **D** They belong to a minority religion.

4. The Refugee Convention is
   - **A** a policy designed to protect refugees in Australia.
   - **B** an Australian government policy for dealing with refugees.
   - **C** an international agreement designed to protect refugees.
   - **D** Australian law.

5. After World War II many refugees came to Australia from
   - **A** Bosnia and Croatia.
   - **B** Vietnam.
   - **C** Africa.
   - **D** Poland and Germany.

6. Why is it illegal for Australia not to protect refugees?

   ....

   ....

   ....

   ....

Answers and explanations on p. 98

Fact-finding questions

Use the **Step-by-step guide** on pages 28–31 to help you read the text and **find facts** to answer the questions below. Circle the correct answers or write your answers on the lines.

THE PERTH TRIBUNE

21 NOVEMBER 1978

The Last Whale

A female sperm whale harpooned yesterday will be the last whale killed by the Australian whaling industry.

Cheynes Beach Whaling Station is Australia's last whaling station. Operating since 1952 it is now being decommissioned. This brings an end to whaling activity that has forced humpback, southern right whales and sperm whales to the brink of extinction in Australian waters.

Improved technology such as the harpoon cannon, the toggle harpoon, deck cannons, faster chase boats and later factory ships and the use of aircraft to spot whale pods increased the efficiency of whaling and led to the rapid depletion of whale stocks. This forced the Australian government to ban all commercial whaling before whales become extinct in Australian waters.

Tangalooma in Queensland was once the largest land-based whaling station in the southern hemisphere. It closed in 1962 after decimating the number of humpbacks off the east coast of Australia from an estimated 15 000 to 500 whales in ten years. Humpbacks have been protected under Australian law since 1963.

The first Greenpeace campaign in Australia saw protestors involved in actions against Cheynes Beach Whaling Company vessels last year, drawing international attention to the industry at that time.

Whaling was one of Australia's first industries. Whale oil was a lucrative export business in the early colonies and used for lighting and candle making. Whale baleen was used for women's corsets. Later the oil was used in cosmetics while whale meat was used for animal food.

The value of the industry varied greatly over the years as the price of whale oil was affected by market influences. The introduction of vegetable oil and the advent of commercial drilling for petroleum oil in USA in the late 1850s reduced the world's reliance on whale oil.

Sixteen thousand sperm whales have been killed in Australia waters since 1952. The final season's catch for the Cheynes Beach station was 698 sperm whales.

1. When was the last sperm whale killed by the Australian whaling industry?

   A 1962 **B** 1952
   C 1978 **D** 1963

2. Why was whale oil valuable in the early colonies?

   A It was used for lighting, candle-making and women's corsets.
   B It was used for export, lighting and candle-making.
   C It was used for cosmetics and animal food.
   D It was used for export.

3. How long did it take Tangalooma to decimate humpback numbers off Queensland?

   A from 1952 to 1978 **B** 500 years
   C 1963 **D** ten years

4. When did Greenpeace first campaign in Australia?

   A against Cheynes' Beach Whaling Company
   B 1963
   C 1977
   D when 698 sperm whales were killed

5. Which three whale species were important to the Australian whale industry?

   ....

6. How did technology impact on whale numbers?

   ....
   ....
   ....
   ....

Answers and explanations on p. 99

Step-by-step guide to **synthesis** questions

Synthesis questions involve connecting ideas and information from across the text.

Use this **Step-by-step guide** to help you read the text and **synthesise** information to answer the questions below. Circle the correct answers or write your answer on the lines.

STEP ①	**Skim** the text to see what it is about and how it is organised.	**Read** the title, *Jane Goodall: conservationist.* Notice the illustration and the use of paragraphs. Make **predictions** about the subject and purpose of the text.
STEP ②	**Read** the text. **Monitor** your reading to make sure you understand the text.	**Visualise** and **connect** with the ideas in the text. **Think** about what you already know about the subject and the type of text, a biography. Make **predictions.** Make **inferences**. Reflect on meanings and make **judgements**.

Jane Goodall: conservationist

Some people devote their lives to helping animals. Jane Goodall is a person who is famous world-wide for her work with chimpanzees. She spent many years in Africa studying chimpanzees in the wild and has campaigned tirelessly for their conservation and the conservation of their habitat, particularly in the Gombe Stream National Park in Tanzania.

Goodall's work with chimpanzees dates back to 1960 when she began her now famous research study of chimpanzees in the wild. She lived with a chimpanzee troop in Gombe for twenty-two months, studying them and interacting with them. Her research proved to her the similarities between humans and chimps in intellectual capacity, family life and social attachments. She was the first official researcher to note that chimps modify twigs and blades of grass to use as tools, for example when collecting termites to eat from inside a termite mound. Previously, scientists had believed that humans were the only animals to make or use tools.

Goodall established the Jane Goodall Institute in 1977. As well as promoting conservation, one of the Institute's goals is to help raise African people out of poverty. The institute has offices around the world, including in Australia and works to educate people about the interdependence of people, animals and the environment. Goodall believes in action, no matter how small. She said, "The greatest danger to our future is apathy"*.

Goodall has received numerous awards including the J Paul Getty Wildlife Conservation Prize (1984) and a Lifetime Achievement Award presented by International Fund for Animal Welfare.

Extract from Chapter 4 of *Defenders of Animals,* unpublished

**Apathy* is a lack of caring, interest or involvement.

Question 1 **Which of the following chapters might also be suitable in the book, *Defenders of Animals*?**

A Chimpanzee behaviour

B Sir Peter Scott, J Paul Getty Conservation Prize winner

C Peter Jackson, film-maker, *King Kong*

D Amanda Hayes, Wildlife Photography Award Winner

STEP 3	**Read** the question. **Think** about what type of question it is. Work out what you need to do to answer it.	✪ This is a **synthesis** question. You need to use your understanding of the role of chapter titles to work out which chapter belongs in the book, *Defenders of Animals*.
STEP 4	**Think** about the text. Remember what you have read and **visualised**.	✪ **Think** about the text as a whole and **connect** ideas from across the text. **Think** about the main ideas in the text.

B is correct. Notice that this text is a biography: it gives information about Jane Goodall's life. The text is Chapter 4 of a book. Combine this with your own knowledge about the way individual chapters work in a book of biographies. You read *Chapter 4 of Defenders of Animals* ***(see line 23)***. You read *Goodall has received numerous awards including the J Paul Getty Wildlife Conservation Prize* ***(see line 21)***. You can work out from the book's title *Defenders of Animals* that the book will have chapters about people who defend animals. Peter Scott and Jane Goodall have both won the J Paul Getty Prize, which is a prize for conservation.

Check the other options to confirm why they are incorrect. **A** is incorrect because it is about chimpanzees, so it doesn't belong in a biographical book. **C** is incorrect because it is about a filmmaker, Peter Jackson, and his film involving the fictional character King Kong. **D** is incorrect because it is about a person who has won an award for wildlife photography; photographing wildlife does not necessarily mean that the photographer is a defender of wildlife.

Question 2 Instead of *Defenders of Animals* an alternative title for the book could be

A The Gombe Stream National Park.

B People and their Pets.

C People Who Protect Animals.

D Protecting Chimpanzees.

STEP 3	**Read** the question. **Think** about what type of question it is. Work out what you need to do to answer it.	✪ This is a **synthesis** question. You need to select an alternative title to suit the contents of a whole book based on your understanding of a sample chapter.
STEP 4	**Think** about the text. Remember what you have read and **visualised**.	✪ **Think** about the text as a whole and **connect** ideas from across the text. Remember that this text is a biography.

C is correct. The text gives information about Jane Goodall's life. You should work out that the whole book will consist of chapters about people who are *Defenders of Animals*. *Defender* is a word that means 'protector'. A suitable alternative title could be 'People Who Protect Animals'.

Check the other options to confirm why they are incorrect. **A** is incorrect because *The Gombe Stream National Park* ***(see line 6)*** is a place and the focus of a biography is people. **B** is incorrect because the text is about wild chimpanzees and not about pets. **D** is incorrect because the book title includes the word *Animals* ***(see line 23)*** so you should predict that the book will not just be about protecting chimpanzees.

Question 3 Number the statements in chronological order, starting with what happened first.

A Goodall has devoted her life to helping animals.

B Goodall founded the Jane Goodall Institute.

C Goodall won The J Paul Getty Wildlife Conservation Prize.

D Goodall studied chimpanzees in Gombe.

STEP 3	**Read** the question. **Think** about what type of question it is. Work out what you need to do to answer it.	✪ This is a **synthesis** question. You need to organise the statements into chronological (time) order.
STEP 4	**Think** about the text. Remember what you have read and **visualised**.	✪ **Scan** the text. Re-read sections of text if necessary. **Think** about the text as a whole and **connect** ideas from across the text in a time sequence.

The answer sequence is **D, B, C, A.** Each event listed in the question relates to each of the four paragraphs in the text. Goodall's work with chimpanzees dates back to 1960. Goodall established the Jane Goodall Institute in 1977. Goodall won The J Paul Getty Wildlife Conservation Prize in 1984. The first sentence in paragraph one says that Goodall has devoted her life to helping animals. Even though this is the first sentence in the text, it is not the first event in Goodall's life but acts as a summation of her entire life. It is used as a thesis statement to introduce the text.

Synthesis questions involve connecting ideas and information from across the text.

Jane Goodall: conservationist

Some people devote their lives to helping animals. Jane Goodall is a person who is famous world-wide for her work with chimpanzees. She spent many years in Africa studying chimpanzees in the wild and has campaigned tirelessly for their conservation and the conservation of their habitat, particularly in the Gombe Stream National Park in Tanzania.

Goodall's work with chimpanzees dates back to 1960 when she began her now famous research study of chimpanzees in the wild. She lived with a chimpanzee troop in Gombe for twenty-two months, studying them and interacting with them. Her research proved to her the similarities between humans and chimps in intellectual capacity, family life and social attachments. She was the first official researcher to note that chimps modify twigs and blades of grass to use as tools, for example when collecting termites to eat from inside a termite mound. Previously, scientists had believed that humans were the only animals to make or use tools.

Goodall established the Jane Goodall Institute in 1977. As well as promoting conservation, one of the Institute's goals is to help raise African people out of poverty. The institute has offices around the world, including in Australia and works to educate people about the interdependence of people, animals and the environment. Goodall believes in action, no matter how small. She said, "The greatest danger to our future is apathy"*.

Goodall has received numerous awards including the J Paul Getty Wildlife Conservation Prize (1984) and a Lifetime Achievement Award presented by International Fund for Animal Welfare.

Extract from Chapter 4 of *Defenders of Animals,* unpublished

**Apathy* is a lack of caring, interest or involvement.

Question 4 **The text is an extract from a chapter in a book. What extra information could the chapter include?**

A information about colobus monkeys in Gombe

B information about Goodall's work to conserve chimpanzee habitat

C information about ways to help African people living in poverty

D information about famous donors to the Goodall Institute

STEP 3 **Read** the question. **Think** about what type of question it is. Work out what you need to do to answer it.	This is a **synthesis** question. You need to **connect** ideas across the whole text to work out which of the suggested topics belongs in the text.
STEP 4 **Think** about the text. Remember what you have read and **visualised**.	**Scan** the text. Re-read sections of text if necessary. **Think** about the information you have read and the ideas suggested in the question to work out which one is relevant to the theme of the chapter *Jane Goodall: conservationist*.

B is correct. Information about Goodall's work to conserve chimpanzee habitat could belong in a biographical chapter about Jane Goodall.

Check the other options to confirm why they are incorrect. **A** is incorrect because it is about monkeys. **C** is incorrect because it focuses on African people living in poverty. **D** is not about Jane Goodall but about the Institute and its donors or benefactors.

Question 5 **Which statement best fits with the theme of the text?**

A Goodall thinks it is important to study animals.
B Goodall thinks it is important to win conservation prizes.
C Goodall works to protect animals and the environment.
D Goodall proved chimps are clever.

STEP 3 **Read** the question. **Think** about what type of question it is. Work out what you need to do to answer it.

- of the suggested statements best fits the theme of the text.

STEP 4 **Think** about the text. Remember what you have read and **visualised**.

- **Scan** the text. Re-read sections of text if necessary. **Think** about what the information means in relation to Goodall's attitude to the environment, winning prizes, helping wildlife and about chimps. Use a process of elimination to work out the answer.

C is correct. It is the best fit for the theme of the text. The general theme of the text is Goodall's attitude towards wildlife and conservation.

Check the other options to confirm why they are incorrect. **A** relates to Goodall's study of chimps which was significant in her life but not Goodall's lifetime priority. There is nothing in the text to support **B**. **D** may be true but it is not the theme of the text as a whole.

Question 6 **"We shan't save all we should like to, but we shall save a great deal more than if we had never tried." Would Jane Goodall agree or disagree with this quote about conservation by Sir Peter Scott? Explain your reasoning.**

....

....

....

STEP 3 **Read** the question. **Think** about what type of question it is. Work out what you need to do to answer it.

- This is a **synthesis** question. You need to use your understanding of ideas across the text to work out whether Jane Goodall would agree with the quote.

STEP 4 **Think** about the text. Remember what you have read and **visualised**.

- **Scan** the text. **Think** about the text as a whole and **connect** ideas from across the text.

You can connect Goodall's statement, "*The greatest danger to our future is apathy*" ***(see lines 19–20)***, to Peter Scott's statement. *Apathy* means 'a lack of caring, interest or involvement'. You can work out that Goodall worried about people doing nothing. Your answer should explain that Goodall would agree with Scott's statement. You should recognise that Goodall would want people to take action, become involved and do something rather than sit back and do nothing.

Synthesis questions

Use the **Step-by-step guide** on pages 36–39 to help you read the text and **synthesise** information to answer the questions below. Circle the correct answers or write your answer on the lines.

BURGER SHACK

Grand Opening across Australia May 1st

Come on in. Be the first to TRY our delicious mouth-watering BURGERS

--- home-made vegan burgers, flame grilled while U wait ---

Sample

- **Byron Bay Burger**—with avocado on a wattle seed bun
- **Bondi Burger**—with caramelised onions
- **Mediterranean Burger**—with field mushrooms, capsicum, zucchini
- **Tropical Burger**—with pineapple, coconut and lime

Try

- our home-made potato and corn patties
- and our crispy fried tofu with soy and ginger on a rice bun
- or our lemon myrtle rice with stir fried greens.

Natural

- Fresh market produce daily
- Wholesome healthy ingredients—no preservatives or additives
- All burgers made with compassion for animals
- Gluten-free available

Our burgers are not super-sized. We promise not to super-size you!

Our slogan: Eat for health. Eat with compassion. Live well. Enjoy life.

No animals are killed to procure or produce our food.

PRESENT THIS ADVERTISEMENT AND RECEIVE one freshly pressed juice **FREE** with every burger purchased.

Open 7 am–10 pm 7 days a week • Dine in or takeaway • Phone 0400 399 999 • www.burgershack.com.au

1. What is the purpose of the text?
   - **A** to encourage people to eat more burgers
   - **B** to offer people a free juice
   - **C** to tell people Burger Shack makes burgers *while U wait*
   - **D** to attract customers

2. How are ideas linked in the text?
   - **A** through introduction, body of text, conclusion
   - **B** by adding information
   - **C** in a time sequence
   - **D** through cause and effect

3. What is the main idea in the text?
   - **A** There is a Grand Opening.
   - **B** The owners love chickens.
   - **C** Burger Shack sells delicious food.
   - **D** You can get a free freshly pressed juice for every burger purchased.

4. Which item could be added to the menu?
   - **A** Flame grilled chicken burgers
   - **B** All beef patties
   - **C** Free range bacon and egg rolls
   - **D** Wild rice dumplings

5. What does this mean? *We promise not to super-size you!* (line 24)
   - **A** Customers are only allowed one burger each.
   - **B** Burger Shack does not sell French fries.
   - **C** The food is in healthy portion sizes.
   - **D** The food is very tasty.

6. There is no street address in the text. Why might this be?

   ....

   ....

   ....

Answers and explanations on pp. 99–100

Synthesis questions

Use the **Step-by-step guide** on pages 36–39 to help you read the text and **synthesise** information to answer the questions below. Circle the correct answers or write your answers on the lines.

Citizenship

Australian citizens are people who were born in Australia or people who immigrated to Australia and later applied to become citizens. People who were born in Australia are automatically citizens. People who live and work in Australia but are not citizens are called residents. People who have lived and worked in Australia for a long time but are not citizens are referred to as permanent residents. Everyone living in Australia (citizens, residents and tourists) must comply with Australian law.

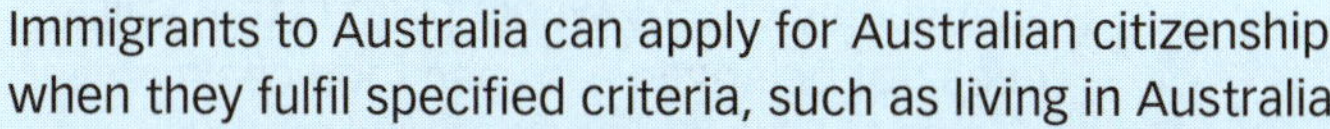

Immigrants to Australia can apply for Australian citizenship when they fulfil specified criteria, such as living in Australia for four years. When they become Australian citizens they receive an Australian passport and are entitled to all the rights, privileges and responsibilities of citizenship.

Some people who are permanent residents choose not to become Australian citizens. This is most likely because they have strong ties to their countries of birth. For other people, becoming a citizen is very important and they feel immense pride in being awarded citizenship.

Citizens have the right to vote and stand for parliament. These rights are also privileges; they bring with them the responsibility to do what each citizen believes is best for Australia as a nation and for the Australian people. Australian society values freedom of speech and of religion, equality and tolerance, democracy and the law, respect for the individual and compassion for others. This set of values is one reason Australia is sometimes referred to as the 'lucky country'.

Australia is recognised as a multicultural country. More than seven million people have settled in Australia since World War II. These seven million people represent more than 260 languages and ancestries, and it is this diversity of culture that contributes to the richness of life in Australia today.

1 What is the purpose of the text?

- **A** to give instructions
- **B** to explain a citizen's point of view
- **C** to provide information on a topic
- **D** to advise people about becoming citizens

2 How are ideas connected across the text?

- **A** The paragraphs are connected chronologically.
- **B** Each paragraph adds new information about an aspect of the topic.
- **C** The paragraphs all have information.
- **D** Each paragraph gives an opinion and evidence after a topic sentence.

3 What can citizens of Australia do? Choose all that apply.

- **A** vote in elections
- **B** be elected to parliament
- **C** practise their religion
- **D** break the law

4 Which of the following is a right, as well as a responsibility, of a citizen?

- **A** having a passport
- **B** obeying the law
- **C** having freedom of religion
- **D** voting

5 Use ideas in the text to explain the meaning of the term 'lucky country'.

....

....

6 Explain the differences between these categories of people living in Australia: citizens, residents and tourists.

....

....

....

....

Answers and explanations on p. 100

Synthesis questions

Use the **Step-by-step guide** on pages 36–39 to help you read the text and **synthesise** information to answer the questions below. Circle the correct answers or write your answer on extra paper.

Krill

Transcript of a radio interview.

Radio host: Today on our program we welcome Lee Cheung from the organisation 'Sustaining the Oceans.' Lee's going to tell us about krill. Welcome to the program, Lee.

Lee: Thank you for having me.

Radio host: Lee, I believe you're campaigning to stop people from buying krill oil.

Lee: Yes! I am. People consume krill oil for its reported heart health benefits, but the important fact to remember is that marine creatures such as fish, penguins and whales rely on krill for survival. Krill is a basis of the marine food chain, and now we have huge factory ships scooping up all the wild krill they can find to make health food tablets for people. It is ridiculous and it makes me very angry because it's so irresponsible.

Radio host: What in particular makes you so angry about it?

Lee: The health food industry is worth billions of dollars, in Australia alone. People want to improve their health but they want to do it the lazy way—by swallowing what they hope is a 'magic' pill. But that so-called 'magic' ingredient is being stolen from whales and other marine creatures that will starve to death without this food source. Krill is a finite resource. Krill fishing for a health food tablet is simply not sustainable.

Radio host: Is any krill sustainable?

Lee: Some brands claim their krill is fished sustainably but my whole point is that krill does not belong in a human food chain. People need to stop and think about the planet when they make shopping choices. Krill is harvested right alongside whale feeding areas. Some experts suggest that wild krill numbers have declined by 80 per cent over recent decades. The advertising from suppliers of krill oil makes people believe they have to eat it. This just puts company profits ahead of the planet, yet again.

Radio host: Do you have any final words before we conclude the interview?

Lee: Yes. My final point is to beg people to think before they buy. Think about how a product has been sourced and produced and decide whether or not it's sustainable and ethical.

1 What is the purpose of the text?
- **A** to provide factual information about krill
- **B** to present a point of view about krill
- **C** to persuade people that krill oil is good for whales
- **D** to explain the marine food chain

2 How are ideas connected in the interview?
- **A** through cause and effect
- **B** in chronological order
- **C** through thesis statement and supporting evidence
- **D** through question and answer

3 What is Lee's main message?
- **A** Stop buying krill oil tablets.
- **B** Krill might be good for people's health.
- **C** Krill is the basis for the marine food chain.
- **D** People should only buy sustainably fished krill.

4 The opposite point of view to Lee's would be:
- **A** Krill oil is a healthy product for people to consume.
- **B** There's plenty of krill in the sea for everyone.
- **C** Companies put profits ahead of the environment.
- **D** Make sure all products are sustainably sourced.

5 Which newspaper headline would suit Lee's message in the text?
- **A** People benefit from 'magic' pill
- **B** Whales starve to death
- **C** Spokesperson urges people to fish sustainably
- **D** Lee Cheung denies value of krill oil

6 Draw four conclusions about krill from the text. Write your answer on extra paper.

Answers and explanations on pp. 100–101

Synthesis questions

Use the **Step-by-step** guide on pages 36–39 to help you read the text and **synthesise** information to answer the questions below. Circle the correct answers or write your answers on the lines.

Suffrage

The United Nations Convention on the Elimination of All Forms of Discrimination Against Women (1979) identifies suffrage as a basic right. Suffrage means the right to vote. Women in Australia were granted the right to vote in Federal elections as well as the right to stand for election to Federal Parliament in 1902. This combination was a world first but it took another 41 years for a female politician to actually be elected to parliament, the worst record of any democratic western nation.

The different States in Australia awarded women the right to vote at various other times, before or after the Federal right to vote became law. In 1893 New Zealand became the first country in the world to allow women to vote. America did not grant women the right to vote until 1920, England 1928, France 1944, Italy 1946 and Greece in 1952.

Suffragette is the term used for a woman who campaigned for women to be allowed to vote. The experience of suffragettes around the world has often been difficult and sometimes violent. In England, for example, up to 1000 suffragettes were sent to jail. In jail many of the women went on hunger strikes to draw attention to their cause. Hunger strikers were sometimes force-fed, a painful process where food is pumped into a person's stomach via a stomach or nostril tube.

Australian suffragettes used legal and peaceful means to campaign for women's rights. One of the most amazing feats was a petition presented to the Victorian Parliament in 1891. Unrolled, the petition is 260m long. It is nicknamed the 'Monster Petition' and includes signatures of almost 30 000 Victorian women. Some of the campaigners in Australia were Rose Scott, Henrietta Dugdale, Marie Kirk, Annette Bear-Crawford, Vida Goldstein, Edith Cowan and Adela Pankhurst Walsh.

1 What is the purpose of the text?

- **A** to name Australian suffragettes
- **B** to explain why Australian women won the vote
- **C** to provide general information about suffrage
- **D** to convince readers of the importance of suffrage

2 Which of the following might have been found in Vida Goldstein's monthly journal *The Australian Women's Sphere*?

- **A** A woman's place is in the home.
- **B** Women don't want the vote—they are busy looking after their children.
- **C** Votes for women!
- **D** Vote *No* on suffrage because 90 per cent of women eligible to vote are married and can only annul or double their husband's vote.

3 Sequence the events in chronological order, starting with what happened first.

- **A** New Zealand women gain suffrage.
- **B** The United Nations officially recognises suffrage as a right.
- **C** Australian women gain the right to vote in Federal elections.
- **D** People in Australia campaign for women's suffrage.

4 Choose an alternative title for the text.

- **A** Women in politics
- **B** Women denied the vote
- **C** Women's suffrage
- **D** Voters' rights

5 Which statement represents a key conclusion drawn from the text?

- **A** Suffrage has always been recognised as a human right.
- **B** Most Australians did not want to give women the vote in 1902.
- **C** Society was largely prejudiced against women in the late 1800s.
- **D** Men and women were treated equally under Australian law in the late 1800s.

6 Write a comment that an Australian politician might have made in 1902 about suffrage.

....

....

....

Answers and explanations on pp. 101–102

Step-by-step guide to **inferring** questions

Inferring questions involve reading between the lines to work out an answer that is not stated directly in the text.

Use this **Step-by-step guide** to help you read the text and make **inferences** to answer the questions below. Circle the correct answers or write your answers on the lines.

STEP 1	**Skim** the text to see what it is about and how it is organised. Notice the series of emails.	**Read** the subject heading or title of each email, **Easter**. Make **predictions** about the purpose of the emails.
STEP 2	**Read** the text. **Monitor** your reading to make sure you understand it.	**Visualise** and **connect** with the ideas in the text. **Think** about what you already know about the subject and the type of text, emails. Make **predictions.** Make **inferences**. Make **judgements**.

Easter

New | Reply | Delete | Archive | Junk | Sweep | Move to

Easter
To: Liza cc: Emily

21 February

Hi Girls

I can't believe all the chocolates and Easter eggs in the shops—it's not even Easter for another month. Chocolate manufacturers surely must love Easter. You know, people in Australia spend more than $150 million on chocolates every Easter. I can think of better ways to spend that money. We could immunise children in developing countries against childhood disease or pay for hospital equipment or buy farming equipment for communities in Africa. It's disgraceful really that so much money is spent on chocolate. Sorry about my rant. Love you both, Aunty K

New | Reply | Delete | Archive | Junk

Easter
To: Katy cc: Emily

Hi Aunt Katy

I know what you mean. Mum stopped buying me chocolates at Easter when I was 8. She said too much chocolate is unhealthy. She gave me music vouchers instead for a few years. Now she just boycotts Easter altogether. Love Liza

New | Reply | Delete | Archive | Junk | Sweep | Move to

Easter
To: AK

Hi Aunt Katy

We're getting virtual Easter gifts this year. Mum said that money she would have spent on eggs is going to the World Wildlife Fund and we can choose our own virtual gifts. It's pretty cool. Mum sends her love. Miss you, Emily

New | Reply | Delete | Archive | Junk | Sweep | Move to

Easter
To: Liza

Hi Liza

Sorry can't stay at your place Saturday. Easter Sunday is the one day of the year my parents insist we go to church. I have an Easter bilby for you. I'll bring it to school next week ☺ Sally.

New | Reply | Delete | Archive | Junk | Sweep | Move to

Easter
To: Aaron

Hi Aaron

I know your family doesn't celebrate Easter but I have a chocolate bilby for you anyway. I'll bring it to school next week ☺ Sally.

New | Reply | Delete | Archive | Junk | Sweep | Move to

Easter
To: Sally H

Hi Sally

Mum's banned us from contributing to the 'chocolatisation' of Easter. Ha ha! You can help me eat the bilby. Liza

Question 1 **What can you infer about Aunty Katy? Choose all that apply.**

A She is concerned about people living in poverty.
B She won't buy Easter eggs.
C She doesn't like chocolate.
D She is not religious.

STEP 3 **Read** the question. **Think** about what type of question it is. Work out what you need to do to answer it.

✪ This is an **inferring** question. The answer is not stated directly in the text. You can make **inferences** about Aunty Katy by reading between the lines.

STEP 4 **Think** about the text. Remember what you have read and **visualised**.

✪ You can work out the answer using the clues in the text.

You can infer that **A** and **B** are correct. You read *I can think of better ways to spend that money. We could immunise children in developing countries against childhood disease or pay for hospital equipment or buy farming equipment for communities in Africa* *(see lines 9–12)*. You can infer that Aunty Katy cares about people living in poverty or living in less fortunate circumstances than she does (**A**). You read *It's disgraceful really that so much money is spent on chocolate* *(see lines 12–13)*. You can infer (**B**) that she won't buy Easter eggs because she thinks they are a waste of money.

Check the other options to confirm why they are incorrect. **C** and **D** are incorrect. These statements could well be true but there is nothing in the text to support the inferences that she doesn't like chocolate or that she is not religious.

Question 2 **Which inference can you make from the text?**

A Liza and Emily are cousins.
B Liza and Emily are sisters.
C Aunty K and Sally are sisters.
D Aunty Katy is a school teacher.

STEP 3 **Read** the question. **Think** about what type of question it is. Work out what you need to do to answer it.

✪ This is an **inferring** question. The answer is not stated directly in the text. You can make **inferences** about the people by reading between the lines of their emails.

STEP 4 **Think** about the text. Remember what you have read and **visualised**.

✪ You can work out the answer using the clues in the text.

A is correct. Liza says her mum *boycotts Easter altogether* *(see lines 23–24)*. Emily says her mum gives money to World Wildlife Fund instead of buying chocolates. Both girls reply to Aunty K or Aunty Katy. You can infer that Liza and Emily are cousins (**A**).

Check the other options to confirm why they are incorrect. **B** is incorrect. The girls have different mothers so they are not sisters. **C** is incorrect. It is unlikely that Sally and Aunty K are sisters because Sally is Liza's school friend. **D** is correct. There is nothing in the text to support an inference that Aunty Katy is a school teacher.

Question 3 **What inferences can you make from the information in the text? Choose all that apply.**

A Sally 's family is the most religious.
B Sally's family is the only religious family.
C Aarons' family has no religion.
D Emily's mum cares about animals.

STEP 3 **Read** the question. **Think** about what type of question it is. Work out what you need to do to answer it.

✪ This is an **inferring** question. The answer is not stated directly in the text. You **infer** information about the people by reading between the lines of their correspondence.

STEP 4 **Think** about the text. Remember what you have read and **visualised**.

✪ You can work out the answer using the clues in the text.

D is the only correct answer. You read Emily's email: *Mum said that money she would have spent on eggs is going to the World Wildlife Fund* *(see lines 28–30)*. You can infer that Emily's mum cares about animals.

Check the other options to confirm why they are incorrect. **A** and **B** are incorrect. You cannot infer that Sally's family is the only religious family or the most religious as no information is given about the religion of other families in the text. The text only states that Aunty Katy and the families of Liza and Emily are not buying chocolates; not that they are not religious. Answer **C** is incorrect. Aaron's family doesn't celebrate Easter but that could be because he is from a non-Christian religion.

Step-by-step guide to **inferring** questions *continued*

Inferring questions involve reading between the lines to work out an answer that is not stated directly in the text.

Easter

New | Reply | Delete | Archive | Junk | Sweep | Move to

Easter
To: Liza cc: Emily

21 February

Hi Girls
I can't believe all the chocolates and Easter eggs in the shops—it's not even Easter for another month. Chocolate manufacturers surely must love Easter. You know, people in Australia spend more than $150 million on chocolates every Easter. I can think of better ways to spend that money. We could immunise children in developing countries against childhood disease or pay for hospital equipment or buy farming equipment for communities in Africa. It's disgraceful really that so much money is spent on chocolate. Sorry about my rant. Love you both, Aunty K

New | Reply | Delete | Archive | Junk

Easter
To: Katy cc: Emily

Hi Aunt Katy
I know what you mean. Mum stopped buying me chocolates at Easter when I was 8. She said too much chocolate is unhealthy. She gave me music vouchers instead for a few years. Now she just boycotts Easter altogether. Love Liza

New | Reply | Delete | Archive | Junk | Sweep | Move to

Easter
To: AK

Hi Aunt Katy
We're getting virtual Easter gifts this year. Mum said that money she would have spent on eggs is going to the World Wildlife Fund and we can choose our own virtual gifts. It's pretty cool. Mum sends her love. Miss you, Emily

New | Reply | Delete | Archive | Junk | Sweep | Move to

Easter
To: Liza

Hi Liza
Sorry can't stay at your place Saturday. Easter Sunday is the one day of the year my parents insist we go to church. I have an Easter bilby for you. I'll bring it to school next week ☺ Sally.

New | Reply | Delete | Archive | Junk | Sweep | Move to

Easter
To: Aaron

Hi Aaron
I know your family doesn't celebrate Easter but I have a chocolate bilby for you anyway. I'll bring it to school next week ☺ Sally.

New | Reply | Delete | Archive | Junk | Sweep | Move to

Easter
To: Sally H

Hi Sally
Mum's banned us from contributing to the 'chocolatisation' of Easter. Ha ha! You can help me eat the bilby. Liza

Question 4 What can you infer from Liza's reply to Sally? Choose all that apply.

A Liza loves to eat chocolate.
B Sally loves to eat chocolate.
C Liza will not buy Sally chocolate.
D Liza is not greedy.

STEP 3 **Read** the question. **Think** about what type of question it is. Work out what you need to do to answer it.

- This is an **inferring** question. The answer is not stated directly in the text. You can work out the answer by reading between the lines of Liza's email.

STEP 4 **Think** about the text. Remember what you have read and **visualised**.

- You can work out the answer using the clues in the text.

C is correct. You read *Mum's banned us from contributing to the 'chocolatisation' of Easter (see lines 50–51)*. You can infer that Liza will not buy Sally chocolates. **D** is correct. You read *You can help me eat the bilby (see lines 51–52)* and you can infer that Liza is happy to share the chocolate with her friend and that she is not a greedy person.

Check the other options to confirm why they are incorrect. There is nothing in the text to support inferences **A** or **B**.

Question 5 Why do you think Sally tells her friends she has a bilby for them?

....

....

STEP 3 **Read** the question. **Think** about what type of question it is. Work out what you need to do to answer it.

- This is an **inferring** question. The answer is not stated directly in the text. You can work out the answer by reading between the lines of Sally's emails to her friends and classmates.

STEP 4 **Think** about the text. Remember what you have read and **visualised**.

- You can work out the answer using the clues in the text.

Sally emails two people to advise them of her intention to give them each a gift. You might infer that she does this because she is keen to share the news of her gift with her friends and can't wait to surprise them. You might also infer that she hopes that by informing them that she has gifts for them, they will get her gifts in return. Either answer could be correct.

Question 6 *Sorry about my rant (line 13)*. Why do you think Aunty K says this?

....

....

....

STEP 3 **Read** the question. **Think** about what type of question it is. Work out what you need to do to answer it.

- This is an **inferring** question. The answer is not stated directly in the text. You need to read between the lines to **infer** the answer.

STEP 4 **Think** about the text. Remember what you have read and **visualised**.

- A *rant* is a long-winded talk someone gives when they feel passionate about a topic.

You should infer that Aunty K is passionate about the subject of money wasted on chocolates at Easter. She apologises to Liza and Emily for ranting at them because she is their Aunt and she didn't intend to spoil their happiness or excitement at Easter.

Use the **Step-by-step guide** on pages 44–47 to help you read the text and make **inferences** to answer the questions below. Circle the correct answers, write your answer on the lines or use extra paper.

Landmines

Landmines are bombs that are laid across an area of ground or hidden in the ground. They explode when someone steps on them or a vehicle drives over them. They are used during war or conflict because they are easy and cheap to lay. Landmines are a particularly brutal weapon because they kill and maim indiscriminately, injuring civilians, children and animals.

After a conflict has ended unexploded land mines need to be removed before the land can be returned to normal safe use. However, landmines are very difficult, dangerous and expensive to remove. In developing countries they are left lying around long after wars are over. Landmines kill and injure hundreds of people somewhere in the world every week. People commonly have feet and legs blown off or are blinded by shrapnel and mine fragments. People in developing countries sometimes take risks and use mined fields because of economic necessity.

It is estimated that there are currently 100 million landmines in the ground and 100 million more stockpiled in warehouses around the world. Many countries, such as Australia, are signatories to an international convention against landmine use (the Convention on the Prohibition of the Use, Stockpiling, Production and Transfer of Anti-Personnel Mines and on their Destruction, 1997, also known as the Mine Ban Treaty) but some countries (not signatories to the Convention) are still producing landmines.

Humanitarian demining is a term used to refer to the removal of mines from land or waterways. Humanitarian demining is a time-consuming job because the area needs to be totally safe before local people can start to use it again. Demining typically involves metal detectors, mine detection dogs and specifically designed vehicles. The mine detection armour-plated vehicles drive back and forth across an area using a huge rotating barrel to pound the land and set off any explosive devices. The driver sits well back and is heavily protected.

An important aspect of the humanitarian effort is educating people to stay out of any area suspected of having landmines until the area is officially declared safe. Humanitarian groups also provide prosthetic limbs and other medical support.

1. What might *normal safe use* (line 8) be in an area cleared of landmine? Choose all that apply.
   - **A** growing food
   - **B** as a transport route
   - **C** grazing livestock
   - **D** removal of mines from waterways

2. Why would countries produce landmines? Choose all that apply.
   - **A** to stockpile them in warehouses
   - **B** to use in war or conflict
   - **C** to sell to other countries
   - **D** to sell to their enemies

3. What is the worst thing about landmines?
   - **A** They remain after conflict is finished.
   - **B** They kill and maim civilians and children.
   - **C** They are sneaky and hidden.
   - **D** They make lands unusable.

4. A mine detection vehicle clears mined fields by:
   - **A** carrying mine detection dogs to the site.
   - **B** finding the mines so they can be deactivated.
   - **C** blowing up the mines.
   - **D** identifying the placement of mines by driving back and forth.

5. *People in developing countries sometimes take risks and use mined fields because of economic necessity.* (lines 11–12)

   What does this imply?

   ....

   ....

6. Why would countries like Australia sign a convention on the prohibition of landmines? Write your answer on extra paper.

Answers and explanations on p. 102

Inferring questions

Use the **Step-by-step guide** on pages 44–47 to help you read the text and make **inferences** to answer the questions below. Circle the correct answers, write your answer on the lines or use extra paper.

Palm oil

Lily Wong (age 12) spoke at her school assembly about being an ethical consumer.

Good morning. My topic is sustainable palm oil.

Palm oil is a vegetable oil. It is used in thousands of products including shampoo, ice cream, margarine, chips, biscuits, toothpaste, chocolate, lipstick and candles. It's the most widely used vegetable oil in the entire world because the oil palm tree is quicker and cheaper to grow than other oil-producing plants.

The problem with palm oil is that oil palm trees grow where rainforests grow so large areas of rainforest in Indonesia and Malaysia have been cleared indiscriminately and the land converted to palm oil plantations. This has led to large-scale habitat loss for endangered species like orang-utans, rhinos, elephants and tigers. It has also meant that some indigenous people have had their land and livelihoods taken from them and sometimes also their homes.

The solution to deforestation is to grow palm oil sustainably. This would mean that no more wild forests are chopped down. Manufacturers that use certified sustainable palm oil in their products can label their products with the palm tree logo that states 'Certified Sustainable Palm Oil' and has RSPO certification. RSPO stands for 'Roundtable on Sustainable Palm Oil'. As well as making sure the palm oil is sustainably sourced the RSPO certification ensures that traditional landowners' interests are protected, that workers' rights are respected and that other aspects of the environment are safeguarded, including reducing the use of pesticides.

Yet another problem associated with palm oil use is the fact that many manufacturers that use palm oil don't label it on their packaging as palm oil. The product labels just say 'vegetable oil', so consumers don't even know that they are buying palm oil. The only way to be sure is for government to pass legislation that forces companies to label their products properly and for consumers to use their purchasing power to buy products that have RSPO certification.

Become an ethical consumer. Find out how your products are sourced or made, and tell companies to do the right thing environmentally or you won't buy their products.

1 Why do manufacturers need to use palm oil?

- **A** It's the most widely used vegetable oil in the entire world.
- **B** It is important for a range of products.
- **C** It grows quickly and cheaply.
- **D** It's more sustainable than other oils.

2 How does palm oil hurt rhinos? Choose all that apply.

- **A** It is poisonous to rhinos if they eat it.
- **B** Palm oil plantations have replaced rhino habitats.
- **C** People don't leave enough food for rhinos in the rainforest.
- **D** Palm oil trees grow all over the rainforest habitats.

3 What can you infer about Lily's family's attitude to grocery shopping? Choose all that apply.

- **A** They don't shop in supermarkets.
- **B** They read product labels.
- **C** They try to buy sustainable products.
- **D** They like to buy shampoo, ice cream, margarine, chips, biscuits, chocolate, lipstick and candles.

4 What does Lily suggest her listeners do to help wildlife? Choose all that apply.

- **A** Donate money to wildlife charities.
- **B** Check labels and shop for products that don't use non-certified palm oil.
- **C** Use products labelled RSPO.
- **D** Only buy products that use canola oil.

5 What does Lily say has caused deforestation in Indonesia and Malaysia?

....

....

6 How does product-labelling impact on the environment? Write your answer on extra paper.

Answers and explanations on pp. 102–103

Use the **Step-by-step guide** on pages 44–47 to help you read the text and make **inferences** to answer the questions below. Circle the correct answers or write your answer on the lines.

THE STIRLING CHRONICLE

Giant slain, goose gone!

Police are searching for a 12-year-old boy wanted in connection with the slaying of a giant late yesterday. The giant was descending a tree when the tree was felled. The giant died instantly. Police have confiscated an axe found at the scene and are having it tested for fingerprints. Police suspect that the tree was felled deliberately to kill the giant and would like to speak with a boy known only as Jack. Witnesses say they saw Jack running from the scene with a goose tucked under his arm.

Jack's mother is distraught. She says her son is a gentle, loving boy and not a giant killer. "He wouldn't hurt a fly," she said, "but he was obsessed with that tree, claiming it would solve all our financial problems and that he would be able to care for me better. I don't know where he could be hiding. I'd tell the police if I knew he was hiding in the cupboard."

A news crew in a helicopter interviewed the giant's wife who accused Jack of stealing her favourite pet goose and offered a reward for the goose's return. She commented, "Jack kept turning up on my doorstep. I gave him some food because he looked hungry. I felt sorry for him and look how he has repaid my kindness. I think he was after my goose the whole time. My husband warned me. He said Jack smelt funny. I should have listened to him. I am very upset. I miss my goose dreadfully."

Jack's neighbours report seeing a large bean tree growing from Jack's front yard over recent weeks. Emma Wishbone, who lives two doors down from where the giant died, stated "It was like the tree grew overnight. We went to bed and everything was normal. The next morning I took my little dog Walter for a walk and there was this enormous tree. The top of it was in the clouds."

Jack's mother insists Jack is a quiet boy who always does what he's told except when he doesn't. She refused an extended television interview, saying she had to go and buy goose food.

1 How did the giant die?

A He was killed with an axe.
B A tree fell on him.
C He fell to the ground.
D He was descending a tree.

2 What is the giant's wife's main concern?

A The giant is dead.
B Jack took advantage of her kindness.
C She should have listened to her husband.
D Her goose is gone.

3 What do you think has happened to Jack?

A He has run away with the goose.
B He is hiding at home.
C He has climbed back up the tree to search the giant's home for treasures.
D He has been murdered.

4 What did the giant think of Jack?

A He liked him.
B He wanted to be his friend.
C He didn't trust him.
D He was frightened of him.

5 What do you think motivated Jack?

A He hated the giant.
B He hated the giant's wife.
C He loved his mother.
D He loved the goose.

6 What might Jack say to police? Explain the reason for your answer.

....

....

....

Answers and explanations on p. 103

Inferring questions

Use the **Step-by-step guide** on pages 44–47 to help you read the text and make **inferences** to answer the questions below. Circle the correct answers and write your answer on the lines or on extra paper.

My grandparents

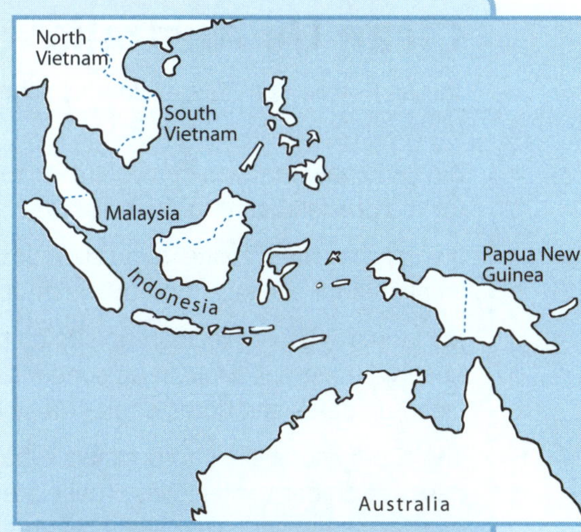

The map shows Vietnam split into North and South. In 1976 North and South Vietnam reunited as the Socialist Republic of Vietnam.

My grandparents are my heroes. They came to Australia from Vietnam in 1977 when they were in their early twenties. My father came with them but he was only three years old at the time so he doesn't really remember anything. My grandparents fled from Vietnam because they were fearful about life in Saigon after the fall of the South Vietnamese Government in 1975. They lived in a refugee camp in Malaysia for eighteen months before being permitted to immigrate to Australia.

My grandparents settled in Sydney and have worked hard since their arrival in Australia to make sure their two sons have a good life and a good education. My dad became a pharmacist and his brother is a doctor. I think that is so amazing! My grandparents are Buddhist and every day they tell their sons to do good things and create a bright future. They are extremely proud of both their sons. My dad is the eldest so he is responsible for the welfare of his parents and will look after them dutifully in their old age.

There is a strong and vibrant Vietnamese community in Sydney, but my grandparents told me that when they first arrived in Australia it was very difficult. They spoke no English and had no possessions. They said that many Australian people helped them settle so they do feel very fortunate. They had access to English language classes, settlement services and other migrant services.

My family is proud of its Vietnamese heritage. The most important celebration of the year for us is Tết or Vietnamese New Year. Tết is celebrated on the same day as Chinese New Year. My family starts cleaning the house and cooking special foods at least two weeks before Tết. We always spend New Year's Day with the whole family. We are given new clothes to wear. Our home is filled with the wonderful smells of flowers and foods. My parents and grandparents and uncle give me 'lucky money'. I love it.

Tam, Age 12

1 Where was the writer's father born?

A 1975
B Australia
C Vietnam
D Malaysia

2 Why did the writer's grandparents move to Australia?

A They wanted their sons to become doctors or pharmacists.
B They wanted a better future.
C They wanted to be looked after in their old age.
D They didn't like the refugee camp in Malaysia.

3 *My parents and grandparents and uncle give me 'lucky money'.* **(line 27)**

Why is it called 'lucky money'?

A You are lucky to be given money.
B It is given at New Year for good luck.
C They kiss it to make it lucky.
D It's money they found so it was lucky.

4 What is implied by the custom of cleaning the house for New Year?

A so the house is clean for guests
B because the whole family visits
C to get every family member doing jobs
D so that the year starts with a clean slate

5 How do the writer's grandparents show pride in their heritage?

....

....

....

6 Why does the writer refer to his grandparents as heroes? Write your answer on extra paper.

Answers and explanations on pp. 103–104

Inferring questions

Use the **Step-by-step guide** on pages 44–47 to help you read the text and make **inferences** to answer the questions below. Circle the correct answers or write your answer on the lines.

Clean Up Australia

Jordan Potter, age 12, spoke at his school assembly about volunteering. The following text is a transcript of his speech.

Did you know that you can volunteer to help clean up Australia any time you like? You don't have to wait for the official Clean Up Australia Day.

If you go on the website www.cleanupaustraliaday.org.au you can join a volunteer clean-up group in your local area for a special one-off clean-up project or for scheduled regular clean-ups.

My Mum registered a clean-up site on behalf of her netball club. Because she registered the group she became the group's 'clean-up supervisor'. She received a Clean Up Kit in the post. She advertised our clean-up dates and times on the Clean Up Australia Day website, inviting others to join us.

The supervisor's job is to organise rubbish collection with the local council and to make sure everyone has rubbish bags and gloves. These are provided in the Clean Up Kit. The kit also included recycling bags, a supervisor's vest, volunteer registration forms and safety information. Mum also requested a sharps container.

We clean up at the beach near my home on the second and fourth Saturdays of the month from 4 pm till 6 pm (3 pm to 5 pm during daylight savings times). Twenty-eight people are registered volunteers for our site. We clean up along the beach, the dunes, paths and walkways. It's very upsetting to see how much rubbish accumulates in the environment each fortnight.

Before the clean-up starts mum gets everyone to sign on and then she gives a safety briefing to warn people about risks like snakes and spiders, and she tells people not to handle dangerous items like syringes. Mum is a fanatic about sun safety so she takes sunscreen and reminds people that they should 'slip, slop, slap and slide'. Volunteers are also advised to wear sturdy shoes and drink plenty of water.

After each session mum submits a report, the signed volunteer forms and any accident or incident reports from the day. We sometimes send in photos too.

After Clean Up Saturdays we always have an easy dinner at home, usually home-made pizzas and salad.

If you have a site you think needs cleaning up you can register it, as an individual or for your group, school, class, club or organisation. It is fun and you meet people and it's a really good cause.

1 How did Jordan get involved in Clean Up Australia?

A because of the netball club
B because his mum did
C to meet people
D it's a really good cause

2 How does Jordan feel about volunteering?

A annoyed **B** happy
C bored **D** upset

3 What can you infer about Jordan?

A He annoys people in the clean-up group.
B He is a show-off.
C He is bossy.
D He likes to share his enthusiasm.

4 What can you infer about the twenty-eight people who registered for Jordan's site?

A They are from Mum's netball club.
B They have a lot of free time.
C They care about the environment.
D They are all Mum's friends.

5 What can you infer about Jordan's mother? Choose all that apply.

A She's a good organiser.
B She is confident in public speaking.
C She likes to be in charge.
D She tries to keep fit.

6 *It's very upsetting to see how much rubbish accumulates in the environment each fortnight.* **(lines 17–18)**

What does Jordan imply in this statement?

....

....

....

Answers and explanations on pp. 104–105

Use the **Step-by-step guide** on pages 44–47 to help you read the text and make **inferences** to answer the questions below. Circle the correct answers or write your answer on the lines.

Camping with Grandpa

Last school holidays I went on a camping holiday with my family: Grandpa and his new girlfriend Deborah, my mum and dad, and my younger sister Hayley. It was Deborah's first camping trip ever!

My grandpa rented two camping sites in the national park. People book it twelve months in advance to get the same site every year at the same time. Grandpa has been camping there every September for at least 15 years so he knows everyone. The national park is a great location. There's a short track through the scrub to the beach.

Grandpa set up his caravan and annexe, then Mum and Dad set up our tent on the site next to Grandpa's. Mum, Dad, Hayley and I have sleeping bags and inflatable mattresses. Grandpa has a lot of gear. His annexe has roll-down mosquito screens. He has an aluminium fold-up dining table and six folding chairs, a gas BBQ with a hood as well as a three-burner stove. Mum says camping with Grandpa could never be described as 'roughing it'. She says Grandpa goes glamping rather than camping.

Grandpa loves fishing. He took Deborah and Hayley fishing in the dinghy one day while Mum, Dad and I went surfing. Deborah caught a few bream and threw them back. Grandpa accidently caught a stingray which he said was difficult to set free but eventually he got it off the hook and it swam safely away. My sister caught seaweed.

A kangaroo came into our tent late one afternoon and started rustling through a bag of food. I would have liked to pat it but Mum said you have to be careful with wild animals. She shooed it off. After that we stored the food bag in the caravan.

Mira, age 12

1 *Grandpa and his new girlfriend …* **(line 3)** What does this imply?

- **A** that Grandma has died
- **B** that Grandpa has had previous girlfriends
- **C** that Grandpa is quite young
- **D** that Grandpa gets lonely on his own

2 *Mum says camping with Grandpa could never be described as 'roughing it'.* **(lines 15–16)** What does this imply?

- **A** Grandpa has a lot of gear.
- **B** Grandpa has most of the comforts of home when he goes camping.
- **C** Grandpa has a spirit of adventure.
- **D** Grandpa sleeps under the stars.

3 What can you infer about Grandpa's attitude to camping?

- **A** He likes roughing it.
- **B** He likes solitude.
- **C** He likes to be well set-up and comfortable.
- **D** This is a new way of holidaying for him.

4 What can you infer about meals when camping with Grandpa?

- **A** Grandpa likes to cook and eat.
- **B** Grandpa eats everything that people cook for him.
- **C** Grandpa usually catches his own fish to cook.
- **D** Grandpa doesn't enjoy cooking.

5 Why would mum have said you have to be careful with wild animals?

- **A** The kangaroo was searching for food.
- **B** You can't predict what a wild animal will do if it's startled or frightened.
- **C** Wild animals don't like people in the national parks.
- **D** You might catch a disease or germs.

6 *It was Deborah's first camping trip ever!* **(lines 4–5)** What does this imply about the writer?

....

....

....

Answers and explanations on p. 105

Inferring questions

Use the **Step-by-step guide** on pages 44–47 to help you read the text and make **inferences** to answer the questions below. Circle the correct answers or write your answer on extra paper.

Aliens attack Earth!

Giant aliens are attacking major cities across the globe and stretching giant webs across whole suburbs.

Artist sketch

In a coordinated attack from the aliens, every major city on Earth was hit at the same time, 5am AEST yesterday. Space craft hovered above the cities spewing out giant gossamer webs. At the same time all military installations were blanketed with the sticky webs.

Television broadcasts have been interrupted. At this stage news from the major cities is sporadic and coming via the internet and social network sites only.

Available information suggests that the aliens look like giant spiders. They stand two storeys tall. Their heads have eight eyes in a circle. They have a thorax with eight legs, and an oversized abdomen. Eyewitness reports suggest the aliens seem to have an exoskeleton made of resin, wax or a plastic-like substance. Twitter traffic from around the world largely confirms this description.

Scientists have yet to determine whether these spiders are an intelligent life form themselves or merely a method of transport and destruction operated by aliens either internally or by remote control.

All attempts by international defence forces to stop the spiders have failed. All attempts at communication with the spiders have also failed at this stage.

World leaders are urging people to remain calm and refrain from civil unrest, raiding and looting. Harsh penalties will apply for crimes committed while Earth is under attack.

So far there are no confirmed deaths directly attributed to the aliens.

1 What do *attack, attacking* and *destruction* imply? Choose all that apply.

- **A** People should be very frightened.
- **B** The aliens intend to destroy Earth.
- **C** The aliens are killing people.
- **D** The aliens might be on Earth to make friends.

2 What does *largely confirms* (line 22) imply?

- **A** Witnesses confirm that the aliens are large.
- **B** Most witnesses describe the aliens the same way.
- **C** Every eyewitness says the same thing about the aliens.
- **D** Twitter users have confirmed what the aliens look like.

3 What does *at this stage* (line 12) imply?

- **A** It is impossible to communicate with the aliens.
- **B** The aliens have no desire to communicate.
- **C** Humans will continue attempting to communicate with the aliens.
- **D** Humans will never know how to communicate with aliens.

4 Regarding the law, the text implies that

- **A** people are allowed to break the law when aliens attack.
- **B** the police have to shut down criminals.
- **C** criminals will help the aliens steal from Earthlings.
- **D** people commit crimes when they think they can get away with it.

5 *Scientists have yet to determine* (line 24) means that scientists

- **A** are determined to find out more about the aliens.
- **B** are determined to examine the spiders.
- **C** haven't yet decided how to capture a spider.
- **D** haven't been able to prove anything about the spiders.

6 What does the final paragraph imply? Write your answer on extra paper.

Answers and explanations on pp. 105–106

Use the **Step-by-step guide** on pages 44–47 to help you read the text and make **inferences** to answer the questions below. Circle the correct answers or write your answer on the lines.

Celebrity interview

Interviewer: Welcome to the program, Kirra Lee.

Kirra Lee: Thank you. It's a pleasure to be here.

Interviewer: Firstly I'd like to ask you: how do you feel about your fame?

Kirra: Being famous is a huge responsibility. I feel I owe it to my fans—and their parents—to be a positive role model. I try not to take my success for granted. I've been lucky but I do also work very hard.

Interviewer: Many of your songs have social or environmental messages …

Kirra: Yes. One thing I can't accept is discrimination. My brother and I suffered because of racism at school. One particular boy continually made racist remarks about us. And you know what? When the school contacted his parents they too made racist comments about First Nations Australians. My songs share my opinions about issues such as discrimination and prejudice. I think the lyrics resonate with young people from all walks of life.

Interviewer: Were your school experiences the inspiration for your song 'Walk in my Shoes'?

Kirra: I believe that you can't make judgements about a person's life unless you've walked in their shoes. You don't know what a person's been through or what makes them behave the way they do unless you can empathise with them—put yourself in their shoes. I think everyone could use a little more empathy and compassion in their lives. Everyone is so judgemental and so quick to condemn. That's why my lyrics say 'Walk in my shoes. Try being me. Feel what I feel. Be me for a day.'

Interviewer: Do you think you use your fame wisely?

Kirra: I try. I have particular charities that are close to my heart such as children's charities. I believe education is the key to everything. Education can help lift people out of poverty. If we can educate children then they can have better lives and it will be a better future for everyone. I like to help the Red Cross in Australia and overseas, especially for its humanitarian work in countries where there is conflict.

Interviewer: Kirra Lee, thank you for your time and your candid responses today.

Kirra: Thank you for having me on your program.

1 Why is Kirra famous?
- **A** She broke the law.
- **B** She is a celebrity.
- **C** She is a singer.
- **D** She appears on television.

2 You can infer that Kirra
- **A** had problems at school.
- **B** loved school.
- **C** did well at school.
- **D** left school at a young age.

3 Which statements are likely to be true? Choose all that apply.
- **A** Kirra regularly gets into trouble with police.
- **B** Kirra takes her career seriously.
- **C** Kirra plays guitar as well as sings.
- **D** Kirra says her success is all due to luck.

4 You can infer that Kirra
- **A** lives in Sydney.
- **B** is a First Australian.
- **C** is American.
- **D** lives overseas.

5 What does the interviewer mean by *candid responses* (line 51)?
- **A** secretive
- **B** lengthy and thorough
- **C** entertaining
- **D** open and honest

6 Kirra's song 'Walk in my Shoes' has a social message. Name five other topics Kirra might sing about.

....

....

....

....

Answers and explanations on pp. 106–107

Step-by-step guide to **language** questions

Language questions involve examining how language is used in a text.

Use this **Step-by-step guide** to help you read the text and examine the way **language** is used to answer the questions below. Circle the correct answers or draw your answers in the box.

STEP 1	**Skim** the text to see what it is about and how it is organised.	**Read** the title, *White Fang*. Look at the illustrations. Notice that the text is written in paragraphs. Make **predictions** about the subject and purpose of the text.
STEP 2	**Read** the text. **Monitor** your reading to make sure you understand it.	**Visualise** and **connect** with the ideas in the text**. Think** about what you already know about the subject and the type of text, a narrative. Make **predictions.** Make **inferences**. Reflect on meanings and make **judgements**.

White Fang

In advance of the dogs, on wide snowshoes, toiled a man. At the rear of the sled toiled a second man. On the sled, in the box, lay a third man whose toil was over, a man whom the Wild had conquered and beaten down until he would never move nor struggle again. It is not the way of the Wild to like movement. Life is an offence to it, for life is movement; and the Wild aims always to destroy movement. It freezes the water to prevent it running to the sea; it drives the sap out of the trees till they are frozen to their mighty hearts; and most ferociously and terribly of all does the Wild harry and crush into submission man—man who is the most restless of life, ever in revolt against the dictum that all movement must in the end come to the cessation of movement.

But at front and rear, unawed and indomitable, toiled the two men who were not yet dead. Their bodies were covered with fur and soft-tanned leather. Eyelashes and cheeks and lips were so coated with the crystals from their frozen breath that their faces were not discernible. This gave them the seeming of ghostly masques, undertakers in a spectral world at the funeral of some ghost. But under it all they were men, penetrating the land of desolation and mockery and silence, puny adventurers bent on colossal adventure, pitting themselves against the might of a world as remote and alien and pulseless as the abysses of space.

Extract from *White Fang* by Jack London, 1906, Chapter 1

Question 1 **What were the men wearing?**

A snowshoes

B snowshoes, fur and leather

C snowshoes, warm coats, warm hats and scarves

D masques like ghosts

STEP 3	**Read** the question. **Think** about what type of question it is. Work out what you need to do to answer it.	This is a **language** question. You need to think about the meanings of the words and phrases used in the text to work out the answer.

STEP		
STEP 4	**Think** about the text. Remember what you have read and **visualised**.	**Re-read** the text if necessary, and make sure you form a mental picture of the men. The parts of the text that tell you what the men are wearing are in paragraph one (*In advance of the dogs, on wide snowshoes*) and paragraph two (*Their bodies were covered with fur and soft-tanned leather*).

B is correct.

Check the other options to confirm why they are incorrect. **A** and **C** are each only partly incorrect. You could presume that the men were probably wearing hats of some kind but the text does not specifically say that the men were wearing hats and scarves, so be careful about making assumptions that aren't fully supported by the text. **D** is incorrect. The men were not wearing ghost-like masques (masks).

Question 2 Why were the faces of the men *not discernible* (*line 18*)?

A Their eyelashes and cheeks and lips were covered by their coat collars.

B They were on a sled in the Wild.

C They looked like ghosts.

D They had ice hanging off their eyelashes, cheeks and lips.

STEP		
STEP 3	**Read** the question. **Think** about what type of question it is. Work out what you need to do to answer it.	This is a **language** question. You need to **think** about the meanings of the words and phrases used in the text to work out the answer.
STEP 4	**Think** about the text. Remember what you have read and **visualised**.	**Scan** the text to find the key words *not discernible*. Re-read the part of the text around the words to understand the way the words are used.

D is correct. You read *Eyelashes and cheeks and lips were so coated with the crystals from their frozen breath that their faces were not discernible (see lines 16–18)*. You can work out that the men's breath was freezing in the cold and this ice was forming on the men's faces. The text says their faces were *so coated that* their faces were *not discernible*. It means that you could barely make out their features because they were covered with ice.

Check the other options to confirm why they are incorrect. **A** is not true in the text. **B** is true in the text but not the reason their faces were not discernible. **C** is partially true, as the men were ghost-like in appearance, but this is not the reason their faces were *not discernible*.

Question 3 Choose the description for the two men that best fits the meaning of the extract.

A not yet dead **B** puny adventurers **C** frozen toilers **D** restless and weary

STEP		
STEP 3	**Read** the question. **Think** about what type of question it is. Work out what you need to do to answer it.	This is a **language** question. You need to **think** about the meaning of the whole text and the way the men are described to work out the answer.
STEP 4	**Think** about the text. Remember what you have read and **visualised**.	**Scan** the text to find the relevant parts. You might need to re-read the text.

B is correct. These words can be found in the final paragraph: *puny adventurers bent on colossal adventure, pitting themselves against the might of a world (see lines 21–22)*. The men faced harsh circumstances but were toiling on. They were tiny in an immense lifeless wilderness.

Check the other options to confirm why they are incorrect. **A** is true in that the men *were not yet dead (see line 15)* but it is not the best description of the men under their circumstances. **C** is partially true in that the men were toiling and they were in a frozen wilderness, but they were not frozen themselves. **D** is partially correct: you might assume that the men were weary but they are not described as 'restless'.

Language questions involve examining how language is used in a text.

White Fang

In advance of the dogs, on wide snowshoes, toiled a man. At the rear of the sled toiled a second man. On the sled, in the box, lay a third man whose toil was over, a man whom the Wild had conquered and beaten down until he would never move nor struggle again. It is not the way of the Wild to like movement. Life is an offence to it, for life is movement; and the Wild aims always to destroy movement. It freezes the water to prevent it running to the sea; it drives the sap out of the trees till they are frozen to their mighty hearts; and most ferociously and terribly of all does the Wild harry and crush into submission man—man who is the most restless of life, ever in revolt against the dictum that all movement must in the end come to the cessation of movement.

But at front and rear, unawed and indomitable, toiled the two men who were not yet dead. Their bodies were covered with fur and soft-tanned leather. Eyelashes and cheeks and lips were so coated with the crystals from their frozen breath that their faces were not discernible. This gave them the seeming of ghostly masques, undertakers in a spectral world at the funeral of some ghost. But under it all they were men, penetrating the land of desolation and mockery and silence, puny adventurers bent on colossal adventure, pitting themselves against the might of a world as remote and alien and pulseless as the abysses of space.

Extract from *White Fang* by Jack London, 1906, Chapter 1

Question 4 **The attitude of the two toiling men is described as *indomitable* (line 14). What does this mean?**

A undefeated	**B** useless	**C** dominating	**D** ready to give up

STEP 3	**Read** the question. **Think** about what type of question it is. Work out what you need to do to answer it.	This is a **language** question. You need to **think** about the meanings of the words and phrases used in the text to work out the answer.
STEP 4	**Think** about the text. Remember what you have read and **visualised**.	**Scan** the text to find the relevant parts and the key word *indomitable*.

A is correct. Re-read the part of the text around the words to understand the way the word is used: *But at front and rear, unawed and indomitable, toiled the two men who were not yet dead (see lines 14–15).* The root or base of the word *indomitable* is from the word family 'dominate/dominated/dominating', which are words that deal with controlling. The prefix *in-* is a negative prefix. Placed at the front of a word it means 'without' or 'not'. So you can work out that *indomitable* must mean something like 'not able to be controlled'. Read the answer options and decide which one comes closest in meaning to your understanding of the word *indomitable.*

Check the other options to confirm why they are incorrect. **B** and **C** are incorrect because you can work out that the men aren't useless or ready to give up. You can work out that **C** is incorrect because of the prefix *in-*. *Indomitable* cannot mean 'dominating'. Domitable actually means 'able to be tamed or controlled', so *indomitable* in the context of the story extract means that the men can't be tamed or subdued by nature; they simple toil on.

Question 5 ... *as remote and alien and pulseless as the abysses of space* (*line 22*). What does this simile mean?

A The men are a long way from anywhere.
B Nothing lives in the desolate area.
C The men are in a far-off, lifeless area of wilderness.
D The third man's toil is over as he has no pulse.

STEP 3 **Read** the question. **Think** about what type of question it is. Work out what you need to do to answer it.

- This is a **language** question. You need to **think** about the meanings of the words and phrases used in the text to work out the answer.

STEP 4 **Think** about the text. Remember what you have read and **visualised**.

- **Scan** the text to find the relevant parts and the simile from the question. Re-read that section of text.

C is correct. The simile compares outer space with the landscape of the *Wild* (*see line 4*): both are far from civilisation (*remote*); both are absent of living creatures (*pulseless*); and both are foreign (*alien*) environments to people.

Check the other options to confirm why they are incorrect. **A** and **B** are both partly correct but are not the best answers. **D** is true in the text but is not the meaning of the simile.

Question 6 Draw the scene as it is described.

STEP 3 **Read** the question. **Think** about what type of question it is. Work out what you need to do to answer it.

- This is a **language** question. You need to **think** about the meanings of the words and phrases used in the text to work out the answer.

STEP 4 **Think** about the text. Remember what you have read and **visualised**.

- **Visualise** the scene described in the extract in your mind. **Think** about the meanings of the words used.

You should have drawn: the first man ahead of the dogs; the dogs pulling a sled with a box (coffin) on it; the second man at the rear of the sled; the rest of the scene should be empty because the author describes the frozen *Wild* as devoid of life. You read *Life is an offence to it, for life is movement; and the Wild aims always to destroy movement* (*see lines 6–8*).

Language questions

Use the **Step-by-step guide** on pages 56–59 to help you read the text and examine the way **language** is used to answer the questions below. Circle the correct answers or write your answer on the lines.

The man in a boy

The boy looked like his father
tall as a mountain ash,
centurion,
legs planted on the ground
solid and dependable.
At sixteen he hadn't even finished growing.
Big-hearted:
rescuing injured birds and lizards
he'd nurse them to health
or cart them to the vet
on his bicycle
mindful of the bumps along the way.
A smart boy.
A reader.
A thinker.
Not one to challenge or argue
but watchful,
eyes alert to hypocrites and bullies.
He could speak his mind
to defend an underdog—
someone or something
smaller or weaker.
That's who the boy was.
The boy was not his father.
Yet,
he'd taken to stooping,
his shoulders hunched
as if to hide
as if ashamed
not wanting to stand out.
Walk tall,
I'd admonish.
Be proud.
Wear your skin well.
It's not easy standing out,
he'd say.
It's not easy being different.
No it's not.
But
don't let others
define who you are.
You are you.
You are not your father.
March to your own drum.

by Tanya Dalgleish

1 What might the boy get angry about?

A injured animals
B his height
C his father
D bullies

2 What does *admonish* (line 33) mean?

A scold
B yell
C praise
D approve

3 The narrator believes the boy to be

A kind but loud.
B smart but proud.
C watchful but thoughtless.
D solid but gentle.

4 *March to your own drum.* (line 45)

What does this mean?

A Listen to the beat of your footsteps.
B Play the drums and march to the beat.
C Be true to yourself.
D Don't let others call you names.

5 How does the narrator feel about the boy?

A annoyed
B frustrated
C ashamed
D proud

6 How does the narrator feel about the boy's father? Explain.

....

....

....

....

....

....

Answers and explanations on p. 107

Language questions

Use the **Step-by-step guide** on pages 56–59 to help you read the text and examine the way **language** is used to answer the questions below. Circle the correct answers or write your answers on the lines.

Enviro-holidays

Are you passionate about the environment?

Enviro-holidays

Travel with a conscience and help make the world a better place.

Program:

Travel to Kun yuu tee nai CHANG Reserve in **Thailand**

Work in the rescue and rehabilitation of **elephants**

Stay from two weeks ($1800) to three months ($3500). Fees for a good cause: animal rescues, elephant medical care, habitat restoration, and supporting local communities in education and conservation.

Just book and pay for your own return flight.

All meals provided.

For anyone over 18.

You'll love the locals

Experience the real Thailand. Accommodation is homestay so you get to live with the locals.

Meet like-minded people from around the world, all enthusiastically helping elephants.

We'll meet you at the airport and take you to the Wildlife Centre. You'll be trained to support the work of vets, rangers and wildlife carers.

Testimonials

Tui (New Zealand): I spent a month in 2014. Worked hard and loved every minute. The elephants are wonderful. Staff do a great job. Met people from all over the world. Breaks my heart that elephant habitats are shrinking.

Jarrod (USA): Definitely recommend this type of holiday. So worthwhile.

Sebastiaan (the Netherlands): Enviro-holidays staff were really helpful. Elephants amazing.

Contact us at www.enviro-holidays.com
ENVIRO-HOLIDAYS
Make a difference to wildlife on your next holiday!

1 *We'll meet you at the airport.* (line 22)
Who is *we* in *we'll*?

- **A** Enviro-holidays staff
- **B** the people who wrote the advertisement
- **C** other holiday travellers
- **D** Tui, Jarrod and Sebastiaan

2 What is a *testimonial*?

- **A** a test
- **B** a recommendation
- **C** advice
- **D** an advertisement

3 *Are you passionate about the environment?* (line 2) What is the purpose of this question? Choose all that apply.

- **A** to get the reader's attention
- **B** to promote environmental issues
- **C** to attract the interest of people who are interested in environmental issues
- **D** to make the reader want to read the advertisement

4 How long can you stay at Kun yuu tee nai CHANG?

- **A** two weeks or three months
- **B** any length of stay
- **C** any time less that 3 months
- **D** between two weeks and three months

5 Why do you have to pay a fee?

....

....

....

6 *Travel with a conscience …* (line 4)

What does this mean?

....

....

....

Answers and explanations on pp. 107–108

Language questions

Use the **Step-by-step guide** on pages 56–59 to help you read the text and examine the way **language** is used to answer the questions below. Circle the correct answers or write your answer on the lines.

1 Which of the following is true?

- **A** The supermarket cares about animals.
- **B** The products won't hurt animals.
- **C** The products were manufactured without hurting animals.
- **D** The products are all cruelty free.

2 Which of the following is most likely to be true? Super 'S' Supermarkets

- **A** only buy Fair Trade produce.
- **B** might stock some Fair Trade produce.
- **C** don't have Fair Trade products.
- **D** stock some Fair Trade products.

3 *Super 'S' Supermarkets discourage the use of pesticides in the production of our products.* (lines 24–27) What does this mean?

- **A** All products sold are pesticide free.
- **B** The supermarket encourages producers to avoid pesticides.
- **C** All products sold are chemical free.
- **D** The supermarket tells producers not to use pesticides.

4 What is the purpose of the text?

- **A** to make fun of an advertisement
- **B** to advertise a supermarket chain
- **C** to tell shoppers about sustainable shopping
- **D** to provide information about supermarkets

5 Which product is sold in the supermarkets?

- **A** pets
- **B** pesticides
- **C** plastic bags
- **D** reuseable bags

6 What is the impact of repeating the 's' sound in *The Super 'S' in Super 'S' Supermarket stands for Super Sustainable* (lines 7–8) and elsewhere in the ad?

....

....

....

....

....

Answers and explanations on pp. 108–109

Language questions

Use the **Step-by-step guide** on pages 56–59 to help you read the text and examine the way **language** is used to answer the questions below. Circle the correct answers or write your answers on the lines.

My sister

My little sister is spoilt rotten. She gets away with murder. She has Dad wrapped around her finger. If I had done or said some of the things that she does when I was her age I would have been in big trouble. Not her—she's Daddy's girl. She's three.

An example: Dad asked her to fetch his glasses from the kitchen. My sister said, "You've got legs. You get them." When he asked again, she said, "Benny's got legs. He can get them." Mum and Dad thought she was funny. I just thought she was rude and cheeky.

She is so spoilt. One night she had a bad dream. She woke Dad and said she dreamed that "Benny was foughting a witch." Mum and Dad let her sleep in their bed the rest of the night. I never slept in their bed—not that I would have wanted to.

One time at the beach after she'd been playing in the surf with mum, my sister whinged that an "octopus's tentacles" had bitten her. Dad laughed his head off. It wasn't that funny. She was obviously imagining that a blue-ringed octopus had bitten her. I knew that's what she thought as I'd done a project on venomous animals for school.

She likes to do homework when I do mine. She sits at the dinner table next to me and pretends to write pages of homework. It's just scribbled, pretend handwriting and random letters such as the letters in her name that she repeats for row after row. Mum says she's just trying to be like me but it drives me crazy when I'm trying to concentrate on my work.

She took her favourite book, *Animalia,* to Kindy this morning. It used to be mine. When Dad and I collected her from Kindy this afternoon a boy had taken her book out of her locker and was being really rough with the pages. She was sitting with him but I could tell she didn't like him having her book. I took the book off him and told him not to take other people's things and to treat books nicely. My sister looked very happy.

Later my Dad told me that my sister adores me. I guess that's pretty cool.

1 *She gets away with murder.* (line 2)

What does this mean?

- **A** She always gets into mischief.
- **B** She could kill someone and get away with it.
- **C** She could be a murderer and not go to jail.
- **D** She never gets into trouble even when being very naughty.

2 How does the sister feel about her brother?

- **A** She wants to be him.
- **B** She idolises him.
- **C** She is jealous of him.
- **D** She wants his attention all the time.

3 *wrapped around her finger* (line 2)

What does this mean?

- **A** The sister can tell Dad to do anything.
- **B** Dad will do whatever the sister asks of him.
- **C** The sister makes Dad bend and do exercises.
- **D** Dad will never be angry with the sister.

4 The narrator is

- **A** jealous, protective and proud.
- **B** hurt, angry and jealous.
- **C** resentful, envious and annoyed.
- **D** jealous, angry and loving.

5 *I guess that's pretty cool.* (line 24)

What does *that's* refer to?

....

....

6 *that an "octopus's tentacles" had bitten her* (lines 11–12)

Why did Dad think this was funny?

....

....

....

Answers and explanations on p. 109

Language questions

Use the **Step-by-step guide** on pages 56–59 to help you read the text and examine the way **language** is used to answer the questions below. Circle the correct answers or write your answers on the lines.

Uluru

Go there
but
don't go there.
Stand apart.
Reflect.
Do not trample;
cause erosion;
step on sacred ground.
Created
at the beginning of time.
Place of spirits:
ancestral beings.
9 k round 6 k down—
more hidden than in sight.
Monumental.
Wondrous.
Sandstone monolith.
Red with rusted iron.
Weathering.
Eroded.
By time, wind and rain.
By footsteps.
Constantly changing,
always the same.
Deceptively barren,
yet here are birds
and reptiles
—lizards, snakes, and frogs,
wallabies and kangaroos.
Some are few.
Some are threatened.
All connected to this land.
Plants, by the hundreds—
shrubs, flowers, grasses, fruits:
medicine, tools, fuel,
ornaments for ceremonies,
food.
A landscape filled with life.
If—you have the time to look
If—you have the eyes to see.
Anangu Country.
Taken and then handed back.
Central to culture
—a people's history:
follow the songlines.
Listen in the quiet.
Pay attention.
Try to understand.

by Tanya Dalgleish

1 *Go there / but / don't go there.* **(lines 2–4)**

What does the poet mean by this?

....

....

....

....

2 *Deceptively barren.* **(line 26)**

What does this mean?

A a dry red desert
B hidden creatures
C looks barren but actually isn't
D a barren area

3 What is the tone of the poem?

A respectful and awed
B playful and humorous
C serious and depressing
D excited and celebratory

4 *more hidden than in sight.* **(line 15)**

What does this mean?

....

....

....

5 What could the poet mean by *Constantly changing, / always the same.* **(lines 24–25)**

....

....

....

6 *If—you have the eyes to see.* **(line 41)**

What does the poet mean by this?

....

....

....

Answers and explanations on pp. 109–110

Language questions

Use the **Step-by-step guide** on pages 56–59 to help you read the text and examine the way **language** is used to answer the questions below. Circle the correct answers or write your answers on the lines.

Biosecurity is so important

Editorial, *The National Times,* March 20

Australia's biosecurity is worth protecting but it seems that the general public travelling into Australia has no understanding of the significance and value of Australia's unique environment.

People entering Australia from overseas, including residents returning after a holiday, have to be careful about animal and plant products they bring into the country. That includes food, timber products and seeds. Border protection is vitally important because pests and diseases brought here from other parts of the world can spread in Australia and destroy any number of agricultural industries as well as native flora and fauna. For example, foot and mouth disease is a disease of cloven-hoofed animals (cattle, sheep, pigs, and so on). If that disease gets into Australia it would be devastating for Australia's livestock industries. People entering Australia by plane or ship are asked by Department of Agriculture officials to declare if they've been on a farm or visited rural areas because they could be bringing back soil with foot and mouth disease virus in it on their shoes.

When you declare that you have in your possession the sorts of items the Department of Agiculture is concerned about, departmental officers check the items. Sometimes the items are declared OK. Sometimes you have to pay for them to be fumigated or irradiated. Sometimes the items are confiscated and destroyed. *That is how it should be!* People should never complain if their items are destroyed because they might have unwittingly caused a terrible plant or animal disease or pest to enter our country. People should support biosecurity measures instead of trying to hide plant or animal matter in their luggage.

Letter to the Editor, March 27

Harsher penalties for smugglers

In response to the Editorial 'Biosecurity is so important' (March 20) I'd like to suggest harsher penalties for people who put Australia's biodiversity at risk. I am sick and tired of reading about people who bring plant and animal matter into Australia and the Department of Agriculture only fines them a few hundred dollars. The law must get tougher on people who threaten our biosecurity.

Tom, Ryde

1 What does *fumigated* (line 22) mean?

- **A** soak in poison to kill pests and diseases
- **B** treat with toxic fumes to kill pests and diseases
- **C** treat with disinfectant to kill pests and diseases
- **D** treat with fumes from wood smoke to kill pests and diseases

2 Why would something be destroyed by Department of Agriculture officers?

- **A** because it has diseases
- **B** because it is illegal, dangerous or a biosecurity risk
- **C** because it was seized, either temporarily or permanently
- **D** because you are doing something wrong

3 Which of these is a cloven-hoofed animal?

- **A** bear
- **B** crocodile
- **C** goat
- **D** chicken

4 What is the tone of the Letter to the Editor?

- **A** outrage
- **B** sadness
- **C** horror
- **D** surprise

5 Why does the Editor state *That is how it should be!* (line 23)?

....

....

....

....

6 What is *biosecurity*?

....

....

....

....

....

Answers and explanations on p. 110

Language questions

Use the **Step-by-step guide** on pages 56–59 to help you read the text and examine the way **language** is used to answer the questions below. Circle the correct answers and write your answer on the lines or on extra paper.

Lost

"He ought to be home," said the old man, "without there's something amiss.
He only went to the Two-mile—he ought to be back by this.
He WOULD ride the Reckless filly, he WOULD have his wilful way;
And, here, he's not back at sundown and what will his mother say?

He was always his mother's idol, since ever his father died;
And there isn't a horse on the station that he isn't game to ride.
But that Reckless mare is vicious, and if once she gets away
He hasn't got strength to hold her and what will his mother say?"

The old man walked to the sliprail, and peered up the dark'ning track,
And looked and longed for the rider that would never more come back;
And the mother came and clutched him, with sudden, spasmodic fright:
"What has become of my Willie?—why isn't he home to-night?"

Away in the gloomy ranges, at the foot of an ironbark,
The bonnie, winsome laddie was lying stiff and stark;
For the Reckless mare had smashed him against a leaning limb,
And his comely face was battered, and his merry eyes were dim.

And the thoroughbred chestnut filly, the saddle beneath her flanks,
Was away like fire through the ranges to join the wild mob's ranks;
And a broken-hearted woman and an old man worn and grey
Were searching all night in the ranges till the sunrise brought the day.

And the mother kept feebly calling, with a hope that would not die,
"Willie! Where are you, Willie?" But how can the dead reply;
And hope died out with the daylight, and the darkness brought despair,
God pity the stricken mother, and answer the widow's prayer!

Though far and wide they sought him, they found not where he fell;
For the ranges held him precious, and guarded their treasure well.
The wattle blooms above him, and the blue bells blow close by,
And the brown bees buzz the secret, and the wild birds sing reply.

But the mother pined and faded, and cried, and took no rest,
And rode each day to the ranges on her hopeless, weary quest.
Seeking her loved one ever, she faded and pined away,
But with strength of her great affection she still sought every day.

"I know that sooner or later I shall find my boy," she said.
But she came not home one evening, and they found her lying dead,
And stamped on the poor pale features, as the spirit homeward pass'd,
Was an angel smile of gladness—she had found the boy at last.

by AB 'Banjo' Paterson

1 What does *without there's something amiss* *(lines 3–4)* mean?

- **A** Things are missing.
- **B** The old man missed seeing someone.
- **C** There's something wrong.
- **D** He ought to be home.

2 Who or what is the old man most concerned about in the poem?

- **A** himself
- **B** the mother
- **C** the boy, Willie
- **D** the Reckless mare

3 What is the *treasure* *(line 73)*?

- **A** precious
- **B** Willie
- **C** the wild horses
- **D** wattle blooms and bluebells

4 What is the old man's attitude towards Willie?

- **A** angry and annoyed
- **B** annoyed but concerned
- **C** worried and frightened
- **D** worried but hopeful

5 What does *an angel smile of gladness* *(lines 99–100)* mean?

....

6 Summarise each stanza of the poem. Then draw a storyboard. In your storyboard show that you have thought about close-ups, mid-shots and long shots as well as perspective and framing. Add dialogue if you wish. Use your own paper.

Answers and explanations on pp. 110–111

Language questions

Use the **Step-by-step guide** on pages 56–59 to help you read the text and examine the way **language** is used to answer the questions below. Circle the correct answers or write your answers on the lines.

Chief THINGS that are in the WORLD

One of the first picture books ever written for children is called *Orbis Sensualium Pictus*. It was written in 1658 to explain the 'Chief THINGS that are in the WORLD'. It was first used in schools in Germany.

Here are some extracts:

Living-Creatures
A living Creature liveth, perceiveth, moveth it self; is born, dieth, is nourished, and groweth, standeth, or sitteth, or lieth, or goeth.

Four-footed Beasts: and First those about the House
The Dog is keeper of the House.

The Cat riddeth the House of Mice.

The Ape and the Monkey are kept at home for delight.

Wild-Beasts
Wild Beasts have sharp paws, and teeth, and are flesh eaters.

The Head
In the Head are the Hair (which is combed with a Comb) two Ears, the Temples, and the Face. The Face are the Fore-head, both the Eyes, the Nose (with two Nostrils) the Mouth, the Cheeks, and the Chin. The Mouth is fenced with a Mustachio and Lips, a Tongue, a Palate and Teeth, in the Cheek-bone.

The Outward and Inward Senses
There are five outward Senses; The Eye, seeth Colours, what is white or black, green or blew, red or yellow.

The Ear heareth Sounds, both natural, Voices and Words; and artificial.

The Nose scenteth smells and stinks.

The Tongue, with the roof of the Mouth, tastes Savours, what is sweet or bitter, keen or biting, sower or harsh.

The Hand, by touching, discerneth the quantity and quality of things; the hot and cold, the moist and dry, the hard and soft, the smooth and rough, the heavy and light.

The inward Senses are three.

The Common Sense, under the forepart of the head, apprehendeth things taken from the outward senses.

The Phantasie, under the crown of the head judgeth of those things, thinketh and dreameth.

The Memory under the hinder part of the Head, layeth up every thing and fetcheth them out: it loseth some, and this is forgetfulness.

Sleep, is the rest of the Senses.

1 What purpose do the Ape and Monkey have?

A They are useful in the house.
B They are entertaining.
C They are dangerous.
D They are wild.

2 Choose all that apply. Why wouldn't a plant fit the definition of a *living Creature* (line 9)?

A It does not 'moveth it self'.
B It is not nourished.
C It does not 'dieth'.
D It cannot 'goeth'.

3 What does *apprehendeth* (line 45) mean in the text?

A dream
B make sense of things
C steal ideas for safekeeping
D worry

4 What does the Sense *Phantasie* (line 47) do?

A sleep **B** taste
C judge **D** forget things

5 What are the outward sensory receptors?

....

....

6 Explain how people's attitudes to cats and dogs have changed from 1658 to now?

....

....

....

....

Answers and explanations on pp. 111–112

Step-by-step guide to **judgement** questions

Judgement questions involve making judgements.

Use this **Step-by-step guide** to help you read the text and make **judgements** to answer the questions below. Circle the correct answers or write your answers on the lines.

STEP 1	**Skim** the text to see what it is about and how it is organised.	**Read** the title, *Childminding*. Look at the photograph. Notice the font style and the layout. Make **predictions** about the subject and purpose of the text.
STEP 2	**Read** the text. **Monitor** your reading to make sure you understand it.	**Visualise** and **connect** with the ideas in the text. **Think** about what you already know about the subject and the type of text, an advertising leaflet. Make **predictions**. Make **inferences.** Reflect on meanings and make **judgements**.

Childminding

CHEAP AND RELIABLE

Hello

My name is **Matt Buchanan**.

I live at number 17 Chester Street, not far from you. I am 14 years old and in Year 8 at North Canberra High School. I am writing to offer my services as a child minder. I am very responsible and reliable. I have been helping my mum look after my brother (age 10) and sister (age 7) since they were born.

I can look after your children for you on Wednesday, Saturday or Sunday nights after 6pm until late, and on Saturdays after 2pm. I can also help your children with their homework.

I work at Ben's Bakery, Arundel, on Tuesdays after school and from 9–5pm on Sundays. I play Aussie Rules on Saturday mornings and have training on Mondays and Thursdays so I am unavailable at those times.

Please give me a call on **6206 0919**. I am really keen.

I look forward to hearing from you.

Referees
Ms Angela Bingham (Head Teacher, North Canberra High School)
Mr Nigel Vukovich (AFL coach)
Mr Benjamin Dumas (Ben's Bakery, owner)
James and Subin Kwon (parents/clients)
Ms Lauren Buchanan (my mum)

Referees' contact details available on request. See reference attached.

Reference

To whom it may concern

I have known Matt Buchanan as a family friend and as his AFL coach since he was 4 years old. He is a very friendly and sensible boy. He does well at school and is a reliable member of our team. He is punctual at training sessions and is a popular team member.

I can confidently recommend him to any prospective employer. I am certain that he will fulfil his obligations to the best of his ability. I can be contacted on 1414 911823.

Kind regards
Nigel Vukovich, Coach

Question 1 Which word best describes Matt's letter? and Why did Matt choose to write the letter this way?

A formal | B friendly | C distant | D official

STEP 3 **Read** the question. **Think** about what type of question it is. Work out what you need to do to answer it.

- This is a **judgement** question. You need to find evidence in the text to **judge** the text and the reason Matt chose to write the letter like this. Note that this question is about the 'tenor' of the text. Tenor relates to the relationships between the people involved in a text; in this case the writer and his audience—his prospective employers.

STEP 4 **Think** about the text. Remember what you have read and **visualised**.

- **Scan** the text or re-read it if necessary. Look for evidence to help you make a judgement.

You can **judge** that the tenor of the text is **B**, friendly. It starts with *Hello (see line 3)*. It addresses the reader as *your* and *you—I can look after your children for you … (see line 9)* It sounds chatty: *Please give me a call … I am really keen (see line 15)*.

Check the other options to confirm why they are incorrect. Answers **A**, **B** and **C** are incorrect because formal (**A**), distant (**C**) and official (**D**) are the opposite of friendly. These kinds of letters would likely start with 'To whom it may concern'. You should judge that Matt chose to write the letter in this way because he wanted to sound friendly and appealing to parents.

Question 2 Which purposes does the text achieve? Choose all that apply.

A It introduces Matt.
B It provides information about Matt.
C It provides information about the times Matt is available.
D It helps readers judge that Matt is a reliable boy.

STEP 3 **Read** the question. **Think** about what type of question it is. Work out what you need to do to answer it.

- This is a **judgement** question. You need to **judge** how successful the text is in achieving the purpose of getting childminding work for Matt.

STEP 4 **Think** about the text. **Remember** what you have read and visualised.

- **Scan** the text or **re-read** it if necessary. Look for evidence to help you make a judgement.

You can **judge** that **A**, **B**, **C** and **D** are correct. The text successfully introduces Matt (**A**), provides some basic information about him (**B**), tells readers what times he is available to mind their children (**C**) and includes enough positive aspects about Matt to help readers judge that he seems a nice, reliable boy (**D**).

Question 3 What does the text make you think about Matt? Choose all that apply.

A He is ambitious and hardworking.
B He is unmotivated and boring.
C He is confident and outgoing.
D He is fun-loving and never serious.

STEP 3 **Read** the question. **Think** about what type of question it is. Work out what you need to do to answer it.

- This is a **judgement** question. You need to find evidence in the text to help you make judgements about Matt's character.

STEP 4 **Think** about the text. Remember what you have read and **visualised**.

- **Scan** the text or re-read it if necessary. Look for evidence to help you make judgements.

You can **judge** that **A** and **C** are correct. You read the information in the text about Matt's work schedule and the comments from the Head Teacher and the AFL coach and you can judge that Matt is both ambitious and hardworking (**A**). You read the information in the text that Matt has written about himself and that the Coach has written about him, as well as the people he lists as referees and you can judge that Matt is confident and outgoing (**C**).

Check the other options to confirm why they are incorrect. Answer **B** is incorrect because you can tell that Matt is highly motivated. The evidence is that he does well at school. He works at Ben's Bakery as well as at childminding. He is committed to his AFL team. **D** is incorrect. You might make the judgement that Matt seems like he is fun-loving because the coach says that he is a popular member of the AFL team but you cannot make the judgement that he is never serious. The evidence suggests that Matt is serious about his commitments.

Step-by-step guide to **judgement** questions *continued*

Judgement questions involve making judgements.

Childminding

CHEAP AND RELIABLE

Hello

My name is **Matt Buchanan**.

I live at number 17 Chester Street, not far from you. I am 14 years old and in Year 8 at North Canberra High School. I am writing to offer my services as a child minder. I am very responsible and reliable. I have been helping my mum look after my brother (age 10) and sister (age 7) since they were born.

I can look after your children for you on Wednesday, Saturday or Sunday nights after 6pm until late, and on Saturdays after 2pm. I can also help your children with their homework.

I work at Ben's Bakery, Arundel, on Tuesdays after school and from 9–5pm on Sundays. I play Aussie Rules on Saturday mornings and have training on Mondays and Thursdays so I am unavailable at those times.

Please give me a call on **6206 0919**. I am really keen.

I look forward to hearing from you.

Referees
Ms Angela Bingham (Head Teacher, North Canberra High School)
Mr Nigel Vukovich (AFL coach)
Mr Benjamin Dumas (Ben's Bakery, owner)
James and Subin Kwon (parents/clients)
Ms Lauren Buchanan (my mum)

Referees' contact details available on request. See reference attached.

Reference

To whom it may concern

I have known Matt Buchanan as a family friend and as his AFL coach since he was 4 years old. He is a very friendly and sensible boy. He does well at school and is a reliable member of our team. He is punctual at training sessions and is a popular team member.

I can confidently recommend him to any prospective employer. I am certain that he will fulfil his obligations to the best of his ability. I can be contacted on 1414 911823.

Kind regards
Nigel Vukovich, Coach

Question 4 **What does Matt want children's parents to think is most important about him?**

A He is a good AFL player.
B He is trustworthy and reliable.
C He has a brother (age 10) and sister (age 7).
D He is popular and friendly.

STEP 3 **Read** the question. **Think** about what type of question it is. Work out what you need to do to answer it.

- This is a **judgement** question. You need to find evidence in the text to **judge** what Matt thinks would be most important to parents (prospective childminding employers) reading his letter.

STEP (4)	**Think** about the text. Remember what you have read and **visualised**.	✪ **Scan** the text or re-read it if necessary. Look for evidence to help you make a **judgement**. You need to find evidence in the text to judge what sort of impression Matt most wants to make on prospective employers. Remember that these would be parents who have children that Matt can be paid to mind.

B is correct. Matt wants readers to believe he is trustworthy and reliable. He says *I am very responsible and reliable (see line 7)*. He cites his childminding experience with his siblings as evidence. *I have been helping my mum look after my brother (age 10) and sister (age 7) since they were born (see lines 7–8)*. He lists clients *James and Subin Kwong (see line 21)* as referees. He lists the Head Teacher at school, his bakery employer and his coach as referees. He tells readers his work schedule to prove that he is reliable and trustworthy.

Check the other options to confirm why they are incorrect. **A** is incorrect because this is not the most important thing that Matt wants parents to know about him. **C** is true and important but not the most important thing about Matt in relation to childminding work. **D** is incorrect. Children might think these qualities are important but parents would not think these qualities are the most important.

Question 5 **Whose reference would be most useful to parents who would be prospective employers? Explain your choice.**

A Ms Angela Bingham (Head Teacher North Canberra High School)

B Mr Benjamin Dumas (Ben's Bakery owner)

C James and Subin Kwon (parents/current clients)

D Ms Lauren Buchanan (my mum)

STEP (3)	**Read** the question. **Think** about what type of question it is. Work out what you need to do to answer it.	✪ This is a **judgement** question. You need to find evidence in the text to help you **judge** the relevance and importance of the references.
STEP (4)	**Think** about the text. Remember what you have read and **visualised**.	✪ **Scan** the text or re-read it if necessary. Look for evidence to help you make a **judgement**.

You can **judge** that **C** is correct. The most useful reference to prospective parent employers would be from an existing employer that hires the worker for the same job or service. James and Subin Kwon are parents and current clients of Matt's. They would be able to provide the most useful and relevant reference to potential parent employers because they use Matt to look after their child or children.

Check the other options to confirm why they are incorrect. Answers **A**, **B** and **D** are incorrect because they are not as relevant or pertinent to other parents. **A** and **B** can attest to Matt's character and reliability and work ethic but they do not employ Matt for childminding purposes. **D** is incorrect as you would judge Matt's mother to be biased and therefore unreliable as a character referee.

Question 6 **If you were a parent of a six-year-old, would you employ Matt for childminding services? Explain your judgement.**

....

....

STEP (3)	**Read** the question. **Think** about what type of question it is. Work out what you need to do to answer it.	✪ This is a **judgement** question.
STEP (4)	**Think** about the text. Remember what you have read and **visualised**.	✪ **Scan** the text or re-read it if necessary. Look for evidence to help you **judge** the truthfulness, relevance and accuracy of the information in the text from the perspective of a parent of a six-year-old.

You would likely **judge** Matt to be a good employee for childminding. He has a number of very useful referees that you could contact for further evidence. You can judge by the photo that he looks responsible. He appears friendly, reliable and hard working. He could help your child do homework. He might be a good role model for your child.

Judgement questions

Use the **Step-by-step guide** on pages 68–71 to help you read the text and make **judgements** to answer the questions below. Circle the correct answers or write your answer on the lines.

A coal seam gas debate

Farmer A

Speaker 1: I have an organic beef farm on land that has been in my family for three generations. The Australian government owns the mineral resources in my land and has approved the applications of two mining companies to mine my land. I have no legal right to tell the mining company to stay off my land and I worry that my beef won't be organic any more.

Farmer B

Speaker 2: I am worried about potential contamination of our fresh water aquifers by chemical residues from the fracking process. I also worry about methane gas leaking into the air. The mining company pays me $3000 per year per well. Initially I thought this was a windfall but I realise now that the money does not make up for the health of my family or the health of my animals. If the land is contaminated forever or all the water gets polluted what will future Australians eat and drink?

Resident of a small town

Speaker 3: I believe that CSG puts our land, water and future at risk. I worry that the technology is so new we really can't say it is safe. I worry about polluted water leaking out of the holding ponds. Coal seam gas is a fossil fuel. Fossil fuels are unsustainable. I believe in clean renewable energy.

CSG company spokesperson

Speaker 4: CSG is important for economic growth and for an assured and affordable power supply to homes and businesses for all Australia. Coal seam gas is more environmentally friendly than using coal as it emits 70 per cent less carbon. Queensland and New South Wales governments have now banned the use of holding ponds for wastewater in all new operations. Those governments have also introduced extra safeguards and regulations to protect agricultural land, towns and communities.

1 What is the most common point of view?

A concern about water pollution
B concern about pollution
C concern for the health of farm animals
D that extra research is needed into the safety of CSG

2 Whose interests does Speaker 1 represent?

A the Australian government
B his or her own
C the people of Australia
D a mining company

3 How does Speaker 2 feel about payment for the wells?

A It's bad for the farm.
B It's worth more money.
C It isn't worth the risk.
D It's a windfall.

4 Which statement best describes Speaker 3's argument?

A shows anger and bias through emotive language and accusations
B uses modal verbs to express the point of view assertively
C uses modal verbs that show less certainty
D uses emotive language to express a strong point of view

5 Whose interests does Speaker 4 represent?

A Queensland and New South Wales governments
B all Australians
C the Coal Seam Gas Company
D his or her own

6 Which speaker's comments do you judge the most relevant to you? Why?

....

....

....

....

....

Answers and explanations on p. 112

Judgement questions

Use the **Step-by-step guide** on pages 68–71 to help you read the text and make **judgements** to answer the questions below. Circle the correct answers or write your answer on extra paper.

Disappointed resident

Doug Williams
1 Bundall Road, Bundall, QLD 4217

Gold Coast City Council
PO Box 5042
Gold Coast Mail Centre 9729

19.3.14

Dear Mayor and Councillors

I am writing to express my disappointment in Gold Coast City Council for allowing an animal circus to operate on a Council Park. The circus currently using Mitchell Park, Southport clearly promotes itself as 'Australia's largest animal circus' advertising use of exotic animals such as lions and monkeys. This is in contravention of Council's own Park Usage Policy, currently displayed on Council's website and dated effective 16 October, 2012. Council Policy covering 'Temporary Commercial Recreation Activities on Council Parks' clearly states that circuses applying to use Council Parks must be 'travelling without animals'.

Animal welfare groups such as the RSPCA and the Animal Welfare League of Queensland are opposed to circuses that use animals. I am appalled that an animal circus is performing on public land. Educated and informed people today do not want to see animals in demeaning circus acts. Investigations into animal circuses have found the stress on circus animals to be unimaginable. Many countries around the world have banned animals in circuses.

I expect Council to uphold its own rules and not allow circuses with animals on Council land.

Awaiting your response.

Yours sincerely

Doug Williams

1. Which statement best summarises the writer's opinion?
   - **A** There is an animal circus in Southport.
   - **B** A circus should not be operating on Council land.
   - **C** The Council has a set of rules about use of its land.
   - **D** Many countries have banned animal circuses.

2. Which idea is the least relevant to the writer's purpose?
   - **A** Council is not complying with its own rules.
   - **B** The circus says it's 'Australia's largest animal circus.'
   - **C** Animal circuses are banned in many countries.
   - **D** The stress on circus animals is unimaginable.

3. What outcome would the writer prefer?
   - **A** a reply from council
   - **B** an explanation from Council
   - **C** an apology from Council
   - **D** Council to uphold its policy

4. Which of the following best describes the tenor of the letter?
   - **A** formal and businesslike
   - **B** friendly and polite
   - **C** personal and chatty
   - **D** official and scientific

5. What judgements could you make about the writer? Choose all that apply. The writer
   - **A** is compassionate about animals.
   - **B** has a lot of time to write letters.
   - **C** uses emotive words and phrases to convince others of a point of view.
   - **D** wants circus owners to lose money.

6. What is your judgement of animal circuses? Explain your opinions. Use your own paper.

Answers and explanations on p. 113

Judgement questions

Use the **Step-by-step guide** on pages 68–71 to help you read the text and make **judgements** to answer the questions below. Circle the correct answers or write your answer on the lines.

Fly like an eagle

1 Who is the target audience for the advertisement?

A girls **B** boys
C all teenagers **D** parents

2 The advertisement says *look cool* (line 11) to make you think the shoes will

A make you a better person.
B help make you popular.
C turn you into a sports star.
D make you look strong.

3 Why do you think the shoe company uses an eagle for its logo?

A Eagles have a hooked beak and talons.
B Eagles are handsome birds.
C Eagles are at the top of the food chain.
D Eagles are fast and powerful.

4 Choose all that apply. The advertisement persuades through use of

A celebrity endorsements.
B expert recommendations.
C science and technology.
D emotive words and phrases.

5 The mood of the advertisement is

A humorous.
B dark and scary.
C strong and masculine.
D light hearted and dreamy.

6 How successful is the advertisement in achieving its purpose?

....

....

Answers and explanations on pp. 113–114

Judgement questions

Use the **Step-by-step guide** on pages 68–71 to help you read the text and make **judgements** to answer the questions below. Circle the correct answers or write your answer on the lines.

Born lucky

Food: some have too much
and some not enough.
In one country
we're fat
in another
malnourished.
We don't get to choose
the place where we're born
or a life of the haves or the haven'ts.
I was born in a land
of hot showers, cold drinks,
lawns and hoses and taps,
and sinks and fridges and bathtubs
and ice;
where food is abundant
and water is pure.
No need to fetch water from far-away streams,
missing school so your family can drink on that day.
I have a roof and a bed.
I have school and can learn.
I have books and games and toys.
I have medicine and doctors,
and the law and my freedom.
I was born in a land
where I'm safe.
I was born
lucky.

by Tanya Dalgleish

1 Identify the main theme of the poem.

A envy
B greed
C wealth
D poverty

2 How does the poet feel about the life of the *haven'ts* (line 10)?

A angry
B lucky
C guilty
D sad

3 What does the poet want the reader to feel?

A ashamed of themselves because they are lucky
B angry that there are *haves* and *haven'ts*
C sympathetic towards people less fortunate
D envious because some people have swimming pools and more toys

4 Why do you think the poet wrote this poem?

A to persuade readers to a point of view
B to encourage people to think about others
C to encourage people to donate to charity
D to tell people how to live better lives

5 What do you think about the ideas in the poem?

A The ideas are biased and deceitful.
B Information in the poem is sensationalised.
C The poem seems heartfelt and accurate.
D Opinions in the poem are not true.

6 *I was born in a land / where I'm safe.* (lines 26–27)

What do you think this means?

....

....

....

....

....

....

Answers and explanations on pp. 114–115

Judgement questions

Use the **Step-by-step guide** on pages 68–71 to help you read the text and make **judgements** to answer the questions below. Circle the correct answers or write your answers on the lines.

Octane Dance

www.octanedance.com.au

OCTANE DANCE

For 12 to 17-year-olds
Classes to suit all dancers/all fitness levels
whether you aim to perform or want to get fit
or you just want to meet other people who love music and dance.
Beginners welcome. First class free. Mention this page.

hip hop | breaking | popping | urban contemporary | contemporary | jazz | lyrical jazz | tap

Great music
Great venue: main room/smaller dance rooms/lounging area.
Funky urban industrial vibe
A range of teaching styles. Our teachers are professional dancers and performers who have a passion for dance and have been dancing themselves since they were very young.
Guest teachers and choreographers—from around Australia and internationally

Your first class is FREE!

Home | teacher bios | class descriptions | class timetables | fees | what to wear
merchandise SHOP | performance schedules | sign up | venue hire | contact us

1 Make a judgement about the main purpose of the text.
- **A** to provide class timetables
- **B** to attract customers or clients
- **C** to sell dance clothes
- **D** to encourage people to get fit

2 Who is the most likely audience for the text?
- **A** parents
- **B** teenagers
- **C** dance teachers
- **D** Year 6 students

3 What judgements can you make about the dance school? Choose all that apply.
- **A** People who belong there have fun.
- **B** It will definitely improve people's dancing.
- **C** The teachers are fantastic.
- **D** It definitely attracts lots of teenagers.

4 Judge which information in the text would be the least important to readers.
- **A** guest teachers
- **B** timetable
- **C** great music
- **D** lounging area

5 Does the text place a greater emphasis on dancing for fun or for fitness? Explain how you reached your decision.

....

....

6 Based on what you read in the text would you choose to attend a class? Explain your decision.

....

....

Answers and explanations on p. 115

Judgement questions

Use the **Step-by-step guide** on pages 68–71 to help you read the text and make **judgements** to answer the questions below. Circle the correct answers or write your answers on the lines.

Animal rights

Ying: Animals have rights just like people.

Sam: Yes, they have rights but not exactly like people.

Ying: What do you mean?

Sam: Well, animals have a right to water, food, shelter, safety, companionship and to live a pain-free life. That's like humans. But some animals are raised for food so they can't be free from captivity in the same way that's a human right. That wouldn't be possible.

Ying: I agree. So animal rights means treating animals ethically.

Isabella: I hate to think of animals suffering at all—any animal, wild or domestic, a worm on a fish hook, a chicken kept in a cage for its eggs, an elephant hunted for its ivory or used in a circus, any animal killed for its fur. I just hate to think of the ways people hurt animals.

Ryan: I know. I'm the same. But I think most people behave ethically.

Sam: I think more people are unethical than ethical.

Ying: Really?

Sam: Yes, I think people put money or their own personal interests ahead of any sort of moral code. My dad's friend has crab pots. He'd catch and eat every mud crab he could. Dad says it's the law to throw the females back but Dad's not sure his friend obeys the law. It's madness to eat all the females because then there's no future for the mud crab but Dad says some people don't think about the future. We know other people who have that same attitude. They are short-sighted and they just think about their own immediate interests.

Ryan: That's terrible.

Isabella: That makes me feel really sad.

Ying: Me too.

Ying: And now there's so many people needing food and the food industry has grown so huge that animal rights often get forgotten.

Isabella: People are becoming more aware. I know we buy organic, free-range and cruelty-free. My Mum is obsessed! She says non-human animals suffer just like human animals do and we should not abuse them and anyway we need to eat vegies rather than meat because meat is not sustainable. I feel guilty when I eat meat for a number of reasons.

1 Which speaker is most informed about the subject of the text?

- **A** Ying
- **B** Sam
- **C** Ryan
- **D** Isabella

2 Which speaker uses the most emotive arguments?

- **A** Ying
- **B** Sam
- **C** Ryan
- **D** Isabella

3 Which statement is untrue?

- **A** Ying feels sad to think about the unethical treatment of animals.
- **B** Sam and Isabella are both concerned about sustainability.
- **C** Sam is more negative about human nature than Ryan.
- **D** Isabella is more concerned about elephants than worms.

4 Does Sam make reasoned arguments? Explain.

....

....

5 Why does Sam think more people are unethical than ethical?

....

....

6 Is Sam or Isabella more hopeful about the future? Explain your judgement.

....

....

....

....

Answers and explanations on pp. 115–116

Use the **Step-by-step guide** on pages 68–71 to help you read the text and make **judgements** to answer the questions below. Circle the correct answers or write your answers on the lines.

Uncle Tom and Little Harry are sold

Very many years ago, instead of having servants to wait upon them and work for them, people used to have slaves. These slaves were paid no wages. Their masters gave them only food and clothes in return for their work.

When any one wanted servants he went to market to buy them, just as nowadays we buy horses and cows, or even tables and chairs.

If the poor slaves were bought by kind people they would be quite happy. Then they would work willingly for their masters and mistresses, and even love them. But very often cruel people bought slaves. These cruel people used to beat them and be unkind to them in many other ways.

It was very wicked to buy and sell human beings as if they were cattle. Yet Christian people did it, and many who were good and kind otherwise thought there was no wrong in being cruel to their poor slaves. "They are only black people," they said to themselves. "Black people do not feel things as we do." That was not kind, as black people suffer pain just in the same way as white people do.

One of the saddest things for the poor slaves was that they could never long be a happy family all together—father, mother, and little brothers and sisters—because at any time the master might sell the father or the mother or one of the children to someone else. When this happened those who were left behind were very sad indeed—more sad than if their dear one had died.

Extract from *Uncle Tom's Cabin (Young Folks' Edition)* by Harriet Beecher Stowe, 1852, Chapter 1

1 The narrator thinks slavery is

- **A** useful because you can buy slaves at the market.
- **B** totally unacceptable.
- **C** acceptable as long as masters are kind.
- **D** a necessary problem.

2 Why did people in the 1850s want to own slaves?

3 According to the narrator, how did people justify being cruel to slaves?

- **A** They gave them food and clothes.
- **B** They bought the slaves at the market.
- **C** Slaves love their masters.
- **D** Black people are different from white people.

4 What do you think about the narrator's assertion that a slave would love a kind master? Explain your response.

5 What does the text imply is the difference between a slave and an employee? List four differences.

6 Why do you think the slaves left behind when a family member was sold would be *more sad than if their dear one had died* (line 17)?

Answers and explanations on p. 116

Judgement questions

Use the **Step-by-step guide** on pages 68–71 to help you read the text and make **judgements** to answer the questions below. Circle the correct answers or write your answers on the lines.

The bogeyman

I eventually got to know the old, old man who lived all alone behind a high fence at the end of our street. He used to sit on his verandah all day and most of the night shouting out at kids who spied on him through knotholes in the fence; shaking his walking stick at them. The children taunted him through the fence. They'd throw pinecones over, then run away squealing. All the children in our town were frightened of him. They'd say he was mean and had a dungeon. They'd call him "The Bogeyman". I had been frightened too when I was small.

He had a big yard with a huge mango tree. His mango tree was the only one for miles around. The bigger kids often dared each other to climb the fence, and get into the mango tree, collecting bucket loads of mangoes in season. They'd call their adventures "the mango raids".

Our teachers chastised us each morning after a raid. They'd tell us that Mr Burns had phoned the principal to complain about children breaking branches off his tree, trampling all over his vegetable garden, then jeering at him; being disrespectful of him and his property. The kids would complain back at the teachers "But he can't even climb the tree to get the mangoes. The possums and bats just eat them. It's not fair." When I got to know the old man better, he said: "All creatures've got a right to eat."

When I started high school I had a community service assignment. My task involved asking Mr Burns to speak at the school about his experiences in World War II. I wasn't confident about getting his help but I knocked at his gate and called out, "Excuse me. Hello!"

He was on his verandah and called back, "Yes—who goes?"

"May I enter?" I asked permission. He nodded.

I walked up to him and I said, "My name's Zac."

He looked at me a moment. I held my breath. Then he held out his hand to shake mine. He smiled and said, "Pleased to meet you, Zac."

I thought he hated children. Turns out he didn't. Turns out he wasn't mean at all. His name was Frank.

1 *I eventually got to know the old, old man who lived all alone behind a high fence at the end of our street.* **(lines 2–3)** What opinion about the old man is revealed in this sentence?

A The narrator is curious about him.
B The narrator feels sorry for him.
C The narrator is frightened of him.
D The narrator is respectful of him.

2 Why had the narrator been frightened of the old man? Choose all that apply.

A The old man was a bogeyman.
B He hadn't got to know him yet.
C He believed what the other children said.
D The old man had a dungeon.

3 What does the narrator think of the other children's behavior?

A He's annoyed and angry with them.
B He took part in mango raids too.
C He doesn't give an opinion.
D He thought their behavior was justified.

4 *The children taunted him through the fence.* **(lines 4–5)** Why do you think the children did this? Choose all that apply.

A They thought it was exciting and daring.
B They knew the old man couldn't run to catch them.
C They couldn't be seen and were confident they wouldn't get caught.
D They liked the perception of danger.

5 What do you think of the town children's behaviour?

....

....

6 What might Zac do to support Frank?

....

....

....

Answers and explanations on p. 117

BRINGING IT ALL TOGETHER

Mixed questions

Use the **Step-by-step guide** on page 4 to help you read the text and answer the questions below. Circle the correct answers or write your answers on the lines.

Going going going gone

This is how it goes:
vulnerable,
endangered,
critically endangered,
extinct.
Going, going, going, gone.
Species disappear
by degrees
until they are
gone.
Animals on the precipice:
the tiger
polar bears,
pandas,
gorillas,
and even our
Carnaby's black cockatoo.
All over the world,
animals
losing habitats.
Killed by poachers.
Declining numbers.
Going, going, going, gone.
How long before they
disappear
altogether?
Will our children's
children
read about
the animals we didn't save?
How will we
be judged?
Will they wonder
why?
Why
there was no
global will to stop
before the end.
To take better care;
to think;
to ACT.
Going, going, going …
going
gone.

by Tanya Dalgleish

1 What is the poet's opinion about animal conservation?

- **A** a waste of time
- **B** too difficult to achieve
- **C** happening all over the world
- **D** very important

2 What is the poet's prediction about the future of endangered animals?

- **A** They will become extinct.
- **B** They will be saved.
- **C** People will act to help them.
- **D** They might disappear.

3 In the text *the precipice* (line 12) means

- **A** a cliff.
- **B** on the brink of disaster.
- **C** the edge of a cliff.
- **D** on the verge of danger.

4 Which word best represents the mood of the poem?

- **A** rage
- **B** peace
- **C** resignation
- **D** awe

5 What does *our* mean in *and even our / Carnaby's black cockatoo* (lines 17–18)?

....

6 What does *global will* (line 38) mean?

....

....

....

....

Answers and explanations on pp. 117–118

Mixed questions

Use the **Step-by-step guide** on page 4 to help you read the text and answer the questions below. Circle the correct answers or write your answers on the lines.

World War II—the bombing of Australia

During World War II there were Japanese air attacks on Darwin and Katherine in the Northern Territory; Broome, Wyndham, Port Hedland and Derby in Western Australia; Townsville and Mossman; Queensland; and Horn Island in the Torres Strait.

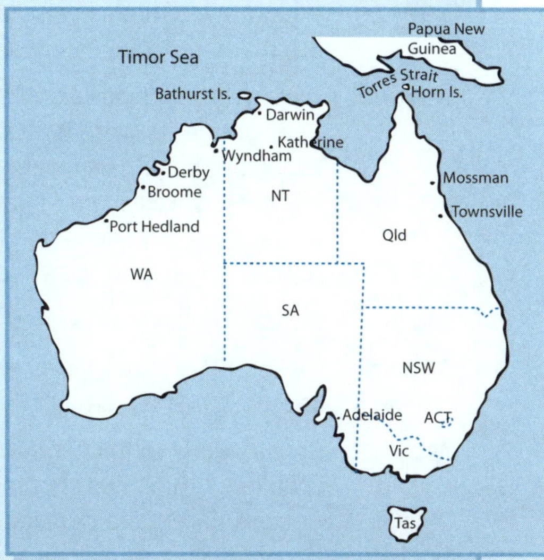

Darwin was bombed on sixty-four occasions between 19 February 1942 and 12 November 1943. The first attacks involved four Japanese aircraft carriers situated in the Timor Sea. Two hundred and sixty planes were launched from the carriers in two waves. The first wave lasted for around forty minutes and bombed the town, the hospital, the military and civilian airports, and the harbour. The second attack lasted an hour and came twenty-five minutes after the first had ended. It focused on the Royal Australian Air Force Base in Parap, a suburb of Darwin. The Japanese planes had been spotted flying over Bathurst Island thirty minutes before the first attack but Darwin RAAF operators presumed these were American planes and so did not sound air raid warnings. As a result of the attacks approximately 250 people died, up to 400 people were wounded, eight ships were sunk and around twenty planes were destroyed.

Darwin and the rest of Australia were taken by surprise by these attacks and Darwin was not prepared for the aftermath of an attack. Immediately after the bombings, Darwin was in civil and military disarray. Neither the military nor local government took effective control. People feared that Darwin was about to be invaded by the Japanese military which was already occupying northern parts of Papua New Guinea right on Australia's doorstep. Half the civilian population of Darwin and even some military personnel fled south towards Adelaide. The scramble to flee from Darwin became known as 'The Adelaide River Stakes'. It was a mass exodus with people carrying whatever possessions they could, and using whatever means of transport they had, to get away from the coast. Some people even walked.

1 Why weren't warnings sounded before Darwin was bombed?

- **A** The American planes were a long way from Darwin.
- **B** The RAAF spotted the planes over Bathurst Island.
- **C** The bombers were thought to be American.
- **D** The bombs landed too far away from Darwin.

2 What does *disarray* (line 21) mean?

- **A** discredit
- **B** disorder
- **C** disbelief
- **D** disagreement

3 What does *exodus* (line 26) mean?

- **A** the way to exit
- **B** a walking departure
- **C** the way out of a city
- **D** evacuation

4 Why did '*The Adelaide River Stakes*' (lines 25–26) occur?

- **A** It was a mass exodus.
- **B** There was a mass scramble to flee Darwin.
- **C** People feared a Japanese invasion.
- **D** The government should have been in control.

5 Why do you think the text uses the words *approximately*, *up to* and *around* in *approximately 250 people died, up to 400 people were wounded … and around twenty planes were destroyed* (lines 17–19)?

....

....

6 How would you have felt living in Darwin the first time it was bombed? Explain.

....

....

Answers and explanations on p. 118

Mixed questions

Use the **Step-by-step guide** on page 4 to help you read the text and answer the questions below. Circle the correct answers or write your answer on the lines.

Bullying

Miyumi: Mum, Becca has this stalker who writes nasty things about her.

Mum: What do you mean a 'stalker' and where are the nasty things written?

Miyumi: Well, maybe it's not a stalker. It's a troll. The comments were written on Becca's Facebook page. They were nasty and mean and they were lies but it was still hurtful. Becca made a printout and then deleted them. She's upset but she doesn't want to tell her parents because they told her she wasn't allowed to have a Facebook page so she'll be in trouble.

Mu: Do you know who this troll is?

Miyumi: We're pretty sure. We've all blocked her. But she pops up under different names and we just know it's her. It's an older girl at school.

Mu: Becca needs to tell her parents but she should also speak to the teachers. This girl has a problem. I think this should be reported to the police, but that will be for the teachers or Becca's parents to decide. Just you make sure Becca knows you all care for her. OK?

Miyumi: Yes of course. That's what we've been saying. This girl is horrible. Nobody likes her. She's a bully in real life too as well as online. She got into trouble last year for cyberbullying. She was emailing hurtful things to another girl. I thought the school should have expelled her but they didn't.

Mu: She must have unresolved issues to be doing it again.

Miyumi: What is her problem?

Mum: Jealousy. Attention-seeking. Problems at home. Difficulty making friends. There's all sorts of reasons someone becomes a bully. Maybe she's been bullied herself. It's up to the school to sort it out. I'd guess she needs counselling.

1 What is a *troll* (line 6) in the text?

- **A** a person who says mean things about you
- **B** an ugly creature from a folktale
- **C** a kind of cyberbully
- **D** someone from Becca's school who is mean

2 Who are *we* in *We've all* (line 13)?

- **A** everyone Becca knows
- **B** Miyumi and Becca
- **C** teachers and students at the school
- **D** Becca's friends

3 Who is *This girl* in *This girl has a problem* (lines 15–16)?

- **A** Miyumi
- **B** the cyberbully
- **C** Becca
- **D** Becca's friend

4 What mistake did Becca make?

- **A** She made a printout of the comments.
- **B** She allowed the bully to hurt her feelings.
- **C** She gave the bully her email address.
- **D** She disobeyed her parents.

5 What does Mum think Becca should do? Choose all that apply.

- **A** Tell her parents.
- **B** Report the incident to the school.
- **C** Tell the police.
- **D** Have the bully expelled from school.

6 Why does Mum say *make sure Becca knows you all care for her* (line 17)?

....

....

....

Answers and explanations on pp. 118–119

Mixed questions

Use the **Step-by-step guide** on page 4 to help you read the text and answer the questions below. Circle the correct answers or write your answers on the lines.

Whale watching

I went on a whale-watching tour when I was on holiday in Hervey Bay. It was amazing. The captain stopped our vessel 100 metres from where two humpback whales were playing and breaching.

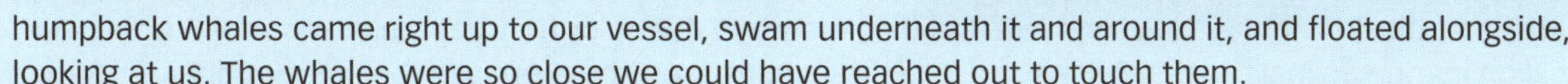

The crew on our whale-watching boat told us, the passengers, to make a lot of noise and wave our arms to attract the whales' interest. It sure did. Two adult humpback whales came right up to our vessel, swam underneath it and around it, and floated alongside, looking at us. The whales were so close we could have reached out to touch them.

We could see other vessels and whales in the Bay. All whale-watch vessels have to follow strict rules to protect the whales. The rules were established by the Environmental Protection Agency. The rules state that if three vessels are within 300 metres of a whale no other boat is allowed to approach the whale. Vessels aren't allowed to approach any whales head-on, get between any whales in a group, or separate a mother from her calf, and they have to be careful not to distress the whales in any other way. Helicopters aren't allowed for whale watching and other aircraft have to stay 300 metres away.

While on the tour I learned that humpbacks travel through Hervey Bay on their way north to warm waters for calving and mating. They pass through Hervey Bay again on their way back south to Antarctica to feed on krill. Apparently the Antarctic winter is too cold for whale calves because they don't have enough blubber yet to survive there. The humpback migration from Antarctica up the Queensland coast is one of the longest migrations in the animal kingdom and the journey to Antarctica is dangerous and arduous for calves. The calf travels in its mother's slipstream and drinks her rich milk to fatten up. Older whales don't usually eat anything as they migrate. They must be very hungry by the time they get back to Antarctica!

Our vessel had a hydrophone so we could hear the males singing. It was incredible. I love whales. They are massive and graceful and playful and inquisitive.

1. Apart from protecting whales why else would there be rules for whale-watching vessels?

   ....

   ....

   ....

2. What is the writer's attitude towards whales?
   - **A** impressed but fearful
   - **B** cautious and concerned
   - **C** interested but cautious
   - **D** interested and admiring

3. What is the writer's attitude towards whale-watching rules?
   - **A** annoyed by the rules
   - **B** respectful of the rules
   - **C** disinterested
   - **D** thinks there are too many rules

4. What is the purpose of the text?
   - **A** describe humpback whales
   - **B** recount events that have occurred
   - **C** advertise a tour
   - **D** promote whale watching

5. Why would the journey to Antarctica be dangerous and arduous for calves?

   ....

   ....

6. Would the writer recommend this particular whale-watching tour? Explain using evidence from the text.

   ....

   ....

   ....

   ....

Answers and explanations on pp. 119–120

Mixed questions

Use the **Step-by-step guide** on page 4 to help you read the text and answer the questions below. Circle the correct answers or write your answers on the lines.

Plastic—it's a problem

Look around your home at all the plastic items. Notice how much of your food and drink comes packaged in plastic. Plastic is a versatile, durable and useful product but plastic also causes huge problems for humans and the environment.

Plastic was invented to last forever but current statistics show that only 5% of plastic is recycled worldwide. Up to 95% of plastic is used only once and then thrown away. Some scientists estimate that up to 80% of plastic ends up washed into waterways and out to sea. Marine animals swallow it, choking on it, or it blocks their digestive system and they starve to death, or they get tangled in it. More than a million marine animals, including sea birds such as albatrosses, die every year because of plastic.

Plastic floating in the ocean absorbs toxic chemicals from the water and conversely toxic chemicals leach from the plastic into the water. They get absorbed into the food chain when fish eat them and then humans consume the fish. Chemicals that leach out of plastic have been found to be detrimental to animal and human health.

Ocean currents take hold of plastic garbage and propel it towards the ocean's five major natural gyres (whirlpools) and several smaller gyres. Over time the action of the sun, waves and wind breaks down the plastic into tiny particles referred to as 'nurdles' or 'mermaids' tears'. These swirl around in massive ocean garbage dumps. It is estimated that plastic particles now outnumber marine plankton in the world's oceans.

Production of plastic uses non-renewable fossil fuels. It takes a quarter of a litre of oil to make one plastic water bottle. We should not be wasting our fossil fuel on disposable plastic. People can reduce their reliance on plastic. In 2010 the Cinque Terre coastal region of Italy banned plastic bottles. The Cinque Terre National Park, a UNESCO World Heritage Site, was becoming a rubbish dump because up to two million plastic bottles were left behind every year by tourists. Tourists now pay a small fee for reusable metal flasks. The flasks can be refilled at water stations throughout the area, saving on plastic usage.

1. What might happen to a marine mammal tangled in plastic?

   ....

   ....

2. What causes mechanical breakdown of plastic?

   ....

   ....

3. What happens in a gyre?

   ....

   ....

4. How can we reduce plastic in the ocean? Choose all that apply.
   - **A** Always recycle plastic containers.
   - **B** Don't use fossil fuel to produce plastic.
   - **C** Use reusable metal flasks instead of plastic water bottles.
   - **D** Buy glass instead of plastic.

5. Why is it a waste to use fossil fuel to make plastic?

   ....

   ....

   ....

6. Is the term '*mermaids' tears*' a good label for plastic in the ocean? Explain.

   ....

   ....

   ....

   ....

   ....

Answers and explanations on p. 120

Mixed questions

Use the **Step-by-step guide** on page 4 to help you read the text and answer the questions below. Circle the correct answers or write your answers on the lines.

The magic seeds

Once upon a time a girl named Arabella lived on a small farm with her mother. Before school each morning Arabella milked the cow. After school each day Arabella picked vegetables for dinner and helped her mother prepare their evening meal of home-grown vegetables and eggs.

One Saturday morning her mother said to Arabella, "We need to trade our cow for seeds so we can grow more vegetables to sell or trade. Take the cow to market today. Make sure you get the best deal you can."

Arabella did not want to sell the old cow whom she had loved since she was a toddler but her mother needed the seeds so she did as she was told and led the cow towards the market. Along the way she passed a seed stall. The vendor had a sign that said 'Magical Bean Tree seeds. Fast growing. Free samples. Try them today!'

Arabella quizzed the vendor. Are the seeds easy to grow? How fast will they grow? Will the beans be tasty? Will she be able to sell them? The vendor promised that the bean trees were easy to grow, that they would grow overnight and that indeed the beans would taste delicious. Arabella decided to try the free seeds and save the cow from the market. She took her sample from the vendor and returned home leading the cow.

Her mother was surprised to see her and the cow. She told Arabella that she had been tricked and that she was disappointed in her. She said, "Why would anyone buy our beans when they can grow their own for free?" She told Arabella to throw the seeds away and not waste her time with them. Arabella was not deterred. She decided that at the very worst she had only lost one day. She could take the cow to the market the next morning so she might as well give the magic seeds a chance. She carefully planted them.

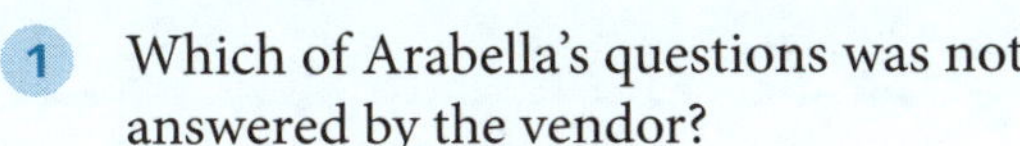

1. Which of Arabella's questions was not answered by the vendor?
   - **A** Will the beans be tasty?
   - **B** Will the beans sell?
   - **C** Are the seeds easy to grow?
   - **D** How fast will they grow?

2. Why didn't Arabella want to sell the cow?
   - **A** Her mother needed the seeds.
   - **B** She loved milk.
   - **C** She'd owned the cow since she was little.
   - **D** She'd owned the cow since it was little.

3. What food does the family grow to eat? Choose all that apply.
   - **A** eggs
   - **B** cows
   - **C** chickens
   - **D** vegetables

4. Why does her mother think Arabella has been tricked?
   - **A** People won't buy beans that they can grow themselves for free.
   - **B** The vendor was a trickster.
   - **C** There's no such thing as magic seeds.
   - **D** It's impossible for a bean tree to grow overnight.

5. What has it cost Arabella to try the beans?

   ....

   ....

   ....

6. What do you think will happen next? Explain.

   ....

   ....

   ....

   ....

   ....

Answers and explanations on pp. 120–121

Mixed questions

Use the **Step-by-step guide** on page 4 to help you read the text and answer the questions below. Circle the correct answers or write your answers on the lines.

The pacifist

Bryan waited fifteen minutes, then peeked out from behind the building. Everyone had gone. He'd missed the school bus home and would now have to walk, but at least he'd avoided a confrontation with Simon.

Simon: school thug. A mean boy who liked to intimidate Bryan and make him look small or stupid in front of classmates.

Classmates: not mates. Just people in the same class. Not friends or friendly. People who laughed at Simon's jokes or avoided looking Bryan in the eye. People who maybe thought bullying was entertaining or maybe just people who didn't want to become victims of bullying.

Bullying: something done to Bryan on a regular basis. He was never physically hurt. Simon wasn't a big boy. Bryan was the larger boy. But Simon had a large need to prove himself a big man all the time. He cornered Bryan and ridiculed him, always in front of an audience.

Audience: witnesses. Passive accepters. Not participants. Not interjectors. Not rejecters. If the audience stepped off the fence there would be no audience, watching Simon taunt Bryan; name-calling.

Name-calling: giving labels to others to tease them or to be mean or cruel—bullying.

Bullying: not acceptable anytime, anywhere. Bryan knew that. He sometimes fantasised about revenge. He wasn't fast-witted or clever with words like Simon but he was big and strong. He could stop Simon's taunts with one good shove. But would that make him a bully? Hitting a smaller boy? No. Bryan decided. He couldn't defeat Simon, verbally or physically. He could only outlast him. It was best to just avoid Simon when he could and wait for Year 6 to be over. He was patient. He could manage that.

Bryan headed home.

1 Whose point of view is given in the text?

A the author's **B** no-one's
C Simon's **D** Bryan's

2 The text ends

A suspensefully. **B** hopefully.
C mysteriously. **D** depressingly.

3 Simon bullies Bryan

A physically.
B with words.
C by shoving and pushing.
D by making him miss the school bus.

4 *If the audience stepped off the fence …* (lines 18–19). What does this mean?

....

....

....

5 *He could only outlast him.* (line 24)

What does this imply?

....

....

....

6 Do you agree with the way Bryan is handling his situation? If you made friends with Bryan, what advice would you give him? Explain.

....

....

....

....

....

Answers and explanations on p. 121

Mixed questions

Use the **Step-by-step guide** on page 4 to help you read the text and answer the questions below. Circle the correct answers or write your answers on the lines.

Urgent! Great Barrier Reef Holiday Sale ON NOW!

Visit before it's too late!

Your last chance to see:

- ★ 2300 kms of World Heritage–listed ecosystem
- ★ Pristine sandy beaches on palm-fringed islands
- ★ Coral atolls
- ★ Amazing wildlife

- One of the world's most important DUGONG populations
- Six of the world's seven MARINE TURTLE SPECIES—these turtles are listed as vulnerable, endangered or critically endangered
- Breeding habitats for SHOREBIRDS, LANDBIRDS and SEABIRDS
- Thirty species of WHALES and DOLPHINS—the Great Barrier Reef Marine Park Area is a nursery for vulnerable HUMPBACK WHALES and an important protection area for the AUSTRALIAN SNUBFIN DOLPHIN and the INDO-PACIFIC HUMPBACK DOLPHIN, numbers of which are in decline

Book your holiday today before climate change and coastal development ruins your opportunity. There's no time to delay! **You must book now!**

- ★ **SNORKEL** coral reefs before the coral is bleached or storm damaged.
- ★ **STROLL** along pristine sandy beaches before the reef's palm-fringed islands disappear under rising sea levels.
- ★ **SWIM** with dugong and turtles before they starve to death because flood plumes, agricultural run-off and dredging spoil have destroyed their seagrass.
- ★ **SEE** seabirds before the next severe storm (becoming more frequent and more destructive due to climate change) destroys their nesting areas.

BOOK your trip today at Last Chance Tours. Call 13000savetheGBR

1 What is the purpose of the text?
- **A** to describe the Great Barrier Reef
- **B** to explain about climate change
- **C** to sell holidays to the Great Barrier Reef
- **D** to raise awareness of threats to the Great Barrier Reef

2 Which of the following would be most likely to create a text like this?
- **A** a water sports equipment manufacturer
- **B** a recreational fishing lobby
- **C** a scientific research lobby
- **D** an environmental lobby

3 Which of the following statements do you believe to be true? Choose all that apply.
- **A** Human activity threatens the area.
- **B** It's a lovely place for a holiday.
- **C** Call 1300savethereef and book a holiday.
- **D** Sea-level rise is a threat to the reef.

4 What effect does agricultural run-off have on turtles and dugongs?

....

5 Why do you think the text starts with the word *Urgent?* Choose all that apply.
- **A** to gain the reader's attention
- **B** to make people believe the information in the text
- **C** to encourage people to book their holidays quickly
- **D** to reinforce the message of urgency to protect the reef

6 How do you know this is a persuasive text? Explain.

....

....

....

Answers and explanations on pp. 121–122

Mixed questions

Use the **Step-by-step guide** on page 4 to help you read the text and answer the questions below. Circle the correct answers or write your answers on the lines.

Bushfires

Bushfires are disasters that occur each year in Australia and in many other parts of the world. Bushfires kill people and animals, and destroy farmland, natural forest and bushland. They destroy people's homes and other buildings, and threaten towns and cities. Bushfires have a devastating effect on families and communities.

Bushfire risk is assessed using information about wind, humidity, temperature, rainfall and vegetation. In Australia bushfires are categorised as grass fires or forest fires. The worst forest fires usually involve eucalypt trees. Eucalypt leaves are highly flammable so eucalypt forest fires are extremely intense. A eucalypt tree can explode in a ball of fire. The most severe and largest bushfires in the world occur in south-eastern Australia during summer and autumn. The north of Australia experiences bushfires during winter, which is the dry season there.

People can accidentally cause bushfires when they leave campfires or barbecues smouldering or unattended, especially on windy days. People also cause fires when they toss burning cigarettes onto the ground where dry grasses can easily catch fire, or when sparks from power tools ignite fires on hot, dry, windy days.

When bushfires are deliberately lit it is called arson. Arson is a criminal offence and if perpetrators are caught and convicted they face long jail sentences, especially if people have died as a result of their deliberately lit fires.

Scientists predict that climate change will cause fire weather conditions to worsen. The south-east of mainland Australia will become hotter and drier in the future. One report, published by the Bushfire Cooperative Research Centre in 2007, using CSIRO simulations, suggests that fire danger could increase by as much as 15 to 70 per cent by 2050. The report found that climate change is causing average temperatures to rise and the number of extremely high temperature days to increase. Bushfire weather is likely to occur earlier in the season than in the past and to last longer—for example from October through to March. The numbers of professional firefighters required in the future is expected to double by 2030.

1 Where do the worst bushfires in the world occur?

A in eucalypt trees
B across northern Australia
C in south-eastern Australia
D from October to March

2 Why do most Australian bushfires occur during summer in the south and winter in the north?

....

....

3 What is an arsonist?

....

4 Find and write two emotive words from the first paragraph, which convey the writer's opinion about bushfires.

....

5 Which of these statements expresses the highest modality?

A The numbers of firefighters needed is expected to double by 2030.
B Fire danger could increase by as much as 15 to 70 per cent by 2050.
C Bushfire weather is likely to occur earlier in the season than in the past.
D The south-east of mainland Australia will become hotter and drier in the future.

6 What do you think about people who accidentally cause bushfires? Explain.

....

....

....

....

....

Answers and explanations on pp. 122–123

Mixed questions

Use the **Step-by-step guide** on page 4 to help you read the text and answer the questions below. Circle the correct answers or write your answers on extra paper.

Tribute

Text 1: Lt William Dawes

Lieutenant William Dawes (1762–1836) arrived in Australia in 1788 on HMS *Sirius* with the First Fleet. His role in the colony was as an astronomer. He established an observatory at Sydney Cove, on a point near The Rocks area that is now known as Dawes Point. Dawes is well regarded in history because of his work to learn and record the language of the First Nations peoples of Sydney. Dawes's notebooks, dating back to 1790–91, were discovered in London in 1972. In the notebooks Dawes records his conversations with First Australians, especially a Cammeraygal woman named Patyegarang, who was largely responsible for teaching Dawes her language and about the ways and customs of her people. This Sydney language was extinct but the Dharug people clan are currently reviving it. Many words used in Australian English today have origins in this language. For example, 'bubuk' which became boobook (owl) in English, 'dingu' which became dingo, and 'warada' which became waratah.

Dawes was the first European on record who attempted to defend First Australian rights. His outspoken defiance of Governor Phillip's punitive actions against First Nations Australians saw Dawes shipped back to England in December 1791.

Text 2: Bangarra Dance Theatre

Bangarra Dance Theatre was established in 1989. It is a First Nations Australian contemporary dance company which celebrates First Nations culture and storytelling though music and dance. The story of *Patyegarang* in 2014 was an amazing and beautiful Bangarra performance. In the performance the young Cammeraygal woman Patyegarang gives the gift of her language to the colonist William Dawes. Through sharing her language she is Dawes's guide to First Australian culture; an educator and a remarkable role model for today in developing cross-cultural understanding.

1 How are the two texts connected?

- **A** They are both about history.
- **B** They connect two First Nations people.
- **C** They both tell about Patyegarang.
- **D** They are both about First Nations people in early NSW.

2 Which statements are true of Dawes? Choose all that apply.

- **A** He respected First Australians.
- **B** He influenced Governor Phillip's treatment of First Australians.
- **C** He was interested to learn about First Australian culture.
- **D** He learned and recorded the Dharug language.

3 Which statements are true of Patyegarang? Choose all that apply.

- **A** Her life is the subject of the Bangarra performance.
- **B** She was a dancer in 1788.
- **C** She did not like European settlers in the colony.
- **D** She was keen to meet new people and share ideas.

4 Why is the title *Tribute*?

- **A** to honour the role of First Australians in the history of Sydney
- **B** to persuade people to see Bangarra Dance because it's a tribute to Patyegarang
- **C** to honour the cultural contributions of Dawes, Patyegarang and Bangarra Dance
- **D** to recognise the role of William Dawes in Australia's history

5 Why is Dawes well regarded in history? Write your answer on extra paper.

6 Would Dawes have been popular with the majority of European settlers in the early days of the colony? Explain. Use your own paper.

Answers and explanations on p. 123

Mixed questions

Use the **Step-by-step guide** on page 4 to help you read the text and answer the questions below. Circle the correct answers or write your answers on the lines.

Adventures of Huckleberry Finn

We went tiptoeing along a path towards the end of the widow's garden. When we was passing by the kitchen I fell over a root and made a noise. We scrouched down and laid still. Miss Watson's big nigger, named Jim, was setting in the kitchen door. He got up and stretched his neck out, listening. Then he says: "Who dah?"

He listened some more; then he come tiptoeing down and stood right between us. Well, likely it was minutes and minutes that there warn't a sound, and we all there so close together. There was a place on my ankle that got to itching, but I dasn't scratch it; and then my ear begun to itch; and next my back, right between my shoulders. Seemed like I'd die if I couldn't scratch. Well, I've noticed that thing plenty times since. If you are anywheres where it won't do for you to scratch, why you will itch all over in upwards of a thousand places.

Pretty soon Jim says: "Say, who is you? Whar is you? Dog my cats ef I didn' hear sumf'n. Well, I know what I's gwyne to do: I's gwyne to set down here and listen tell I hears it agin."

So he set down on the ground, leaned his back up against a tree and stretched his legs out. My nose begun to itch. It itched till the tears come into my eyes. But I dasn't scratch. Then it begun to itch on the inside. Next I got to itching underneath. I didn't know how I was going to set still. This miserableness went on as much as six or seven minutes; but it seemed a sight longer than that. I was itching in eleven different places now. I reckoned I couldn't stand it more'n a minute longer, but I set my teeth hard and got ready to try. Just then Jim begun to breathe heavy; next he begun to snore—and then I was pretty soon comfortable again.

Extract from *Adventures of Huckleberry Finn* (*Tom Sawyer's Comrade*) by Mark Twain, 1884, Chapter II. Note that this is an abridged version of the book text. The story is set in the Mississippi Valley, USA, in around 1840.

1 What does *scrouched* mean?

- **A** shrunk low and kept still
- **B** scooted and bent
- **C** scrunched and crouched
- **D** ducked and hid

2 What judgement can you make about the text when the narrator says *Miss Watson's big nigger, named Jim …* (lines 3–4)?

Choose all that apply.

- **A** That's the way people are likely to have talked in 1840.
- **B** The author is racist.
- **C** The story is set in a different time and place from today.
- **D** The story is not relevant to readers today.

3 Why does the narrator get itchy?

- **A** because he's sitting on an ant's nest
- **B** because he has hives
- **C** because he can't scratch
- **D** all over in upwards of a thousand places

4 Why does Jim say "*Dog my cats*" (line 12)?

- **A** He wants his dog to chase the cats away.
- **B** He's sure he heard something.
- **C** He is questioning whether he heard something or not.
- **D** He means to give up his cats if he's wrong.

5 What is implied when the narrator says *I was pretty soon comfortable again* (lines 19–20)?

....

....

....

6 What might the narrator be up to?

....

....

....

....

Answers and explanations on pp. 123–124

Mixed questions

Use the **Step-by-step guide** on page 4 to help you read the text and answer the questions below. Circle the correct answers or write your answers on the lines.

The further adventures of Toad

The front door of the hollow tree faced eastwards, so Toad was called at an early hour; partly by the bright sunlight streaming in on him, partly by the exceeding coldness of his toes, which made him dream that he was at home in bed in his own handsome room with the Tudor window, on a cold winter's night, and his bedclothes had got up, grumbling and protesting they couldn't stand the cold any longer, and had run downstairs to the kitchen fire to warm themselves; and he had followed, on bare feet, along miles and miles of icy stone-paved passages, arguing and beseeching them to be reasonable. He would probably have been aroused much earlier, had he not slept for some weeks on straw over stone flags, and almost forgotten the friendly feeling of thick blankets pulled well up round the chin.

Sitting up, he rubbed his eyes first and his complaining toes next, wondered for a moment where he was, looking round for familiar stone wall and little barred window; then, with a leap of the heart, remembered everything—his escape, his flight, his pursuit; remembered, first and best thing of all, that he was free!

Free! The word and the thought alone were worth fifty blankets. He was warm from end to end as he thought of the jolly world outside, waiting eagerly for him to make his triumphal entrance, ready to serve him and play up to him, anxious to help him and to keep him company, as it always had been in days of old before misfortune fell upon him. He shook himself and combed the dry leaves out of his hair with his fingers; and, his toilet complete, marched forth into the comfortable morning sun, cold but confident, hungry but hopeful, all nervous terrors of yesterday dispelled by rest and sleep and frank and heartening sunshine.

Extract from *The Wind in the Willows* by Kenneth Grahame, 1908, Chapter 10

1 Why had Toad woken early?

A Toad was called at an early hour.
B A dream woke him.
C The front door of the hollow tree faced eastwards.
D Bright sunlight and cold toes woke him.

2 What does *beseeching* *(line 7)* mean?

A begging **B** abusing
C whispering **D** convincing

3 What had triggered Toad's strange dream?

A The bedclothes had gone to warm themselves by the fire.
B He had slept for weeks on straw over stone flags.
C He had cold toes.
D He had almost forgotten the friendly feeling of thick blankets.

4 What sort of character is Toad?

Use evidence from the text to make your judgement. Choose all that apply.

A egotistical
B fretful and cowardly
C lazy and timid
D spoilt and self-important

5 Why had Toad been sleeping on cold flagstones?

6 Why did Toad feel *confident* and *hopeful* *(line 19)* at the end of the text?

Answers and explanations on pp. 124–125

Mixed questions

Use the **Step-by-step guide** on page 4 to help you read the text and answer the questions below. Circle the correct answers or write your answer on extra paper.

Renewable energy

Compere: [*facing camera*] Good morning viewers. Welcome to the program. Our topic for this week is renewable energy—from sunshine, wind, waves, hot rocks and bioenergy resources. Today we continue the theme and discuss wind farming. I'd like to introduce wind industry expert and government consultant Kath Green. [*facing Kath*] Welcome Kath. Please explain the importance of wind energy to viewers.

Kath: Thank you for having me here. Wind energy is incredibly important to Australia. Wind is a clean, safe, renewable resource. It can help to halt the devastating impact of climate change. I am really excited about the potential of wind energy. The south-western, southern and south-eastern coastlines of Australia have consistently high average wind speeds—perfect for wind farming. Our mountain ranges are also good wind areas. Australia could lead the world in wind energy technology.

Compere: How do we harness the energy in wind?

Kath: We use wind turbines: sleek, modern, aerodynamic windmills. The wind rotates the blades of the turbine. The blades rotate the shaft. The shaft is connected to the electrical generator. The generator converts the kinetic energy into electricity. A single turbine can supply a house or a farm, or rows of turbines can power up whole towns.

Compere: And wind energy doesn't produce greenhouse gases?

Kath: That is correct. Once they become operational wind farms produce negligible greenhouse gases. A typical wind turbine in Australia can produce 6000 megawatt hours of electricity in a year. This saves the atmosphere the 6000 tonnes of CO_2 that would have been produced to provide coal-powered electricity. Wind power is environmentally sustainable.

Compere: But is wind energy reliable?

Kath: Wind energy does work. Around the world there are examples of whole communities that use wind power to generate all the electricity they need. Tocco da Casauria, for example, is a village in central Italy that is 100% wind powered.

Compere: Well that's very exciting. On behalf of all our viewers I wish you success with future projects.

Kath: Thank you very much.

1 What is Kath *really excited about* (*line 16*)?
- **A** the importance of wind energy to Australia
- **B** the potential of wind energy in Australia
- **C** wind being a clean, safe, renewable resource
- **D** Australia leading the world in wind energy technology

2 What is the compere's role? Choose all that apply.
- **A** to ask questions
- **B** to provide information about the topic
- **C** to represent the interests of viewers
- **D** to introduce the guest

3 Why does Kath say that wind energy is important? Choose all that apply.
- **A** It's renewable.
- **B** It's sustainable.
- **C** It produces greenhouse gases.
- **D** It doesn't produce greenhouse gases.

4 Choose all that apply. The information provided by Kath Green
- **A** seems accurate and trustworthy.
- **B** isn't supported by technical details.
- **C** is biased against other renewable energy sources.
- **D** is sensationalised and emotive.

5 Who might disagree with Kath?
- **A** wind turbine manufacturers
- **B** a resident of Tocco da Casauria
- **C** a coalmining company executive
- **D** a renewable energy advocate

6 Does this interview influence your attitude in any way? Explain using evidence from the text. Use your own paper.

Answers and explanations on pp. 125–126

Mixed questions

Use the **Step-by-step guide** on page 4 to help you read the text and answer the questions below. Circle the correct answers or write your answer on extra paper.

Poo

Every animal on earth makes it. It is simply digested waste material.

Food goes IN one end—is processed—the good bits are absorbed—then what's left over goes OUT the other end.

Your poo can tell you a lot about your health.

There is definitely such a thing as **healthy poo.**

Check it out!

Poo should sink. Floating poo can be a sign of a diet too high in fats or gas.

Poo should be brown but healthy poo can change colour, depending on what you've been eating. Beetroot can give you red-coloured poo but generally red or black or yellowy poo is a sign of poor health.

Poo should be well formed and hold its shape. It should not be hard like a soft drink can or dried rabbit pellets.

Poo should come out easily and cleanly, not smearing or splattering.

Poo should not be watery but it should not be dry.

Poo should come out on a regular basis. That usually means every day but some people don't go that often and other people go more than once a day, so what's normal and regular for one person is different from another person.

Better-looking poo = better-looking you.

Poo smells. A diet high in animal foods and processed foods makes smellier poo than a diet of natural whole foods and plant foods. It's a fact: vegetarians have less stinky poos! Especially if they avoid processed foods as well as animal foods.

You can have healthy poo, too! Eat lots of fruit and vegetables, whole-grain cereals and breads, and nuts and seeds, plus drink plenty of water and **TAKE ONE SUPER FOOD PLUS+ CAPSULE DAILY.**

BUY SOME TODAY!

Interesting fact about poo: Some scientists study animal poo (also called scat). Scat can tell researchers what the animals have eaten, their gender, their stress levels, where they've been, and how many of the species are living in the area.

1 What is the purpose of the text?

- **A** to entertain
- **B** to inform
- **C** to sell a product
- **D** to perform a community service

2 What is the most important idea in the text?

- **A** Watery poo is a sign of poor health.
- **B** All animals do poos.
- **C** Healthy poo is important.
- **D** Poo should be brown, firm and well formed.

3 Which is true in the text?

- **A** Vegetarians always have greenish poo.
- **B** Vegetarians don't do poos.
- **C** Vegetarians always have less smelly poo.
- **D** You can have healthy poo.

4 The text sounds

- **A** superior because the writer knows more about health issues than the reader.
- **B** friendly and casual.
- **C** formal, technical and educational.
- **D** educational and serious because health is a serious topic.

5 Which judgements can you make about *SUPER FOOD PLUS+ CAPSULES* (line 25)? Choose all that apply.

- **A** Take one a day and you don't need to eat fruit and vegetables.
- **B** The capsules are essential for healthy poo.
- **C** Everyone should take one capsule a day.
- **D** You don't need them if you eat healthy foods.

6 How successful is the text in achieving its purpose? Write your answer on extra paper.

Answers and explanations on p. 126

Mixed questions

Use the **Step-by-step guide** on page 4 to help you read the text and answer the questions below. Circle the correct answers or write your answers on the lines.

What Sophie was thinking

Sophie was so hungry she could eat a horse. Not literally, of course. She imagined the sight that would make, then shrugged off the image. She didn't even eat cow, let alone horse. Though she knew people somewhere in the world would—people hungry enough will eat anything.

She remembered a television program she'd once watched. It showed a man touring around the world eating weird things like scorpions and crickets. He said dry-toasted crickets tasted like sunflower seeds and katydids tasted like toasted avocado. Sophie was sceptical. Maybe that's what bugs would taste like if you were blindfolded and didn't know you were eating bugs. She remembered he'd said that there are over 1400 species of edible insects. Sophie shook her head in wonderment. How crazy is that!

She pondered some more on the subject. The TV show had shown a village in Thailand that grows insects for all the villagers to eat. The manager of the insect farm had said, via a translator, that insects multiply readily, grow quickly, eat very little, take up very little farming space, are less labour-intensive than farming larger animals and are therefore better for the planet. Some insects are healthier for you than meat. Crickets for example are a better, healthier source of protein than chicken because they are low in fat. Go figure! But you have to eat insects that haven't eaten plants sprayed with pesticides or you'd just be poisoning yourself. And you'd have to eat a lot of insects to fill you up.

Entomophagy! That's what he called it, she recalled: the practice of eating insects. Nothing new, she acknowledged. Indigenous peoples have always eaten what's available to them, like sugar ants and bogong moths and witchetty grubs.

Sophie imagined herself chomping on a grasshopper, crunching into its spiky legs. Erk! Didn't seem particularly appealing to her. She'd rather be vegan.

1. What might Sophie choose to eat?
   - **A** roast beef
   - **B** grasshoppers
   - **C** toasted avocado
   - **D** sugar ants

2. What does Sophie think is *crazy* (*line 15*)?
   - **A** the idea that she could eat a horse
   - **B** the fact that people eat insects
   - **C** the existence of insect farms
   - **D** the number of edible insect species there are

3. Which word means 'the study of insects'?
   - **A** zoology
   - **B** entomophagy
   - **C** entomology
   - **D** entomofauna

4. *Sophie shook her head in wonderment. How crazy is that!* (*line 15*) implies that
   - **A** Sophie is disgusted.
   - **B** Sophie finds the idea sickening.
   - **C** Sophie is amazed.
   - **D** Sophie finds it weird.

5. Which words tell you that the text is going on in Sophie's head? Find and write four of the words.

   ....

   ....

6. What image does Sophie shrug off in paragraph one? You might like to draw the image.

   ....

   ....

Answers and explanations on p. 127

Mixed questions

Use the **Step-by-step guide** on page 4 to help you read the text and answer the questions below. Circle the correct answers and write your answer on the lines or use extra paper.

Tippy taps

Bottlebrush Lane State School Fundraising Newsletter

Dear families and members of our school community

This year our school will continue its fundraising efforts to provide tippy taps to rural areas of Papua New Guinea and promote the importance of hand washing for disease prevention.

Over 3 million children around the world die each year from diarrhoea and pneumonia. These diseases are largely preventable. It's estimated that 1.2 million children would be saved each year if people just washed their hands properly. Our school will continue to provide as many villages as possible with tippy taps and soap. Tippy taps are a hands-free way to wash your hands where there's no running water. When people have to carry water long distances they prioritise water for drinking and cooking and believe they can't afford to use it to wash their hands. The tippy tap is convenient for people who would otherwise have to walk to a river or stream to wash their hands.

The tippy tap is simple and easy to construct. It consists of a recycled plastic container filled with water and attached to a frame. A rope links the water container to a foot lever. Soap is also attached by a rope. People use the foot lever to tip out water and wash their hands after toileting or before preparing food or eating.

During the January school holidays our two Year 6 teachers, Mr Robert Walker and Ms Lynette Fok, travelled to Papua New Guinea to see firsthand the result of last year's fundraising efforts. The teachers filmed tippy taps in use in two remote PNG villages and showed these films at this week's school assembly. Community leaders say that there is less illness in the villages since introducing the tippy taps. Lives are being saved and also children don't miss school due to a preventable disease. That's important for their future.

Our school plans to hold a number of specific fundraising events for tippy taps for PNG over the course of the year. These events will culminate in the school's involvement in Global Handwashing Day in October. We will keep you informed.

Kind Regards
Ms Lana Ceric, Principal

1. Why is proper hand washing important?
   - **A** to use the tippy taps
   - **B** to prevent disease
   - **C** to use soap
   - **D** after going to the toilet and before preparing food or eating

2. What is a tippy tap?
   - **A** a special tap made of plastic
   - **B** a device that washes your hands
   - **C** a tap that tips water
   - **D** a water container attached to a foot lever

3. Why mightn't people wash their hands after going to the toilet? Choose all that apply.
   - **A** They don't know it's important.
   - **B** They forget.
   - **C** They have no running water.
   - **D** They spread disease.

4. Why did the teachers travel to PNG?
   - **A** to see the results of school fundraising
   - **B** to make a film
   - **C** for the school holidays
   - **D** to raise more funds

5. Why does the tippy tap have a foot lever?

   ....

   ....

   ....

6. Have tippy taps worked so far in PNG rural villages? Explain. Use your own paper.

Answers and explanations on pp. 127–128

Mixed questions

Use the **Step-by-step guide** on page 4 to help you read the text and answer the questions below. Circle the correct answers or write your answer on the lines.

Rabbit-Proof Fence

Students in Year 6 were placed in groups to share opinions about the plot, soundtrack, cinematography and acting in the film *Rabbit-Proof Fence* (2002).

Ruby: I thought the story was very sad because that sort of thing actually happened back then. First Nations children were taken from their families. That's what happened to the stolen generations.

Oliver: Yes. Unbelievable! And it went on for decades!

Jack: I can't imagine what that would have been like back then for the stolen children or their families.

Charlotte: I thought the plot was suspenseful. The girls' characters in the story were so brave and smart and resourceful, especially Molly. The film made me believe that they really could have survived for all that time in that outback environment.

Jack: Yeah, the acting was terrific and the cinematography was awesome—the vast Australian outback. I loved the landscape.

Oliver: The soundtrack was amazing, too. It really suited the landscape.

Ruby: I think the film did a great job of showing the audience part of Australia's history. A part that was terrible. I honestly can't believe the authorities treated First Nations people like that. It makes me feel ashamed.

Jack: Some white people tried to help the girls in the film. Some people in real life would have tried to …

Charlotte: Yes, but they really couldn't do much or they would have been breaking the law. Really, the stolen generations were the fault of government policy.

Ruby: And also, organisations like the church believed that they were actually helping the children by taking them from their families.

Oliver: I liked the idea of the fence; what the fence sort of represented. Rabbits were introduced by white people. The fence was built to contain the rabbits. Ms Jenkins said that they finished building the fence in 1907 and at that time it was the longest fence in the world.

Jack: Yeah but a fence wouldn't have been needed if the rabbits hadn't been introduced in the first place.

Charlotte: I like the symbolism of the fence. The girls knew that if they followed the fence they'd make their way towards their home.

Ruby: Ms Jenkins said we need to consider if the fence is a metaphor.

1 What is the consensus of opinion about the stolen generations?

A There is disbelief that it happened.
B It was part of Australia's history.
C It was very sad.
D It was shameful.

2 What is the consensus of opinion about the film?

A factual and amazing
B worthwhile and interesting
C sad but true **D** suspenseful

3 Cinematography is to do with

A the soundtrack. **B** visual aspects.
C the outback. **D** cinema history.

4 What themes can you infer that the film explores?

A family, the outback and environmental issues
B authority, rabbits, family and belonging
C Australia today, family and belonging
D authority, determination, family and belonging

5 Do you think members of the group enjoyed the film?

A No. It's informative but not enjoyable.
B Yes. It has a suspenseful plot, good acting and cinematography.
C No. It's too sad even though the soundtrack is amazing.
D No. It was just too real.

6 Why was a rabbit-proof fence built?

....

....

....

Answers and explanations on p. 128

ANSWERS

Fact-finding questions

Australia's highest military award (page 33)

1 C **2** C **3** B **4** B **5** C **6** See below

Explanations

1. This is a **fact-finding** question. **C** is correct. The answer is stated directly in the text. You read *The Victoria Cross for Australia is Australia's highest military award* (see line 2). **A** and **B** are incorrect because they were names previously used to refer to Australia's highest military honour. **D** is incorrect because, although it is a medal, Australia's highest military award is called The Victoria Cross for Australia to differentiate it from other medals and awards.
2. This is a **fact-finding** question. **C** is correct. The answer is stated directly in the text. You read in paragraph one *It* [the Victoria Cross of Australia] *was established in 1991 to replace the original Victoria Cross … The Imperial Victoria Cross dates back to 1856* (see lines 3–5). You can work out that the VC was the highest military award between 1856 and 1991. **A** is incorrect because the Imperial Victoria Cross was replaced in 1991. **B** is incorrect. These are the dates where the Victoria Cross was awarded during these years, but it was the relevant award right up until 1991. **D** is incorrect because these are the years that the Victoria Cross for Australia has been the highest award.
3. This is a **fact-finding** question. **B** is correct. The answer is stated directly in the text. You read *The Victoria Cross for Australia is Australia's highest military award. It is awarded to military personnel …* (see line 2). **A** is incorrect because the award can be presented to living recipients as well as posthumously. **C** is incorrect because Commonwealth military personnel are not eligible. **D** is incorrect because the text says that the award is for all military personnel and not just for the army.
4. This is a **fact-finding** question. **B** is correct. The answer is stated directly in the text. You read *The Imperial Victoria Cross dates back to 1856 when Queen Victoria reigned over the United Kingdom and the British Empire. It was an award of the British Crown to honour soldiers from countries in the Commonwealth* (see lines 4–6). **A** tells how the award came to be named but not its origins. **C** and **D** are incorrect because they only refer to Australian soldiers instead of soldiers from across the Commonwealth.
5. This is a **fact-finding** question. **C** is correct. The answer is stated directly in the text. You read *The last Australian recipient of the Imperial Victoria Cross was Warrant Officer Keith Payne, for gallantry on 24 May 1969 during the Vietnam war* (see lines 18–19). Other dates are incorrect.
6. This is a **fact-finding** question. The answer is stated directly in the text. You read *It* [the Victoria Cross for Australia] *is awarded to military personnel who show extreme bravery, heroism or self sacrifice in the line of duty* (see lines 2–3). Your answer needs to paraphrase this information.

Consumer glossary (page 33)

1 C **2** A, B and D **3** A **4** B **5** C
6 See below

Explanations

1. This is a **fact-finding** question. **C** is correct. The answer is stated directly in the text. You read *Fair Trade labels on products mean that producers or growers have been paid a fair price for their goods* (see lines XX–XX). **A** is incorrect because growers do not swap coffee for tea. **B** is true but does not explain what Fair Trade means. **D** is incorrect as this is not what Fair Trade means.
2. This is a **fact-finding** question. **A**, **B** and **D** are correct. The answer is stated directly in the text. You read *A carbon price is a price paid by businesses for producing carbon emissions. A price on carbon helps to prevent pollution* (see lines 3–5). Pricing carbon encourages businesses to produce

less carbon pollution. **C** is incorrect because it does not make sense.

3 This is a **fact-finding** question. **A** is correct. The answer is stated directly in the text. You read *A sweatshop is a workplace where workers work in poor or unsafe conditions for low wages (see lines 42–44)*. **B** confuses the word *sweet* with *sweat*. **C** is incorrect. The text does not describe sweatshops as places where workers sweat. **D** is incorrect because it contradicts the information in the text about Ethical Clothing Australia.

4 This is a **fact-finding** question. **B** is correct. The answer is stated directly in the text. You read *A sustainable product is one that regrows or is renewable and whose use has minimal negative impact on the environment (see lines 38–40)*. **A** is only part of the answer. **C** might be true in some homes but does not answer the question. **D** contradicts the meaning of the term in the text.

5 This is a **fact-finding** question. **C** is correct. The answer is stated directly in the text. You read that organic food is *produced without the use of synthetic pesticides, herbicides, additives, fertilisers, hormones or processes such as chemical ripening, genetic modification, nanotechnology and irradiation (see lines 31–35)*. **A** is incorrect because the eggs are not labelled organic. **B** is incorrect as the use of growth hormone is not organic. **D** is incorrect because the product includes artificial preservative.

6 This is a **fact-finding** question. You read *Sustainable means 'able to be maintained.' A sustainable product is one that regrows or is renewable and whose use has minimal negative impact on the environment (see lines 37–40)*. Your answer needs to paraphrase this statement. For example: Sustainability is important because sustainable products can be replaced so their use has minimal impact on the environment.

Asylum seekers (page 34)

1 C **2** C **3** A, C and D **4** C **5** D
6 See below

Explanations

1 This is a **fact-finding** question. **C** is correct. The answer is stated directly in the text. You read *Asylum seekers, therefore, are people who leave their own countries because they seek places of safety (see lines 2–4)*. **A** is incorrect because only some asylum seekers flee due to war or conflict. **B** is incorrect because most asylum seekers would not choose to live in another country unless their own is unsafe for them. **D** is incorrect as not all asylum seekers arrive by boat.

2 This is a **fact-finding** question. **C** is correct. The answer is stated directly in the text. You read *Asylum seekers apply for refugee status and are labelled refugees once officials can confirm that their claims are genuine (see lines 10–11)*. Other answers are incorrect because they do not define the term *refugee*. **A** is incorrect because countries and not refugees signed the Refugee Convention. **B** and **D** are true in the text but do not answer the question and define what a refugee is.

3 This is a **fact-finding** question. **A**, **C** and **D** are correct. The answer is stated directly in the text. You read *Some asylum seekers seek political sanctuary, others seek religious sanctuary. Some are persecuted in their own country because of their race, their social group, their views or their gender. Asylum seekers are at risk in their own countries because the government of their own country cannot or will not protect them (see lines 4–7)*. **B** does not make sense.

4 This is a **fact-finding** question. **C** is correct. The answer is stated directly in the text. You read *The Refugee Convention is the key international document by which refugees are identified. As a signatory to the Convention, Australia has moral, legal and humanitarian obligations under international law to protect refugees (see lines 13–15)*. Other answers are incorrect because they are not supported by the way the Refugee Convention is defined in the text.

5 This is a **fact-finding** question. **D** is correct. The answer is stated directly in the text. You read *Refugees from … Germany and Poland came after World War II (see lines 16–17)*. Other answers are incorrect as those waves of refugees came to Australia at other times after other major events.

6 This is a **fact-finding** question. The answer is stated directly in the text. You read *Australia is a signatory to the Refugee Convention of 1951 and the revisions made to the Convention in 1961 … As a signatory to the Convention, Australia has moral, legal and humanitarian obligations under international law to protect refugees (see lines 12–15)*. Your answer needs to paraphrase these facts in the text. For example: It is illegal for Australia not to protect refugees because Australia signed the Refugee Convention of 1951 and the revisions made to the Convention in 1961.

The Last Whale (page 35)

1 C **2** B **3** D **4** C **5** See below
6 See below

Explanations

1 This is a **fact-finding** question. **C** is correct. The answer is stated directly in the text. You read that the date of publication of the newspaper article is *21 November 1978* (see line 2). You further read *A female sperm whale harpooned yesterday will be the last whale killed on behalf of the Australian whaling industry* (see lines 4–5). **A**, **C** and **D** are incorrect because the dates are wrong.

2 This is a **fact-finding** question. **B** is correct. The answer is stated directly in the text. You read *Whale oil was a lucrative export business in the early colonies and used for lighting and candle making* (see lines 35–37). **A** is only partly correct. Whale oil was not used to make corsets. **C** is incorrect as whale oil was [*l*]*ater* (see line 38) used for cosmetics and animal food. **D** is only partly correct and is not the full answer.

3 This is a **fact-finding** question. **D** is correct. The answer is stated directly in the text. You read *It closed in 1962 after decimating the number of humpbacks off the east coast of Australia from an estimated 15,000 to 500 whales in ten years* (see lines 24–27). Other answers are incorrect. **A** gives dates that apply to sperm whales off Cheynes Beach. **B** tells how many humpback whales were left off Tangalooma after ten years. **C** is the date that commercial whaling was banned by the Australian government.

4 This is a **fact-finding** question. **C** is correct. The answer is stated directly in the text. You read *The first Greenpeace campaign in Australia saw protestors involved in actions against Cheynes Beach Whaling Company vessels last year* (see lines 29–32) . You notice that the newspaper was published in 1978 so you can work out that *last year* was 1977. **A** and **D** are incorrect as they are not dates and do not tell when. **B** is incorrect because this is the date that whaling was banned in Australian waters.

5 This is a **fact-finding** question. The answer is stated directly in the text. You read … *whaling activity* [in Australia] *that has forced humpback, southern right whales and sperm whales to the brink of extinction in Australian waters* (see lines 9–12). Your answer should name: humpback, southern right and sperm whales.

6 This is a **fact-finding** question. The answer is stated directly in the text. You read *Improved technology such as the harpoon cannon, the toggle harpoon, deck cannons, faster chase boats and later factory ships and the use of aircraft to spot whale pods increased the efficiency of whaling and led to the rapid depletion of whale stocks. This forced the Australian government to ban all commercial whaling before whales become extinct in Australian waters* (see lines 13–21). Your answer should paraphrase this paragraph. For example: Technological advances that made it easier to find and kill whales impacted on whale numbers. This included the use of aeroplanes, faster boats, factory ships, and more efficient cannons and harpoons.

Synthesis questions

Burger Shack (page 40)

1 D **2** B **3** C **4** D **5** C **6** See below

Explanations

1 This is a **synthesis** question. **D** is correct. Think about the information across the whole text. The text is an advertisement. The design of the text and all the information included is meant to attract customers. The text uses high modality commands (*Sample; Try*) (see lines 5 and 12), descriptive phrases (*Grand Opening; delicious mouth-watering*) (see lines 2–3) and persuasive devices (*Be the first; juice **FREE** with every burger purchased*) (see lines 3 and 30) to influence readers and persuade them to go to Burger Shack. **A** is incorrect because Burger Shack sells other items as well as burgers. **B** is incorrect because offering free juice is not the purpose of the ad. **C** is incorrect. It is a statement made in the text but it is not the purpose of the text.

2 This is a **synthesis** question. **B** is correct. Think about the information across the whole text and how ideas are connected. Ideas are included by adding information. Other answers apply to different types of texts.

3 This is a **synthesis** question. **C** is correct. Think about the ideas across the whole text. The main idea in the text is that the restaurant sells delicious food. **A**, **B** and **D** could be true but they are not the main idea of the text.

4 This is a **synthesis** question. **D** is correct. Think about the information across the whole text and decide which item could be added to the menu.

You read *home-made vegan burgers* (see line 4) and *No animals are killed to procure or produce our food* (see line 26). You can work out that the wild rice dumplings do not appear to use animal products while **A**, **B** and **C** all involve animals and so would not be sold at a vegan restaurant.

5 This is a **synthesis** question. **C** is incorrect. It makes sense in the context of the text. It would not make sense for a restaurant to limit the amount of food a customer is allowed to purchase (**A**). **B** is true in the text but is not an answer to the question. **D** is advertised in the text but is not an answer to the question.

6 This is a **synthesis** question. Think about the information across the whole text. You read *Grand Opening across Australia* (see line 2) and should recognise that numerous venues are opening on the same day across the country. Your answer should state: The text does not include an address because a number of Burger Shacks are opening on the same day across Australia so customers would phone or go online to find an address or they might have noticed a Burger Shack being set up near them. This saves Burger Shack printing different flyers for each region.

Citizenship (page 41)

1 C **2** B **3** A, B and C **4** D **5** See below **6** See below

Explanations

1 This is a **synthesis** question. **C** is correct. Think about the ideas across the whole text and how the ideas are presented. The text provides information on the topic of citizenship. **A**, **B** and **D** are incorrect as the text is not instructional (**A**), it does not give advice (**D**) and it does not explain a citizen's point of view (**B**).

2 This is a **synthesis** question. **B** is correct. Think about the ideas across the whole text and how they are connected. Each paragraph adds new information about the topic. **A** is incorrect as the text is not sequenced chronologically. **C** does not answer how. **D** is incorrect as the text does not present an argument.

3 This is a **synthesis** question. **A**, **B** and **C** are correct. You read paragraph four. This paragraph tells readers what citizens can do. **D** is incorrect because you read *Everyone living in Australia (citizens, residents and tourists) must comply with Australian law* (see lines 8–10).

4 This is a **synthesis** question. **D** is correct. Think about the ideas across the whole text and how they are connected. You read *Citizens have the right to vote and stand for parliament. These rights are also privileges; they bring with them the responsibility to do what each citizen believes is best for Australia as a nation and for the Australian people* (see lines 18–20). You can work out that only Answer **D**, voting, is both a right as well as a responsibility. Other answers are only partly correct. **A** and **C** are rights. **B** is a responsibility.

5 This is a **synthesis** question. Think about and synthesise ideas from across the whole text. A lucky country is a country where people have the right to vote and stand for election, freedom of speech and of religion, equality and tolerance, democracy and the law, respect for the individual and compassion for others.

6 This is a **synthesis** question. Think about the information across the whole text. Your answer should state that citizens, residents and tourists must all respect and obey Australian law. According to the Australian Electoral Commission website, 'The only non-Australian citizens who are eligible to vote are British subjects who were on the Commonwealth electoral roll immediately before 26 January 1984, at which time the eligibility requirements were altered. The following Australians not entitled to enrol and vote are people who are incapable of understanding the nature and significance of enrolment and voting: prisoners serving a sentence of five years or longer; and people who have been convicted of treason and not pardoned.'

Krill (page 42)

1 B **2** D **3** A **4** B **5** B **6** See below

Explanations

1 This is a **synthesis** question. **B** is correct. Think about the ideas across the whole text and how they are presented. You can tell that the text presents a point of view. The speaker, Lee, makes a thesis statement: *marine creatures such as fish, penguins and whales rely on krill for survival* (see lines 12–14), and then provides supporting evidence and arguments in the rest of the text. She uses emotive words and phrases (*survival; starve*) (see lines 14 and 28) and high modality (*it's so irresponsible; krill does not belong in a human food chain*) (see lines 19 and 34–35) to present her point of view on the topic. **A** is incorrect. There is some factual information in the text but the text largely consists of opinions so its purpose is not to present facts. **C** is incorrect because this is not the purpose of the text. **D** is incorrect. The text does include some information about the marine food chain but explaining how it works is not the purpose of the text.

2 This is a **synthesis** question. **D** is correct. Think about the structure of the text. The interviewer controls the structure of the text through the pattern of question and answer. **A** is incorrect because cause and effect does not provide a framework for the text. **B** is incorrect as ideas in the text are not sequenced in time. **C** is incorrect because the text is an interview rather than a speech or argument.

3 This is a **synthesis** question. **A** is correct. Think about the ideas across the whole text. Lee's main message is for people to stop buying krill oil. **B** might be true but is not the point Lee wants to get across to listeners. **C** is a fact in the text but not the main message. **D** is not something that Lee would agree with. While Lee states that some krill might be sustainably fished she says that *krill does not belong in a human food chain* (see lines 34–35).

4 This is a **synthesis** question. **B** is correct. Think about the ideas across the whole text. Lee's key point is that people who consume krill oil products are depriving marine animals of their food and therefore causing them to *starve to death* (see lines 28–29). The opposite point of view to this would be to state that there's plenty of krill in the sea for everyone—people and animals. **A** is incorrect because Lee does say in the text that krill oil has *reported heart health benefits* (see line 11). **C** and **D** are incorrect because these ARE Lee's opinions.

5 This is a **synthesis** question. **B** is correct. Synthesise the ideas and point of view presented in the text and match this with a suitable headline. 'Whales starve to death' is a headline that will capture readers' attention because it is sensational and emotive like Lee's comments. It represents Lee's point of view. Other answers are not what Lee is arguing for.

6 This is a **synthesis** question. Synthesise ideas across the whole text. You should conclude that: Krill is a basis of the marine food chain. Adequate krill in the ocean is vital for marine life. Krill is a finite resource. Krill fished unsustainably will run out.

Suffrage (page 43)

1 C **2** C **3** DACB **4** C **5** C
6 See below

Explanations

1 This is a **synthesis** question. **C** is correct. The text provides general historical information about suffrage. **A** is incorrect as the purpose of the text is not to simply name well-known Australian suffragettes. **B** and **D** are incorrect because the text is not an explanation nor is it a persuasive text.

2 This is a **synthesis** question. **C** is correct. You read that Vida Goldstein was an Australian suffragette *(see line 20)* so you should realise her publication would support suffrage. **A**, **B** and **D** are opposed to women's suffrage.

3 This is a **synthesis** question. **DACB** is the correct sequence. You read *One of the most amazing feats was a petition presented to the Victorian Parliament in 1891* (see lines 16–17). You can work out that campaigning started before 1891, so **D** happened first. New Zealand women being given the right to vote in 1893 was second. Australian women gaining the right to vote in Federal elections in 1902 came third in chronological order. Last in the sequence was The UN declaring suffrage a basic human right in 1979.

4 This is a **synthesis** question. **C** is correct. The text is about women's suffrage. **A** is incorrect as the text is not about women in politics. **B** is incorrect as women being denied the vote is the opposite focus to what the text is about. **D** is incorrect as the text is not about voters' rights.

5 This is a **synthesis** question. **C** is correct. Synthesise ideas from across the whole text. You can draw the conclusion that people in Australia were largely prejudiced against women in the late 1800s, otherwise women would not have had to campaign so hard and for so long to gain suffrage. **A** is incorrect as suffrage was only recognised by the United Nations as a basic right in 1979. **B** is incorrect as the fact that women were given the vote in 1902 means that **B** is untrue. **D** is untrue based on all the evidence in the text.

6 This is a **synthesis** question. Think about and synthesise the ideas in the text. You need to recognise that as a politician it would have been in your best interests to be positive about suffrage as women were now voters. Your answer could express the following idea: I am very pleased that women have now gained the right to vote. I look forward to the next election where they will have the opportunity to caste their inaugural votes. I hope they recognise that I will represent their interests and I hope that they vote for me.

Inferring questions

Landmines (page 48)

1 A, B and C **2** B and C **3** B **4** C
5 See below **6** See below

Explanations

1 This is an **inferring** question. **A**, **B** and **C** are correct. Work out the answer using the clues in the text and by reading between the lines. Normal use for land would be farming (**A** and **C**) and as a transport route such as a road, track or pathway (**B**). **D** does not answer the question.

2 This is an **inferring** question. **B** and **C** are correct. Work out the answer using the clues in the text and by reading between the lines. You read the full title of the Convention: *the Convention on the Prohibition of the Use, Stockpiling, Production and Transfer of Anti-Personnel Mines and on their Destruction* (see lines 15–16). You can work out that countries make landmines to use themselves or as exports to sell to other countries. **A** is incorrect as there is no benefit in manufacturing an item for the purpose of stockpiling it. **D** does not make sense as a country would not knowingly sell landmines to its enemies.

3 This is an **inferring** question. **B** is correct. Work out the answer by reading between the lines. Each answer is true in the text but paragraph one states that landmines *are a particularly brutal weapon because they kill and maim indiscriminately, injuring civilians, children and animals* (see lines 5–6). You should infer that this aspect is the worst thing about landmines.

4 This is an **inferring** question. **C** is correct. You can work out the answer using the clues in the text and by reading between the lines. A mine detection vehicle works to trigger the mine to explode. Other options are incorrect.

5 This is an **inferring** question. Work out the answer using the clues in the text and by reading between the lines. The text implies that people in poor communities need to use their land to grow food for their own use, or for sale or trade. They simply can't afford to leave the land unused so they continue to use their fields and risk stepping on mines. Mines can also be laid in fields or on tracks that local villagers use as short cuts to their destinations.

6 This is an **inferring** question. Work out the answer using the clues in the text and by reading between the lines. You can infer that Australia is signatory to the Mine Ban Treaty because morally or ethically it's the right thing to do. Landmines are military weapons that kill or maim innocent people for many years after a war is over.

Palm oil (page 49)

1 C **2** B **3** B and C **4** B and C
5 See below **6** See below

Explanations

1 This is an **inferring** question. **C** is correct. Work out the answer using the clues in the text and by reading between the lines. You read that palm oil is *the most widely used vegetable oil in the entire world because the oil palm tree is quicker and cheaper to grow than other oil-producing plants* (see lines 5–6). You can infer that this is exactly why the world needs it. **A** and **B** are incorrect because, even though they are statements of fact in the text, they do not answer the question. **D** is not a fact in the text. The text says that palm oil can be sustainably grown but not all palm oil is grown sustainably.

2 This is an **inferring** question. **B** is correct. Work out the answer using the clues in the text and by reading between the lines. Much of the world's palm oil is grown in plantations that have replaced wild rainforest so rhinos have lost habitat as a result. **A** and **C** do not make sense. **D** is incorrect as palm oil trees are not grown all over rainforests.

3 This is an **inferring** question. **B** and **C** are correct. Work out the answer using the clues in the text and by reading between the lines. You can infer that Lily's family has a similar attitude to Lily. You can infer that they will read labels and buy sustainable products such as products with RSPO certification. There is nothing in the text to lead you to infer that **A** or **D** are correct.

4 This is an **inferring** question. **B** and **C** are correct. Work out the answer using the clues in the text and by reading between the lines. You read that Lily urges listeners to become ethical consumers. She says *Find out how your products are sourced or made, and tell companies to do the right thing environmentally or you won't buy their products* (see lines 24–25). You can infer that **B** and **C** are correct. There is nothing in the text to lead to an inference that **A** or **D** are correct.

5 This is an **inferring** question. Work out the answer using the clues in the text and by reading between the lines. You read *The solution to deforestation is to grow palm oil sustainably (see line 12)*. Relate this statement to the information in paragraph two. You can infer that Lily believes that the indiscriminate clearing of rainforests in order to plant palm oil trees is what has caused deforestation in Indonesia and Malaysia.

6 This is an **inferring** question. You can infer that accurate labelling gives people the information they need when making purchasing decisions. It enables people to use their purchasing power to choose more environmentally friendly or sustainable products. Your answer should take account of the following idea: accurate product labelling enables people to read exactly what's in a product and choose not to buy it if it has unsustainable ingredients.

Giant slain, goose gone! (page 50)

1 C **2** D **3** B **4** C **5** C **6** See below

Explanations

1 This is an **inferring** question. **C** is correct. Work out the answer using the clues in the text and by reading between the lines. You read in paragraph one that an axe was used to fell the tree that the giant was descending. You can infer that the fall to the ground is what killed the giant. The giant was not killed with the axe (**A**) or because a tree fell on him (**B**). **D** is a fact in the text but does not answer the question.

2 This is an **inferring** question. **D** is correct. Work out the answer using the clues in the text and by reading between the lines. You read paragraph three and can work out that the giant's wife is most concerned about her goose. She does not imply that she is sorry about the giant's death (**A**). She does express regret that Jack took advantage of her kindness (**B**) and that she didn't heed her husband's advice about Jack (**C**), but these are not her main concerns.

3 This is an **inferring** question. **B** is correct. Work out the answer using the clues in the text and by reading between the lines. You read Jack's mother's statement *"I'd tell the police if I knew he was hiding in the cupboard" (see lines 20–21)* and that she had to buy goose food *(see lines 45–46)*. The author has used irony to let readers know where Jack is hiding, letting readers in on a secret the rest of the characters in the story don't know and at the same time showing readers that Jack's mother is not very bright. You use these clues in the text to work out that **B** is correct. You read that witnesses saw Jack *running … with a goose tucked under his arm (see lines 12–13)* so you know that **A** is true but the question asks what you think has happened. **C** is impossible as the tree has been felled. **D** is incorrect because there is no evidence to imply that Jack has been murdered.

4 This is an **inferring** question. **C** is correct. Work out the answer using the clues in the text and by reading between the lines. You read that the giant's wife says her husband warned her about Jack: *"He said Jack smelt funny. I should have listened to him" (see lines 30–31)*. There is nothing in the text to imply that other options are correct.

5 This is an **inferring** question. **C** is correct. Work out the answer using the clues in the text and by reading between the lines. You read that Jack's mother says *her son is a gentle, loving boy and not a giant killer. "He wouldn't hurt a fly," she said, "but he was obsessed with that tree, claiming it would solve all our financial problems and that he would be able to care for me better" (see lines 14–19)*. You should infer that Jack's motivation was his love for his mother. There is nothing in the text to support an inference that Jack hated the giant (**A**) or the giant's wife (**B**), or that he took the goose because he loved it (**D**).

6 This is an **inferring** question. Work out a suitable answer using the clues in the text. You should infer that it was Jack who chopped down the tree and caused the giant to die. You can infer that when Jack is captured by police he will declare that he did not intend to kill the giant, just to chop down the tree so that the giant could not follow him home. Jack might also use the excuse that he was rescuing the goose rather than stealing it.

My grandparents (page 51)

1 C **2** B **3** B **4** D **5** See below
6 See below

Explanations

1 This is an **inferring** question. **C** is correct. Work out the answer using the clues in the text and by reading between the lines. You can infer that the writer's father was born in Vietnam because you read *My grandparents are my heroes. They came to Australia from Vietnam in 1977 when they were in their early twenties. My father came with them but he was only three years old at the time (see lines 2–5)*. **A** is incorrect as the question asks where

not when. **B** is incorrect as the father was three when he came to Australia. **D** is incorrect because you read *They lived in a refugee camp in Malaysia for eighteen months before being permitted to immigrate to Australia* (see lines 7–9), so you can infer that the writer's father was born before the family fled to Malaysia.

2 This is an **inferring** question. **B** is correct. Work out the answer using the clues in the text and by reading between the lines. You read that the grandparents were *fearful about life in Saigon after the fall of the South Vietnamese Government* (see lines 6–7) and further that *My grandparents are Buddhist and every day they tell their sons to do good things and create a bright future* (see lines 13–15). The grandparents wanted a better future. **A** is incorrect. The grandparents wanted their sons to get a good education but they did not come to Australia so that the sons would become doctors or pharmacists. **C** and **D** are incorrect. These are not the reasons that the grandparents came to Australia.

3 This is an **inferring** question. **B** is correct. Work out the answer using the clues in the text and by reading between the lines. The statement is included in the paragraph about New Year traditions and Vietnamese heritage. You can infer that '*lucky money*' (see line 27) is given every New Year for good luck. **A** is incorrect as the narrator calls the money lucky, not the receiver of the money. There is nothing in the text to cause you to infer that **C** and **D** are correct.

4 This is an **inferring** question. **D** is correct. Work out the answer using the clues in the text and by reading between the lines. This custom implies that the New Year should start with a clean house. A clean house is a metaphor for a clean start to the year. No problems (dirt) from the old year can be carried into the New Year. **A**, **B** and **C** are not supported by evidence in the text.

5 This is an **inferring** question. Work out the answer using the clues in the text. The grandparents show pride by following customs and traditions, passing these on to their children and grandchildren, continuing cultural celebrations and keeping close family bonds.

6 This is an **inferring** question. Work out the answer using the clues in the text and by reading between the lines. You can infer that the writer respects his grandparents' decision to immigrate to Australia, arriving with nothing and building a good life for their sons. They inspired their sons to study hard and get a good education. They maintained their Vietnamese traditions.

Clean up Australia (page 52)

1 B **2** B **3** D **4** C **5** A, B and D
6 See below

Explanations

1 This is an **inferring** question. **B** is correct. Work out the answer using the clues in the text and by reading between the lines. You can infer that Jordan's mum got involved and therefore Jordan got involved. **A** and **C** are incorrect. There is no evidence in the text to imply that Jordan was introduced to the Clean Up Australia Day activity through any means other than his mother. Answer **D** is incorrect. It justifies his volunteering but does not explain how.

2 This is an **inferring** question. **B** is correct. Work out the answer using the clues in the text and by reading between the lines. You can tell that Jordan is happy to volunteer when he says *It is fun and you meet people and it's a really good cause* (see line 27). There is no evidence in the text to support an inference that he is annoyed (**A**), bored (**C**) or upset (**D**) about volunteering. He only gets upset when he sees *how much rubbish accumulates in the environment each fortnight* (see lines 17–18).

3 This is an **inferring** question. **D** is correct. Work out the answer using the clues in the text and by reading between the lines. The fact that Jordan is enthusiastically speaking on the topic at a school assembly allows you to infer that he likes to share his enthusiasm. There is no evidence in the text to support an inference that he annoys others (**A**), that he is a show-off (**B**) or that he is bossy (**C**).

4 This is an **inferring** question. **C** is correct. Work out the answer using the clues in the text and by reading between the lines. You read that Mum *advertised our clean-up dates and times on the Clean Up Australia Day website, inviting others to join us* (see lines 9–10). You can infer that at least some of the people who registered are strangers to Mum but were interested in helping the environment. The volunteers won't all be from the netball club (**A**) or from Mum's circle of friends (**D**). You also cannot infer that they have a lot of free time (**B**). They might have very little free time but choose to spend it volunteering.

5 This is an **inferring** question. **A**, **B** and **D** are correct. Work out the answer using the clues in the text and by reading between the lines. You can infer that Mum is a good organiser (**A**) because she *registered a clean-up site on behalf of her netball club* … and she *advertised* … *clean-up*

dates and times (see lines 8–10) and she coordinates activity on each clean-up day. You can infer that mum is confident in speaking to people in public (**B**) because she gives a safety briefing to the group of twenty-eight people each clean-up day. You can infer that Mum likes to exercise or keep fit (**D**) because she plays netball. **C** is incorrect. There is no evidence in the text to support an inference that Jordan's mother likes to be in charge. She did not ask to be a supervisor but was automatically made supervisor because she was the person who registered the site.

6 This is an **inferring** question. Work out the answer using the clues in the text and by reading between the lines. You read that volunteers clean up the rubbish *along the beach, the dunes, paths and walkways* (see line 17). Your answer should say that Jordan is upset about people rubbishing the environment and that the work he and the group does each fortnight is undone by careless litterers.

Camping with Grandpa (page 53)

1 B **2** B **3** C **4** A **5** B **6** See below

Explanations

1 This is an **inferring** question. **B** is correct. Work out the answer using the clues in the text and by reading between the lines. You read *Grandpa and his new girlfriend Deborah* (see line 3). You can infer that Grandpa has had previous girlfriends who would be his old girlfriends. **A** is incorrect because you cannot infer that Grandma has died as she is not mentioned at all in the text. **C** is incorrect. The fact that Grandpa has a girlfriend is not evidence that he is quite young. This inference would be ageist as a person can have girlfriends or boyfriends at any age. **D** is incorrect. There is nothing in the text to support an inference that Grandpa gets lonely on his own.

2 This is an **inferring** question. **B** is correct. Work out the answer using the clues in the text and by reading between the lines. To *rough it* is a colloquial expression that means living without modern conveniences. People usually rough it when they go camping. Grandpa has a lot of gear for comfort so he does not have to rough it. **A** is incorrect. Grandpa has a lot of gear but you cannot infer that it is all for comfort—some would be for safety. **C** is incorrect. Grandpa might have a spirit of adventure but this is not what is implied by what Mum said. **D** is incorrect. There is nothing in the text to infer that Grandpa sleeps under the stars and this is not an answer to the question.

3 This is an **inferring** question. **C** is correct. Work out the answer using the clues in the text and by reading between the lines. You read about the equipment Grandpa has and you realise he likes to be comfortable. **A** is incorrect because Grandpa does not rough it. **B** and **D** are incorrect. You read *Grandpa has been camping there every September for at least 15 years so he knows everyone* (see lines 8–10) and you can infer that Grandpa does not seek solitude when he goes camping. You can also infer that camping is not a new way of holidaying for him.

4 This is an **inferring** question. **A** is correct. Work out the answer using the clues in the text and by reading between the lines. You read *He has an aluminium fold-up dining table and six folding chairs, a gas BBQ with a hood as well as a three-burner stove* (see lines 14–15). You can infer that Grandpa likes to cook and eat. **B** is incorrect because there is no evidence that anyone other than Grandpa does the cooking. **C** is incorrect as the text says Grandpa fishes but not that he cooks fish. **D** is incorrect as there is no evidence to suggest that Grandpa dislikes cooking.

5 This is an **inferring** question. **B** is correct. Work out the answer using the clues in the text and by reading between the lines. You can infer that Mum is concerned about the unpredictability of a wild kangaroo if a child approaches it. **A** is a fact in the text and not an answer to the question. There is no evidence in the text to support **C** or **D**.

6 This is an **inferring** question. The statement implies that the writer is surprised that someone old enough to be Grandpa's girlfriend had never been camping in her life before. The fact that the writer thought this fact interesting enough to report in the text and the use of the exclamation mark after the word *ever!* (see line 5) shows that the writer is surprised. You can infer that the writer camps regularly and has done so for many years with her family.

Aliens attack Earth! (page 54)

1 A, B and C **2** B **3** C **4** D **5** D
6 See below

Explanations

1 This is an **inferring** question. **A**, **B** and **C** are correct. Work out the answer using the clues in the text and by reading between the lines. You can infer by the words used in the text that the writer wants to frighten people (**A**). You would also infer that people are being killed and cities destroyed. There is no evidence in the text that the aliens want to make friends (**D**).

2 This is an **inferring** question. **B** is correct. Work out the answer using the clues in the text and by reading between the lines. The adjective *largely* (see line 22) is used to imply that most descriptions of the aliens are the same. **A** is incorrect because *largely confirms* (see line 22) does not mean that the aliens are large. **C** and **D** are incorrect because this is not what the statement implies in the text.

3 This is an **inferring** question. **C** is correct. Work out the answer using the clues in the text and by reading between the lines. The phrase *at this stage* (see line 12) implies that humans will continue attempting to communicate with the aliens. **A** and **B** are incorrect. You can't infer that it is impossible or that the aliens don't want to communicate. **D** is incorrect. You cannot infer that humans won't ever know how to communicate with aliens.

4 This is an **inferring** question. **D** is correct. Work out the answer using the clues in the text and by reading between the lines. You read *World leaders are urging people to … refrain from civil unrest, raiding and looting. Harsh penalties will apply for crimes while Earth is under attack* (see lines 33–36). This paragraph implies that authorities believe some people might use this opportunity to break the law or engage in criminal activity. The police are busy elsewhere so people think can get away with their crimes. **A**, **B** and **C** are incorrect. **A** and **B** contradict the meaning of the paragraph. There is no evidence to imply that **C** is correct.

5 This is an **inferring** question. **D** is correct. Work out the answer using the clues in the text and by reading between the lines. The phrase *yet to determine* (see line 24) means 'waiting to find out' or 'working on finding out'. The phrase implies that scientists haven't decided anything or been able to prove anything about the spiders yet. The phrase does not imply **A**, **B** or **C**.

6 This is an **inferring** question. Work out the answer using the clues in the text and by reading between the lines. The statement is a fact at the end of a sensationalised news report. The implication of the statement is that the aliens haven't killed anyone and possibly don't even intend to destroy earth or kill anyone. It is placed at the end of the text because it is of least newsworthy value. The goal of a newspaper is to capture readers' attention so a highly emotive and sensational text about death and destruction will sell more copies that one that says everyone is safe. You might also infer that people have accidentally died because of panic.

Celebrity interview (page 55)

1 C **2** A **3** B **4** B **5** D **6** See below

Explanations

1 This is an **inferring** question. **C** is correct. Work out the answer using the clues in the text and by reading between the lines. You read *Many of your songs …* (see line 11) and you can infer that Kirra is famous for being a singer (**C**). There is no evidence in the text to imply **A** or **D**. Being famous and being a celebrity are the same thing so **B** is incorrect as it does not answer the question.

2 This is an **inferring** question. **A** is correct. Work out the answer using the clues in the text and by reading between the lines. You read *My brother and I suffered because of racism at school* (see lines 14–15) and you can infer that Kirra had problems at school. The word *suffered* in the text implies that **B** is incorrect. There is no evidence in the text to support inferences that **C** or **D** are correct.

3 This is an **inferring** question. **B** is correct. Work out the answer using the clues in the text and by reading between the lines. You read *I've been lucky but I do also work very hard* (see lines 9–10). There is no evidence in the text to support inferences **A** and **C**. **D** is incorrect because Kirra says her success is partly due to hard work and not all to luck.

4 This is an **inferring** question. **B** is correct. Work out the answer using the clues in the text and by reading between the lines. You read *My brother and I suffered because of racism at school. One particular boy continually made racist remarks … his parents* [also] *made racist comments about First Nations Australians* (see lines 15–19). You can infer that Kirra is a First Australian. There is no evidence in the text to support inferences that Kirra lives in Sydney (**A**), is American (**C**) or lives overseas (**D**).

5 This is an **inferring** question. **D** is correct. Work out the answer using the clues in the text and by reading between the lines. You read all of Kirra's responses to the interview questions and you can infer that the interviewer is thanking Kirra for being open and honest (**D**). **A** and **B** are incorrect because Kirra doesn't seem to be secretive and the brief interview means that answers could not be described as lengthy. **C** is incorrect because you can judge that the interview is frank and serious rather than entertaining.

6 This is an **inferring** question. Work out the answer using the clues in the text and by reading between the lines. You read that many of Kirra's songs *have social or environmental messages* (see lines 11–12). You read that Kirra says she supports children's charities. She says *Education can help lift people out of poverty. If we can educate children then they can have better lives and it will be a better future for everyone. I like to help the Red Cross, in Australia and overseas, especially for its humanitarian work in countries where there is conflict* (see lines 42–49). Your answer should include humanitarian and social issues as likely topics for Kirra's songs as well as First Nations issues, racism and discrimination.

Language questions

The man in a boy (page 60)

1 D **2** A **3** D **4** C **5** D **6** See below

Explanations

1 This is a **language** question. **D** is correct. Work out the answer by examining the way language is used in the text. You read that the boy did not usually like to argue (*Not one to challenge or argue*) (see line 17) but that he was watchful for bullies and could *speak his mind to defend an underdog—someone or something smaller or weaker. That's who the boy was* (see lines 20–24). **A**, **B** and **C** would not make the boy speak out in anger.

2 This is a **language** question. **A** is correct. Work out the answer by examining the way language is used in the text. In the poem the narrator admonishes the boy to *walk tall* (see line 32). You can work out that *admonish* means 'scold, give an instruction, rebuke or tell someone what to do'. You can work out that the narrator is neither yelling at the boy nor praising or giving approval in this part of the poem.

3 This is a **language** question. **D** is correct. Work out the answer by examining the way language is used in the text. The boy is described as *solid and dependable* as well as *[b]ig-hearted* (see lines 6–11) and kind to animals. **A** is incorrect as the boy is kind but there is no evidence in the text that he is loud. **B** is incorrect. The boy is described as *smart* (see line 14) but not proud. The narrator advises him to be *proud* (see line 34). **C** is incorrect. Evidence in the text allows readers to recognise that the boy is *watchful* (see line 18) and thoughtful rather than thoughtless.

4 This is a **language** question. **C** is correct. Work out the answer by examining the way language is used in the text. The expression is idiomatic. It does not literally mean anything to do with drums (**A** and **B**). You can work out that the narrator wants the boy to be true to himself; to be proud of who is. **D** is incorrect as there is no evidence in the text that the boy is called names.

5 This is a **language** question. **D** is correct. Work out the answer by examining the way language is used in the text. The narrator describes the boy using positive term such as *solid and dependable; [b]ig-hearted; mindful;* and *alert to … bullies* (see lines 6, 8, 13 and 19), and a defender of smaller or weaker people or animals. The narrator wants the boy to be proud of himself and accepting of who he is, so you can tell that the narrator is proud of the boy. There is no evidence in the text to support **A**, **B** or **C**.

6 This is a **language** question. Work out the answer by examining the way language is used in the text. The narrator says *The boy looked like his father* (see line 2). Then the narrator says positive things about the boy followed by *That's who the boy was. / The boy was not his father* (see lines 24–25). The narrator further says *don't let others / define who you are. / You are you. / You are not your father* (see lines 41–44). You can work out that the narrator does not have a good opinion of the father and reminds the boy he is not like his father and never has to be.

Enviro-holidays (page 61)

1 A **2** B **3** A, C and D **4** D
5 See below **6** See below

Explanations

1 This is a **language** question. **A** is correct. Work out the answer by examining the way language is used in the context of the text. The pronoun *we* (see line 22) refers to the Enviro-holidays staff. **B** and **C** are incorrect because the creators of the advertisement and other holiday travellers would not collect you at the airport. Tui, Jarrod and Sebastiaan (**D**) wrote the Testimonials. They are previous holiday travellers so they would not be collecting people from the airport.

2 This is a **language** question. **B** is correct. Work out that a testimonial is a recommendation.

Testimonials are written by people who have used a product or a service and will vouch for it. You can tell that **A** is incorrect because there is no test in the text. **C** is incorrect. You can tell that the testimonials do not give readers advice. **D** is incorrect because the testimonials are included or used in the advertisement but are not themselves advertisements.

3 This is a **language** question. **A**, **C** and **D** are correct. Work out the answer by examining the way language is used in the context of the text. The advertisement addresses the reader with a question that is most likely to lead to a 'yes' response from the reader. It addresses the reader as *you* *(see line 2)* to attract the reader's attention. The word *environment* *(see line 2)* is aimed at people who are interested in environmental issues. **B** is incorrect because, even though the content of the ad describes an environmental holiday, the use of a question at the beginning of the ad does not promote environmental issues.

4 This is a **language** question. **D** is correct. Work out the answer by examining the language of the text. You read *Stay from two weeks ($1800) to three months ($3500)* *(see lines 9–10)*. The use of *from* indicates that you can stay for any length of time between two weeks and up to three months. Other answers are incorrect as they do not state the right length of time.

5 This is a **language** question. Work out the answer by examining the language of the text. You read *Fees for a good cause: animal rescues, elephant medical care, habitat restoration, and supporting local communities in education and conservation* *(see lines 10–13)*. The use of the preposition *for* helps you link the information about cost to the ways the money will be spent.

6 This is a **language** question. You can work out the answer by examining the use of the phrase *with a conscience* *(see line 4)*. It means using your sense of right and wrong or your own moral code. Holiday behaviour that is morally right means that you can *help make the world a better place* *(see line 4)* while on holiday instead of leaving a place worse off from your visit.

Super 'S' Supermarkets (page 62)

1 B **2** D **3** B **4** A **5** D **6** See below

Explanations

1 This is a **language** question. **B** is correct. Work out the answer by examining the way language is used. You read *Super 'S' Supermarkets honestly care about being cruelty free. None of our products are harmful to animals* *(see lines 13–17)*. The products won't hurt animals. **A**, **C** and **D** are incorrect. The statement *Super 'S' Supermarkets honestly care about being cruelty free* does not mean that all products are cruelty free or were manufactured without hurting animals. The supermarket spokesperson can claim that the supermarket cares about animals and about being cruelty free but this does not guarantee that any actions will follow.

2 This is a **language** question. **D** is correct. Work out the answer by examining the way language is used. The supermarkets are likely to stock some Fair Trade products. Their spokesperson could not claim to support Fair Trade unless they stocked some products but there is no promise to only stock Fair Trade (**A**). **B** is incorrect because it is a lower modality than **D**. The words 'might stock' mean that they also might not stock, so this is likely to be untrue. **C** is incorrect as a supermarket would want to cater for all its shoppers and so it would need to stock some Fair Trade products for customers to choose.

3 This is a **language** question. **B** is correct. Work out the answer by examining the way language is used in the text. The word *discourage* *(see line 22)* means that the supermarket encourages producers to avoid pesticides. It does not mean that all products are pesticide free (**A**) or chemical free (**C**) or that the supermarket tells producers not to use pesticides (**D**).

4 This is a **language** question. **A** is correct. Work out the answer by examining the way language is used in the context of the text. You should work out that the text is tongue-in-cheek or a send-up. It makes fun of a supermarket advertisement. **B**, **C** and **D** are incorrect because the text is not an actual advertisement nor was it written to provide information about supermarkets or shopping.

5 This is a **language** question. **D** is correct. You read *We encourage all our customers to buy reuseable bags and avoid single-use plastic bags* *(see lines 9–11)*. There is no evidence in the text to support **A**, **B** or **C**.

6 This is a **language** question. Work out the answer by examining the way language is used in the text. Repeating a consonant sound such as 's' is called alliteration. This device can be used for a variety of purposes, including creating a tongue-twister effect or a poetic effect. It can sometimes add to the humour in a text. It has been used here for humour to reinforce the 'super' message by repeating the 's' sound.

My sister (page 63)

1 D **2** B **3** B **4** A **5** See below
6 See below

Explanations

1 This is a **language** question. **D** is correct. You read *My little sister is spoilt rotten. She gets away with murder … If I had done or said some of the things that she does when I was her age I would have been in big trouble* (see lines 2–3). The phrase *gets away with murder* is used figuratively rather than literally. It is an example of idiom. It means that, according to the writer, the sister can be very naughty but not get into trouble. **A** is incorrect because it doesn't specify the fact that the sister doesn't get into trouble. You can tell by the way the phrase is used in the text that the sister is not actually killing (**B**) or murdering anyone (**C**).

2 This is a **language** question. **B** is correct. Work out the answer by examining the way language is used in the text. You can tell by the tone of the text and the things the sister does that she idolises her brother. She copies her brother because she loves him, thinks he's clever and admires him. Dad says she adores her brother. Her nightmare involved her brother fighting off a witch so she was concerned for his safety. Her favourite book used to be her brother's. **A** is incorrect. The sister does not want to be the brother—she wants to be like him. **C** is incorrect. The brother is jealous, not the sister. **D** is incorrect as you can tell that the sister interacts with all family members and does not just seek attention from her brother.

3 This is a **language** question. **B** is correct. Work out the answer by examining the way language is used in the text. The phrase is an example of idiom. You can't literally wrap someone around your finger. The expression is used to mean that a person will do anything for you (bend any way you want) for reasons such as loving you a great deal. **A** is incorrect: it does not mean the same thing as wrapped around her finger. You can tell someone to do something but they might not do it. **C** doesn't make sense. **D** is incorrect because it does not explain the meaning of the expression.

4 This is a **language** question. **A** is correct. Work out the answer by examining the way language is used in the text. The narrator is jealous, protective and proud. The narrator is jealous that his sister has Dad wrapped around her finger but he is also protective such as when he took his sister's favourite book back from the boy at Kindy. He is also proud that his sister adores and looks up to him. **B** and **D** are incorrect as the narrator is never angry with his sister. **C** is incorrect. The answer does not include the feelings of love and pride that the narrator feels towards his sister that are evident in the text.

5 This is a **language** question. Work out the answer by examining the way language is used in the text. The word *that's* (see line 24) is used to refer to information in the previous sentence *my sister adores me* (see line 24). The writer thinks it is cool to have a little sister who adores him.

6 This is a **language** question. You can work out the answer by examining the way language is used in the text. Dad finds it funny because tentacles cannot bite, as they have no teeth.

Uluru (page 64)

1 See below **2** C **3** A **4** See below
5 See below **6** See below

Explanations

1 This is a **language** question. Work out the answer by examining the way language is used in the text. You read *Stand apart … Do not trample; / cause erosion; / step on sacred ground* (see lines 5–9). You can work out that the poet wants you to go to Uluru but not walk on it or climb on it.

2 This is a **language** question. **C** is correct. Work out the answer by examining the way language is used in the text. *Barren* means 'infertile' or 'having no ability to support life'. The poet uses the phrase *[d]eceptively barren* (see line 26) to mean that Uluru gives the appearance of being barren, but that looks can be deceiving. You read *Deceptively barren, / yet here are birds / and reptiles* (see lines 26–28). The word *yet* lets you know that Uluru is not barren. The animals and plants are listed in the rest of the stanza. **A** is incorrect as it gives a description of the desert rather than the meaning of the phrase. **B** is incorrect because this is not a definition of the phrase. **D** is incorrect because it doesn't include the concept of *deceptively*.

3 This is a **language** question. **A** is correct. Work out the answer by examining the way language is used in the text. The tone of a text is related to the way the narrator feels about the subject. You can tell that the poet feels respectful and awed. **B** is incorrect. There is no humour in the poem. **C** is incorrect. The poet takes the subject seriously but the poem is not depressing. **D** is incorrect because the poem does not express excitement.

4 This is a **language** question. The statement means that more of Uluru is underground than the part that is visible above the surface.

5 This is a **language** question. Work out the answer by examining the way language is used in the text. The poet means that Uluru looks unchanged since *the beginning of time* (see line 11) but at the same time is eroding very slowly away because of the effect of the weather and human activity. It is also a monolith that is still in itself but teeming with life and stories.

6 This is a **language** question. Work out the answer by examining the way language is used in the text. The poet means that it is possible for a person to look but not actually see what is before them. The person might only notice superficial things but not use their full powers of observation and empathy to look beyond the surface or develop any deeper understanding.

Biosecurity is so important (page 65)

1 B **2** B **3** C **4** A **5** See below **6** See below

Explanations

1 This is a **language** question. **B** is correct. Work out the answer by examining the way language is used in the text. You read *Sometimes you have to pay for* [items] *to be fumigated* (see lines 21–22) by the Department of Agriculture. You can work out that fumigation is a process to make the items safe to bring into Australia. You can work out that fumigation must be toxic or deadly to kill pests and diseases. *Fumigated* starts with the prefix *fum-*, so you should be able to work out that it means to treat with toxic fumes to kill pests and diseases (**B**). **A** and **C** are incorrect as they do not mention fumes. **D** is incorrect as wood smoke would not be sufficient to kill pests. 'Toxic' fumes are required to fumigate.

2 This is a **language** question. **B** is correct. Work out the answer by examining the way language is used in the text. You read *Sometimes the items are confiscated and destroyed* … [People] *might have unwittingly caused a terrible plant or animal disease or pest to enter our country* (see lines 22–25). You can tell that items are destroyed because they are illegal, dangerous or a biosecurity risk. **A** is incorrect as the items themselves don't necessarily have diseases. They can carry diseases which spread to plants and animals. **C** and **D** do not answer the question which starts with 'Why'.

3 This is a **language** question. **C** is correct. Work out the answer by examining the way language is used in the text. You read that *foot and mouth disease is a disease of cloven-hoofed animals (cattle, sheep, pigs, and so on)* (see lines 12–13). A goat has feet similar to cattle, sheep and pigs. **A** is incorrect because a bear has paws. **B** is incorrect because a crocodile has reptile feet. **D** is incorrect because a chicken has claws.

4 This is a **language** question. **A** is correct. Work out the answer by examining the way language is used in the text. You can tell by the tone of the text that the writer feels outrage. The writer uses high modality to express a strong point of view. Other answers are incorrect. The tone of the letter is not sadness (**B**), horror (**C**) or surprise (**D**).

5 This is a **language** question. Work out the answer by examining the way language is used in the text. The editor uses this high modality statement to express a strong point of view about the importance of confiscating and destroying people's property if it carries a risk to Australia's biosecurity.

6 This is a **language** question. Work out the answer by examining the way language is used in the text. The prefix *bio-* is used in biology which is the study of living things, including all plants, animals and other living organisms such as bacteria and viruses. The term *security* means 'safety'. So *biosecurity* means keeping biology (all people, plants and animals) safe from threats such as pests and diseases.

Lost (page 66)

1 C **2** B **3** B **4** B **5** See below **6** See below

Explanations

1 This is a **language** question. **C** is correct. Work out the answer by examining the way language is used in the text. You read stanza one. The word *without* refers to the previous statement *He ought to be home* (see line 2). This means that without him being home there's something amiss (wrong). You read *He only went to the Two-mile— he ought to be back* (see lines 5–6). In this context *amiss* means 'something is wrong' rather than 'something is missing'. **A** is incorrect because things aren't missing. **B** is incorrect as the old man doesn't say he misses seeing someone. **D** is a statement expressed by the old man. It does not give the meaning of the expression *without there's*

something amiss (see lines 2–4) as it is used in the context of the text.

2 This is a **language** question. **B** is correct. Work out the answer by examining the way language is used in the text. The old man is most concerned about the mother. Evidence of this is in the repetition of the line *what will his mother say?* (see lines 10 and 21) at the end of stanzas one and two. **A** is incorrect as the old man never expresses concern for himself. **C** and **D** are incorrect. You can tell by the language used in the poem that the old man is more worried about the mother than Willie or the Reckless mare.

3 This is a **language** question. **B** is correct. Work out the answer by examining the way language is used in the text. You read *Though far and wide they sought him, they found not where he fell; / For the ranges held him precious, and guarded their treasure well* (see lines 68–73). *Treasure* is the term used to refer to Willy rather than **A**, **C** or **D**. The word *treasure* in the poem is used metaphorically to refer to Willie.

4 This is a **language** question. **B** is correct. Work out the answer by examining the way language is used in the text. You read *"He ought to be home," said the old man, "without there's something amiss.* (see lines 2–4). You can tell the old man is worried and concerned. You read *He WOULD ride the Reckless filly, he WOULD have his wilful way* (see lines 7–8). You can tell the old man is annoyed that the boy was so determined to have his way when he'd obviously been advised not to ride the filly. It is a high modality statement of annoyance, implying 'I told him so!' **A** is incorrect because it doesn't mention the old man's worry or concern. **C** is incorrect because it doesn't take account of the old man's annoyance. **D** is incorrect. You read *But that Reckless mare is vicious, and if once she gets away / He hasn't got strength to hold her* (see lines 17–20). You can tell that the old man is not hopeful.

5 This is a **language** question. Work out the answer by examining the way language is used in the text. You read *But she came not home one evening, and they found her lying dead, / And stamped on the poor pale features, as the spirit homeward pass'd, / Was an angel smile of gladness—she had found the boy at last* (see lines 93–101). You should realise that the poet says the mother had died but she had died with a smile on her face because she had been reunited with her son in the afterlife.

6 This is a **language** question. This question requires you to re-read the poem, identify the main idea in each stanza and then write the main ideas in your own words.

An old man says he's worried about a boy who is not home from a short horse ride.

The old man describes the horse as dangerous.

The worried mother joins the old man at the gate, looking up the track.

The boy, Willie, has fallen off the horse, hit his head on a tree limb and is dead. The horse has run off.

The mother and old man search for the boy all night.

The mother searches all day until the next night.

The mother and old man continue to search but they can't find the boy deep within the bushland.

The mother continues her desperate search for days on end.

The mother, exhausted from searching, dies with a smile on her face.

Make sure you vary the shot types in your storyboard to show the particular perspective important in each scene.

Chief THINGS that are in the WORLD (page 67)

1 B **2** A and D **3** B **4** C **5** See below **6** See below

Explanations

1 This is a **language** question. **B** is correct. Work out the answer by examining the way language is used in the text. The list of animals *about the house* (see line 13) include *The Ape and the Monkey* which *are kept at home for delight* (see lines 16–17). You can work out that these animals are kept at home for the purposes of entertainment. **A** is incorrect as the Cat and Dog are useful. **C** is incorrect as only the Wild-Beasts would be considered dangerous. **D** is incorrect as the Ape and Monkey are not categorised as wild.

2 This is a **language** question. **A** and **D** are correct. Work out the answer by examining the way language is used in the text. You should recognise that plants do not move themselves around or go anywhere under their own power. **B** and **C** are incorrect because plants do take nourishment and they do die.

3 This is a **language** question. **B** is correct. Work out the answer by examining the way language is used in the text. You read *The Common Sense, under the forepart of the head, apprehendeth things taken from the outward senses* (see lines 44–46). You can tell by the way *apprehendeth* is used in the text that it means to make sense of things that the person sees, hears, touches, smells or tastes. **A**, **C** and **D** contradict the definitions in the text.

4 This is a **language** question. **C** is correct. Work out the answer by examining the way language is used in the text. You read that *The Phantasie … judgeth … thinketh and dreameth* (see lines 47–48). **A** is incorrect as you read *Sleep, is the rest of the Senses* (see line 52). **B** is incorrect as you read that taste is an outward sense. **D** is incorrect as forgetting things is part of the function of Memory.

5 This is a **language** question. Work out the answer by examining the way language is used in the text. Read the way that the text categorises The Outward and Inward Senses. The outward sensory receptors are defined as the eye, ear, nose, tongue and hand.

6 This is a **language** question. Work out the answer by examining the way language is used in the text. You read that the text was written in 1658. Note that dogs and cats were regarded as useful household animals in that they had jobs to do. Cats were kept to control vermin and dogs were kept to protect the house and occupants from intruders. The text seems to imply that these are the only reasons people kept dogs and cats in those times. In modern times dogs and cats are primarily kept as pets for companionship.

Judgement questions

A coal seam gas debate (page 72)

1 B **2** B **3** C **4** D **5** C **6** See below

Explanations

1 This is a **judgement** question. **B** is correct. Speakers 1, 2 and 3 express concerns about various kinds of pollution—land, water and air. **A** is only part of the answer. **C** is only part of the answer. **D** is incorrect as none of the speakers asked for extra research into the safety of CSG.

2 This is a **judgement** question. **B** is correct. The speaker is expressing his or her own opinion. The speaker's opinions may be shared by other farmers or members of the community or other people in general but he or she is not representing them here or speaking on their behalf. The speaker is expressing personal concerns.

3 This is a **judgement** question. **C** is correct. You read *I thought this* [$3000 per well] *was a windfall but I realise now that the money does not make up for the health of my family or the health of my animals* (see lines 17–20). You can judge that speaker 2 thinks the money is not worth the risk. **A** is incorrect as the money is not what the speaker feels is bad for the farm. **B** and **D** are incorrect as these are the opposite of what the speaker feels.

4 This is a **judgement** question. **D** is correct. The speaker makes emotive statements (*future at risk, can't say it is safe*) and uses emotive thinking verbs (*believe, worry*) and modal verbs/adverbs (*really can't say*) to express personal concerns. **A** is incorrect. The speaker uses emotive words and phrases (*at risk, can't say it's safe, worry*) but does not make accusations. **B** is partly correct but is not the best description as it omits speaker 3's effective use of thinking verbs which make the speaker's comments seem heartfelt and therefore more persuasive. **C** is incorrect as the speaker does not express ideas with less certainty or in a softer manner.

5 This is a **judgement** question. **C** is correct. Speaker 4 is a representative of the CSG company and so represents that company's interests. **A** is incorrect as speaker 4 talks about what the governments now require the CSG companies to do. **B** is incorrect. The speaker promotes an assured and affordable power supply to homes and businesses for all Australia but does not speak on behalf of all Australians. **D** is incorrect. The speaker does not present personal views. The speaker might have views and opinions that are the same as the company views or that differ from those of the company but as a company employee he or she must limit what is said to what the company policy endorses.

6 This is a **judgement** question. You can choose any speaker as long as you justify your choice by explaining why that speaker's remarks are relevant to you.

Disappointed resident (page 73)

1 B **2** C **3** D **4** A **5** A and C
6 See below.

Explanations

1. This is a **judgement** question. **B** is correct. You read the thesis statement in paragraph one *I am writing to express my disappointment in Gold Coast City Council for allowing an animal circus to operate on a Council Park* (see lines 9–10). You read the rest of the letter and you can judge that the writer believes that Council has a rule about animal circuses that Council is not upholding. You read the final paragraph where the writer restates the thesis of the argument: *I expect Council to uphold its own rules and not allow circuses with animals on Council land* (see line 21). The best summary of the writer's opinion is **B**. **A**, **C** and **D** are incorrect. They are statements of fact in the letter and opinions expressed by the writer but they are not the best summaries of the writer's opinions.
2. This is a **judgement** question. **C** is correct. It is the least relevant to the writer's argument about circuses performing on Council land. Other answers are incorrect. **A** is an important point in the writer's letter. **B** and **D** are relevant because they support the writer's argument that the *circus currently using Mitchell Park, Southport* (see line 10) is an animal circus and animal circuses are not good for animals.
3. This is a **judgement** question. **D** is correct. Read the whole letter and judge which outcome the writer would prefer. The writer would prefer that Council upholds its existing policy and bans animal circuses from its land. **A**, **B** and **C** are incorrect. These options would not achieve the writer's goal.
4. This is a **judgement** question. **A** is correct. The tenor of a text relates to the relationships between the people involved. Read the letter and consider who has written it and to whom the letter is addressed. The letter is formal and businesslike (**A**) It is appropriately addressed to the Mayor and Councillors. **B** is incorrect as the letter is not friendly, even though it is polite. **C** is incorrect as the letter is not personal or chatty. Chatty letters are appropriate when writing to friends or family members. **D** is incorrect because the letter is not from one official to another. Even though the letter does include some factual supporting information it cannot be described as scientific.
5. This is a **judgement** question. **A** and **C** are correct. You read the information and opinions included in the letter about animal circuses as well as the fact that *Animal welfare groups … are opposed to circuses that use animals* (see lines 16–17) and you have enough evidence to judge that the writer is compassionate about animals (**A**). **C** is correct because the writer uses emotive words and phrases such as *I am writing to express my disappointment* (see line 9); *I am appalled … demeaning circus acts* (see lines 17–18); and *the stress on circus animals to be unimaginable* (see line 19). **B** is incorrect. The fact that you have one letter is not sufficient evidence to judge that the writer has a lot of time to write letters or that the writer does write a lot of letters. **D** is incorrect as there is no evidence in the text to support a judgement that this is what the writer wants. You might infer that the writer wants animal circuses to close down, but you might also infer that a compassionate person would not want circuses to lose money but rather that they reform and concentrate on human performances.
6. This is a **judgement** question. You should use ideas and evidence in the text as well as your own knowledge and experiences to form a judgement about the topic. You might agree with the content of the letter and the writer's opinions or you might disagree. Express your opinion and provide supporting arguments. Your opinion cannot be wrong but you need to make sure you have thought about the topic and can justify your opinion.

Fly like an eagle (page 74)

1 B **2** B **3** D **4** B, C and D **5** C
6 See below

Explanations

1. This is a **judgement** question. **B** is correct. Notice the photo of the boy in the advertisement. Judge the style of the ad and the layout. Read the language used. You can judge that the ad is aimed at boys rather than girls (**A**), all teenagers (**C**) or parents (**D**).
2. This is a **judgement** question. **B** is correct. You can judge that the advertisement says this to make you think the shoes will help to make you popular. **A** is incorrect. The ad does not try to persuade people to buy the shoes to become a better person. **C** is incorrect. The ad does use reference to sports stars as part of its strategy to persuade but this is not why the ad says *look cool*

(see line 11). **D** is incorrect because you can judge that looking cool will not make you look strong.

3 This is a **judgement** question. **D** is correct. You can judge that the shoe company chose an eagle logo because the eagle symbolises or represents qualities of speed and power that the shoe company would like people to associate with its shoes. **A** is incorrect as these features won't make an eagle attractive to shoe customers. **B** and **C** could also make the eagle an appealing logo but this symbolism is not as important as speed and strength.

4 This is a **judgement** question. **B**, **C** and **D** are correct. You can judge that the advertisement uses expert recommendations (**B**) when you read *The sports brand endorsed by professional athletes … 9 out of 10 athletes surveyed endorse eagle brand shoes (see lines 12–13)*. The advertisers could make this persuasive claim by specifically interviewing sponsored athletes. The claim may not be a factual representation of the percentage of all athletes who prefer eagle brand shoes. You can judge that the advertisement uses science and technology (**C**) when you read *fly like an eagle—into your future … advanced gel cell technology with cushioning for comfort and stability … scientifically tested to ensure maximum performance-enhancing potential … the future is here today (see lines 2–8)*. You read emotive words and phrases (**D**) *why walk when you can run? why run when you can fly? look cool (see lines 9–11)*. **A** is incorrect. The advertisement does not include celebrity endorsements. You can judge that there are not any available or the advertisers chose not to pay for any. It would need to include the faces and/or names of the particular celebrities as evidence of their endorsements.

5 This is a **judgement** question. **C** is correct. The mood of the text is masculine and strong. You can judge this by looking at the imagery. **A** is incorrect as there is no humour in the advertisement. **B** is incorrect as there's nothing about the advertisement that makes it look scary. **D** is incorrect because the advertisement is not light hearted or dreamy.

6 This is a **judgement** question. You can judge the ad to be successful or unsuccessful based on what you think would appeal to the target audience. Your answer cannot be wrong as long as you justify your opinions using evidence from the text and your own knowledge and experiences.

Born lucky (page 75)

1 D **2** D **3** C **4** B **5** C **6** See below

Explanations

1 This is a **judgement** question. **D** is correct. The main theme of the poem is poverty. The poem compares the poet's life with the lives of people who live in poverty. The poem is not about envy (**A**) or greed (**B**). The poet does not describe a wealthy life (**C**) but a life that would be normal or usual for the majority of people in her country.

2 This is a **judgement** question. **D** is correct. You can judge the tone of the text as sad and concerned that there is such a difference between the life of the *haves* and the *haven'ts* *(see line 10)*. The poet does not express the ideas angrily (**A**). The poet declares that she was *born / lucky (see lines 28–29)* but doesn't seem joyful or gloating about this (**B**). There's no evidence to suggest that the poet feels guilty (**C**).

3 This is a **judgement** question. **C** is correct. You read *We don't get to choose / the place where we're born* and *No need to fetch water from far-away streams, / missing school so your family can drink on that day (see lines 8–9 and 18–19)*. You can judge that the poet would like readers to feel sympathy for people born into less fortunate circumstances than themselves. The poet does not ask readers to feel shame (**A**), anger (**B**) or envy (**D**).

4 This is a **judgement** question. **B** is correct. You can judge that the poet's purpose is to encourage readers to think about others. **A** is incorrect. The poem does not use persuasive devices to persuade readers to a point of view. **C** is incorrect as there is no instruction to donate to charity. **D** is incorrect as the poet does not instruct people to live better lives.

5 This is a **judgement** question. **C** is correct. You can judge that the poet presents personal thoughts, experiences and reflections. You could judge these as heartfelt and accurate for the poet, based on the poet's life experiences. **A** and **B** are incorrect because you should judge that the poet is not being deceitful or sensational in presenting her ideas. **D** is incorrect because personal opinions cannot be judged as untrue. Opinions are always true for the person presenting them even if they are based on inaccurate information.

6 This is a **judgement** question. The poet says she was born in a land *where food is abundant / and water is pure … I have a roof and a bed … I have medicine and doctors, / and the law and my* *freedom* (see lines 16–25). Connect this to your own knowledge about life in various parts of the world. You can judge that the poet refers to the fact that children in some countries are not safe from disease, extreme weather events, famine, drought, war, crime and/or exploitation.

Octane Dance (page 76)

1 B **2** B **3** A **4** D **5** See below
6 See below

Explanations

1 This is a **judgement** question. **B** is correct. The text's main purpose is to attract new clients. The text is the main page of a website. Links are provided to class timetables (**A**) and the merchandise shop (**C**) but these are not the purpose of the main page of the website. **D** is incorrect because encouraging people to get fit is also not the main purpose of the webpage.

2 This is a **judgement** question. **B** is correct. You can judge by the content, design, graphics, style and layout of the webpage that the main audience for the text is teenagers (aged 12 to 17). **A** is incorrect as parents are not the target audience although you read *Guest teachers and choreographers—from around Australia and internationally* (see line 16) and you can judge that the text is also designed to show parents that the dance school is worthwhile. **C** is incorrect although a professional and attractive website will also attract potential dance teachers to the dance school. **D** is incorrect as this target audience is too small and age specific.

3 This is a **judgement** question. **A** is correct. The only judgement that you can confidently make is that people who belong or fit in at the dance school will have fun there. These might be people who are good dancers or people who have friends there. **B** is incorrect as you cannot judge that people's dancing will definitely improve. It's likely to improve but it's not definite. **C** is incorrect because you cannot judge from the text that the teachers are fantastic. They are likely to be very good teachers but it's not definite. **D** is incorrect as you cannot judge from the text that the dance school definitely attracts lots of teenagers. You can judge that this is a possibility but not that it is definite.

4 This is a **judgement** question. **D** is correct. This is the least important information in the text. You can judge that people reading the text are interested in dancing classes so they will want to know about the styles of dance taught, the teachers' credentials (**A**), the music (**C**) and the timetable (**B**). They would be less interested in knowing that the venue has a lounging area.

5 This is a **judgement** question. You should judge that the text places a greater emphasis on dancing for fun rather than for fitness. Getting fit is mentioned once only: *whether you … want to get fit* (see lines 4–5). The rest of the text focuses on fun: *meet other people … Great music …* (see lines 6 and 11) and the variety of dancing styles taught (see line 10).

6 This is a **judgement** question. Whether or not you would choose to attend a dance class is based on your personal judgement of what the text offers and how it appeals to your interests and needs. Your decision cannot be right or wrong as long as you base your judgement on evidence in the text and you can justify your decision.

Animal rights (page 77)

1 B **2** D **3** D **4** See below **5** See below
6 See below

Explanations

1 This is a **judgement** question. **B** is correct. Sam is most informed about the subject of animal rights. He can define the topic and compare animal rights with human rights in a more technical and informed manner than Ying (**A**), Ryan (**C**) or Isabella (**D**).

2 This is a **judgement** question. **D** is correct. You should judge that Isabella uses emotive language. You read *I hate to think of animals suffering. … hunted … killed … I just hate to think of the ways people hurt animals* (see lines 14–19) and *non-human animals suffer just like human animals do and we should not abuse them* (see lines 47–48). Her arguments are more emotive than Ying's (**A**), Sam's (**B**) or Ryan's (**C**).

3 This is a **judgement** question. **D** is correct. You can judge that **D** is untrue. You read Isabella's statements and you can judge that she is equally concerned for all creatures. You read *I hate to think of animals suffering at all—any animal, wild or domestic, a worm on a fish hook … an elephant hunted for its ivory or used in a circus* (see lines 14–18). Other answers are incorrect because they ARE true. **A** is incorrect because it is true: Ying says *Me too* (see line 40) and agrees with Isabella about feeling sad about people behaving unethically towards animals. **B** is incorrect because it is true: Sam and Isabella are both concerned about sustainability. Sam says *some people don't think about the future* (see lines 33–34). Isabella says *meat is not sustainable* (see line 50). **C** is incorrect because it is true. Ryan says *I know. I'm the same. But I think most people behave ethically* (see lines 20–21) and Sam replies *I think more people are unethical than ethical* (see lines 22–23). You can judge that Sam is more pessimistic or negative about people's attitudes than Ryan.

4 This is a **judgement** question. You should judge that Sam makes reasoned arguments. He uses common sense in his arguments, for example *But some animals are raised for food so they can't be free from captivity in the same way that's a human right* (see lines 8–11). He supports his opinions with evidence using factual information. He uses technical terminology. He uses anecdotal evidence based on his father's experiences with their friend and with *other people who have that same attitude* (see lines 34–35).

5 This is a **judgement** question. Sam uses his personal experience of his Dad's friend and the mud crabs to make the judgement that people put *their own immediate interests* (see lines 36–37) ahead of any plan for the future.

6 This is a **judgement** question. You should judge that Isabella is the more hopeful and optimistic for the future. She says *People are becoming more aware* (see line 44) and that her family has taken action to *buy organic, free-range and cruelty-free* (see lines 45–46). You should use evidence in the text to judge that Sam is more negative about the future. He says that people are *unethical* (see line 22) and that *people put money or their own personal interests ahead of any sort of moral code* (see lines 25–27). Based on the discussion in the text you would judge Sam to be less hopeful about the future than Isabella.

Uncle Tom and Little Harry are sold (page 78)

1 B **2** See below **3** D **4** See below
5 See below **6** See below

Explanations

1 This is a **judgement** question. **B** is correct. The narrator disapproves of slavery. You read *It was very wicked to buy and sell human beings as if they were cattle* (see line 10). **A** is incorrect. The narrator states that servants, meaning slaves, could be bought at the market but does not say this in order to condone slavery. **C** is incorrect. Even though you read *If the poor slaves were bought by kind people they would be quite happy* (see line 7), the narrator does not endorse the practice of slavery. **D** is incorrect. There is no evidence in the text to support a judgement that the narrator believed slavery was necessary

2 This is a **judgement** question. You read *Very many years ago, instead of having servants to wait upon them and work for them, people used to have slaves. These slaves were paid no wages. Their masters gave them only food and clothes in return for their work* (see lines 2–4). You should judge that people had slaves because it was cheaper than paying people wages.

3 This is a **judgement** question. **D** is correct. You read that the narrator thought people justified cruelty by saying "*They are only black people ... Black people do not feel things as we do.*" (see line 12). **A** is incorrect as a justification of cruelty. It is how masters felt they paid the slaves for work. **B** is incorrect. Although buying slaves at the market might have allowed some people to justify cruelty on the grounds that slaves were property (see lines 5–6) rather than people this isn't the justification explained by the narrator. **C** is incorrect because this is not an argument that justifies cruelty.

4 This is a **judgement** question. You read *If the poor slaves were bought by kind people they would be quite happy. Then they would work willingly for their masters and mistresses, and even love them* (see lines 7–8). The narrator seems to believe that slaves could be happy being slaves and love kind masters. You should question the assumption that anyone could ever be happy being a slave, even a well-treated one.

5 This is a **judgement** question. Slaves were owned and employees were not. Slaves worked for food and clothes rather than wages. Slaves did not have freedom of choice to leave a master. Slaves could be bought and sold. Family members of a slave were all slaves and did not have the freedom to stay together. Slaves could be beaten and abused because they were treated as property and not people. It was generally acceptable to mistreat slaves, whereas even in those times it would generally have been unacceptable to beat employees.

6 This is a **judgement** question. You can judge that not knowing what had happened to their family members and whether they were suffering under cruel masters was worse for those left behind than the closure of knowing someone was dead. You can judge that the narrator believed that the dead could not suffer any further.

The bogeyman (page 79)

1 B **2** B and C **3** C **4** A, B, C and D
5 See below **6** See below

Explanations

1. This is a **judgement** question. **B** is correct. You can use the evidence in the text to judge that, when the narrator referred to the *old, old man* as living *all alone* (see line 2), he felt sorry for him. *All alone* is an emotive phrase. The prepositional phrase *behind a high fence* (see line 2) is also emotive. It makes readers visualise a lonely old man separated from the world by a high fence. You should judge that the adverb *eventually* (see line 2) is used to imply that the narrator knew of the old man for a long while before he actually met him. You might judge that the narrator feels some regret about this. You can judge that the narrator is sensitive to the old man's aloneness and the way the old man is isolated. **A** is incorrect as the sentence starts with *I eventually got to know …* (see line 2). This does not imply curiosity. **C** is incorrect. You cannot judge that the narrator is frightened. There is no evidence of this in the first sentence. Nor can you judge that the narrator is respectful (**D**). You might presume it but there's no evidence in this first sentence.
2. This is a **judgement** question. **B** and **C** are correct. You can judge from evidence in the text that the narrator did not know the old man at that time and believed the stories the children of the town told him. **A** and **D** are incorrect. You can use your own knowledge and judgement to determine that children delight in scary stories about dungeons and bogeymen but these statements are shown not to be true in the text.
3. This is a **judgement** question. **C** is correct. The narrator neither condones nor condemns the other children. **A** is incorrect. The narrator describes what the children did but does not judge or give any personal comment about it. He leaves it up to the reader to decide how to judge the children's behaviour. **B** is incorrect. There's no evidence that the narrator took part in the mango raids. **D** is incorrect because the narrator does not justify the children's behaviour. To justify means to approve and explain why something is appropriate. The narrator does not do this.
4. This is a **judgement** question. **A**, **B**, **C** and **D** are all correct. Use your own experiences and understanding about children's behaviour in narratives to judge that the children hide behind the fence because they feel safe and confident there, out of sight. They can see the old man but he can't see them and he won't be able to catch them if they run away. They like the thrill of doing something they think or perceive to be dangerous.
5. This is a **judgement** question. You should use your own experiences, empathy for others and understanding to judge that the children behaved badly. Your sympathy should lie with the old man who was taunted. His mangoes were stolen. His vegetable garden was trampled. The children were rude and disrespectful.
6. This is a **judgement** question. Zac might offer to help Frank with the neighbourhood children. He might offer to help him pick his mangoes and tend his vegetable garden. He might offer to visit Frank on a regular basis if this is what Frank wants. Zac might try to make sure that Frank feels he is part of the community.

Mixed questions

Going going going gone (page 80)

1 D **2** A **3** B **4** C **5** See below
6 See below

Explanations

1. This is a **judgement** question. **D** is correct. You can use evidence from the whole text to judge that the poet thinks animal conservation is very important. **A** is incorrect. This is the opposite of the poet's point of view as expressed in the poem. **B** is incorrect. There's no evidence in the text to support this answer. **C** is expressed as a fact in the text, not an opinion.
2. This is an **inferring** question. **A** is correct. You can infer that the poet predicts extinction. The poem starts with a high modality statement *This is how it goes* (see line 22). Further evidence of the poet's prediction is included in the statements *there was no / global will to stop / before the end* (see lines 37–39) and that *our children's / children will be the judges* (see lines 28–33). There is no evidence to support inferences **B**, **C** or **D**.
3. This is a **language** question. **B** is correct. A precipice is a cliff or sheer fall. *Precipice* (see line 12) is used in the poem to mean a dangerous situation or the brink of disaster. When you turn back from a precipice you turn towards safety. **A** and **C** are incorrect because in the poem *precipice* is a metaphor. Animals are not actually on a cliff.

D is incorrect because this is also a more literal definition of *precipice*.

4 This is a **judgement** question. **C** is correct. You can judge that the mood of the poem is resignation. The poet seems resigned to accepting that extinction is inevitable for many animals. There is no evidence in the poem to suggest that the poet feels a sense of peace, rage or awe. The feeling is more one of regret.

5 This is an **inferring** question. You can infer that the poet includes Australia's *Carnaby's black cockatoo* (see line 18) in a list of animals from *All over the World* (see line 19)—polar bears in the northern polar regions, tigers in Asia, giant pandas in China and gorillas from Africa. You would also be correct if you said that *our* means 'you and me' or 'humankind'. You could infer that the poet means humankind because the poet says *Will our children's / children / read about / the animals we didn't save?* (see lines 28–31) The poet means 'everyone'.

6 This is a **language** question. You can work out by the way the poet uses it in the text that the noun group *global will* (see line 38) means the collective will of governments and people around the globe or world. The poet means the will to take action—*to take better care* (see line 40) of the earth and its creatures.

World War II—the bombing of Australia (page 81)

1 C **2** B **3** D **4** C **5** See below
6 See below

Explanations

1 This is a **fact-finding** question. **C** is correct. The answer is stated directly in the text. You read *The Japanese planes had been spotted flying over Bathurst Island thirty minutes before the first attack but Darwin RAAF operators presumed these were American planes and so did not sound air raid warnings* (see lines 14–17). **A** and **B** do not answer the question. **D** is incorrect because it is not true in the text.

2 This is a **language** question. **B** is correct. You can work out the meaning of *disarray* (see line 21) by the information in the rest of the paragraph, which describes people's fear of invasion and the messy disorderly fleeing. Notice the negative prefix *dis-* for *array*/*disarray*. Other answers are incorrect meanings.

3 This is a **language** question. **D** is correct. You can work out the meaning of the word *exodus* by the way it is used in the text. You read *The scramble to flee from Darwin became known as 'The Adelaide River Stakes'. It was a mass exodus with people carrying whatever possessions they could* (see lines 25–26). You can work out that the *exodus* was an evacuation of the city. People fled the city in large numbers as quickly as they could. It was not an orderly or organised evacuation. **A** and **C** are incorrect as they don't make sense. **B** is incorrect because it refers only to walking departures. The text states that people used *whatever means of transport they had* (see line 27).

4 This is a **fact-finding** question. **C** is correct. The answer is stated directly in the text. You read *People feared that Darwin was about to be invaded by the Japanese military … Half the civilian population of Darwin and even some military personnel fled south towards Adelaide. The scramble to flee from Darwin became known as 'The Adelaide River Stakes'* (see lines 22–26). **A** and **B** are incorrect because they tell what and don't answer the question why. **D** is incorrect. This is not the reason the Adelaide River Stakes occurred, although people might not have fled if the government had taken effective control.

5 This is an **inferring** question. You can work out the answer by thinking about the historical time of the events and the chaos that ensued in Darwin after the bombings. You can infer that there are no exact numbers or that numbers differ from one government or military site to another. The words *approximately, up to* and *around* (see lines 17–19) are low modality, indefinite words that allow for approximate numbers rather than definite numbers.

6 This is a **judgement** question. You need to consider the evidence in the text and what the majority of people did at that time. You would also have been concerned about a potential invasion. The people fled Darwin by any means they could. You should judge that your family would most likely have fled Darwin too.

Bullying (page 82)

1 C **2** D **3** B **4** D **5** A and B
6 See below

Explanations

1 This is a **language** question. **C** is correct. You can work out the meaning of *troll* in the text by examining how it is used. The *troll* in the text is a person who writes *nasty things* (see line 5) about Becca on the internet. This behaviour is cyberbullying. **A** is incorrect because it implies face-to-face conversations rather than on the internet. **B** is incorrect as this kind of troll is not the topic of the conversation between Miyumi and her mum. **D** is incorrect because it refers to the person Miyumi thinks is a *troll* but does not give a definition for the word *troll.*

2 This is a **language** question. **D** is correct. *We* in *We've all blocked her* (see line 13) refers to all of Becca's friends because these are the people who would support Becca and also have the power to block a troll from their social media sites. **A** is incorrect because not everyone Becca knows would be involved in personal discussions of this nature. **B** is incorrect as *all* implies more people than just Becca and Miyumi. If Miyumi were only referring to herself and Becca she would have said *we've* blocked her. **C** is incorrect because the teachers have not yet been informed of the problem.

3 This is a **language** question. **B** is correct. You can work out who Mum is referring to when you examine the context of the statement in the text. Mum is referring to *This girl* [who] *has a problem* (see lines 15–16)—the cyberbully. **A** is incorrect as Mum is not referring to her own daughter, Miyumi. **C** is incorrect. Becca does have a problem but she is not the girl who has a problem that Mum is describing. **D** is incorrect as the girl who has a problem is not Becca's friend.

4 This is a **judgement** question. **D** is correct. You can judge that Becca did the wrong thing by disobeying her parents. You read *She's upset but she doesn't want to tell her parents because they told her she wasn't allowed to have a Facebook page so she'll be in trouble* (see lines 10–11). Becca's problem with the troll would not be taking place if she had obeyed her parents. You can judge that Becca's parents decided she was not allowed to have a Facebook page because they believed it was not appropriate for a girl her age and they were concerned about her online safety and welfare. **A** and **B** are true in the text but not mistakes made by Becca. **C** is incorrect. There is no evidence in the text that Becca gave the troll her email address.

5 This is a **fact-finding** question. **A** and **B** are correct. The answers are stated directly in the text. You read *Becca needs to tell her parents but she should also speak to the teachers … I think this should be reported to the police, but that will be for the teachers or Becca's parents to decide* (see lines 15–17). **C** is incorrect. Mum thinks the police should be told but not that Becca should go straight to the police. **D** is incorrect. Miyumi is the one who mentioned expelling the cyberbully from school.

6 This is an **inferring** question. You can infer the answer using the information in the text. It's important for friends to support each other against a bully.

Whale watching (page 83)

1 See below **2** D **3** B **4** B **5** See below **6** See below

Explanations

1 This is an **inferring** question. You could infer that the rules are there to protect people as well as whales because whales are large animals that can crash accidently into small vessels and capsize them or injure people. The answer is to protect people from harm.

2 This is a **judgement** question. **D** is correct. You can use evidence in the text to judge the writer's attitude towards whales. You read the whole text and especially the concluding statements of opinion: *I love whales. They are massive and graceful and playful and inquisitive* (see lines 25–26). You can judge that the writer admires whales and is interested in them and their behaviour. Other answers are incorrect as at no point in the text does the writer express concern, fear or caution regarding the whales.

3 This is a **judgement** question. **B** is correct. You can use evidence in the text to judge the writer's attitude towards the rules. You can tell that the writer is respectful of the rules because the rules are described and explained. You read, for example, *Vessels aren't allowed to approach any whales head-on, get between any whales in a group, or separate a mother from her calf, and they have to be careful not to distress the whales in any other way* (see lines 14–15). You can tell by the use of emotive words like *distress* that the writer believes the rules are important and necessary to protect the whales.

4 This is a **synthesis** question. **B** is correct. When you connect ideas across the whole text you can conclude that the text is a recount. It begins with an introduction to the setting. It tells about events that have occurred. It concludes with a personal remark and opinion. **A** is incorrect. Whales are described as part of the recount but the purpose of the text is not to present information about whales. **C** and **D** are incorrect. The text is not an

advertisement for a tour or a persuasive text to promote whale watching. Although each of these goals could be achieved by parts of the text, these are secondary to the writer's purpose.

5 This is an **inferring** question. The answer is not stated directly in the text. You need to use your own knowledge and understanding to make a considered response to the question. You should infer, for example, that calves can get caught in fishing nets, be injured by boats and shipping, and attacked by killer whales or sharks. Storms can also separate calves from their mothers and cause the carves to starve.

6 This is a **judgement** question. You have to work out the answer using evidence in the text. You can judge that the writer would recommend this particular tour operator or vessel. The writer says *It was amazing* (see line 3) when referring to the whale-watching tour. The writer speaks positively about the crew in writing *The crew on our whale-watching boat told us … to make a lot of noise and wave our arms to attract the whales' interest. It sure did* (see lines 6–8). The writer tells of things learnt about whales while on the tour. The final paragraph provides another positive statement about an aspect of the tour: *Our vessel had a hydrophone so we could hear the males singing. It was incredible* (see line 25).

Plastic—it's a problem (page 84)

1 See below **2** See below. **3** See below
4 A, C and D **5** See below **6** See below

Explanations

1 This is an **inferring** question. You should infer that an animal tangled in plastic might be unable to swim, fly or eat. The animal could drown or starve.

2 This is a **fact-finding** question. The answer is stated directly in the text. The physical action of the sun, waves and wind breaks up the plastic into smaller and smaller pieces.

3 This is a **synthesis** question. Connect information from across the text to work out that gyres are whirlpools of swirling ocean currents. Pollution in the ocean is drawn towards these gyres and collects there swirling around in circles.

4 This is a **synthesis** question. **A**, **C** and **D** are correct. You can connect information from across the text to work out that recycling plastic (**A**), using metal instead of plastic (**C**) and using glass instead of plastic (**D**) will reduce the amount of plastic in the oceans. **B** is incorrect as this does not make sense or answer the question.

5 This is a **synthesis** question. You need to connect information from across the text. You read *only 5% of plastic is recycled worldwide* (see lines 6–7) and *Production of plastic uses non-renewable fossil fuels. It takes a quarter of a litre of oil to make one plastic water bottle. We should not be wasting our fossil fuel on disposable plastic* (see lines 20–21). You should draw the conclusion that once fossil fuel is used it's gone forever so to use it to make plastic, especially if that plastic is used only once and then thrown away, is wasteful.

6 This is a **judgement** question. You need to consider the meaning and use of the term *mermaids' tears* (see line 17) and then judge whether it does a good job as the label for a tiny particle of plastic in the ocean. Think for yourself. A tear is small and transparent. The tears of mermaids would be found in the ocean. Figuratively speaking, mermaids could cry oceans of tears about plastic pollution. You might therefore judge the term to be useful and appropriate. You could also judge the term to be inappropriate because plastic is toxic pollution in the ocean and a mermaid's tears would not be toxic. Make your own judgement and justify it.

The magic seeds (page 85)

1 B **2** C **3** A and D **4** A **5** See below
6 See below

Explanations

1 This is a **synthesis** question. **B** is correct. Read paragraph four to work out which question the vendor does not answer. **A**, **C** and **D** are incorrect because you read *The vendor promised that the bean trees were easy to grow, that they would grow overnight and that indeed the beans would taste delicious* (see lines 16–17).

2 This is a **fact-finding** question. **C** is correct. The answer is stated directly in the text. You read *Arabella did not want to sell the old cow whom she had loved since she was a toddler* (see lines 11–12). **A** is incorrect as this is a reason in favour of selling the cow. **B** is incorrect. There is no evidence in the text that Arabella drank milk. **D** is incorrect as the text says Arabella had loved the cow since she was little rather than since the cow was little.

3 This is an **inferring** question. **A** and **D** are correct. You read *Arabella picked vegetables for dinner and helped her mother prepare their evening meal of*

home-grown vegetables and eggs (see lines 4–6). **B** and **C** are incorrect. There is no evidence in the text that Arabella and her mother eat chickens or cow meat. They keep chickens for eggs to eat. They keep the cow for her milk and not to eat her.

4 This is a **fact-finding** question. **A** is correct. The answer is stated directly in the text. You read *She said, "Why would anyone buy our beans when they can grow their own for free?"* (see lines 21–22). **B** is incorrect. Although the vendor might be a trickster this is not how the mother explains that Arabella was tricked. **C** and **D** are incorrect. There may be no such thing as magic seeds and bean trees might not be able to grow overnight but this is not the reason the mother gave.

5 This is a **fact-finding** question. The answer is stated directly in the text. You read *She decided that at the very worst she had only lost one day. She could take the cow to the market the next morning so she might as well give the magic seeds a chance* (see lines 23–24). The answer: it has cost Arabella one extra day to try the beans.

6 This is an **inferring** question. You need to predict or infer the likely outcomes of the story using evidence in the text. This is a narrative based on a fairytale that you might be familiar with about a boy called Jack and a beanstalk that grew overnight. You should predict that magic occurs in fairytales so the beans will grow overnight. You can elaborate on your prediction in any way you like.

The pacifist (page 86)

1 D **2** B **3** B **4** See below **5** See below **6** See below

Explanations

1 This is a **language** question. **D** is correct. You read *Bryan waited fifteen minutes, then peeked out …* (see line 2). The text presents Bryan's point of view. It is a third-person narrative that tells what Bryan is thinking. **A** is incorrect as the author's point of view is not evident in the text. **B** is incorrect because there is a point of view in the text, Bryan's. **C** is incorrect as readers learn what Simon does but not what he thinks.

2 This is a **judgement** question. **B** is correct. You read *He could only outlast him. It was best to just avoid Simon when he could and wait for Year 6 to be over. He was patient. He could manage that. Bryan headed home* (see lines 24–26). You can judge that Bryan has resolved within himself a way to deal with Simon that he feels confident about and he heads home feeling positive about his ability to outlast Simon. **A** and **C** are incorrect because they do not make sense in this kind of text which is a realistic narrative. **D** is incorrect. You can't read the final sentences and feel that the mood is depressing.

3 This is a **synthesis** question. **B** is correct. You connect information from across the text and conclude that Simon's bullying is verbal. He uses words to taunt, tease, intimidate and ridicule Bryan. **A** and **C** are incorrect. You read Bryan *was never physically hurt* (see lines 13–14). **D** is incorrect. Paragraph one tells readers that it was Bryan's decision to miss the school bus.

4 This is a **language** question. The expression 'sit on the fence' means 'not take sides'. The narrator infers that the audience is sitting on the fence by watching Simon bully Bryan and doing nothing to intervene. The audience is referred to as *[p]assive accepters* (see line 18) of the bullying. You can infer from the narrator's choice of language that the narrator thinks the audience should get off the fence and side with Bryan to stop the bullying.

5 This is an **inferring** question. The statement implies that Bryan is hoping Simon will grow tired of bullying him. It tells you that Bryan thinks that if he does not respond to Simon's taunts then Simon will grow bored and move on to a different victim or Bryan will leave for high school.

6 This is a **judgement** question. Your judgement will be based on your own background experiences and the ways you connect with the ideas in the text. You need to justify your answer. You should advise Bryan to tell his teachers or parents/caregivers. You should not advise him to physically hurt Simon because you should judge that action would be inappropriate but also out of character for Bryan. You read *He could stop Simon's taunts with one good shove. But would that make him a bully? Hitting a smaller boy?* (see lines 22–23). You can judge that Bryan would not hit anyone. You cannot advise Bryan to call Simon names because that is also out of character for Bryan. You read *He* [Bryan] *wasn't fast-witted or clever with words like Simon* (see line 22).

Urgent! Great Barrier Reef Holiday Sale (page 87)

1 D **2** D **3** A, B and D **4** See below **5** A and D **6** See below

Explanations

1 This is a **judgement** question. **D** is correct. You can judge by the evidence across the text that even

though it appears to be a travel advertisement it is not. The text is an example of irony. It's saying one thing while meaning something else. Its purpose is to raise awareness of the impact of climate change and coastal development on the Great Barrier Reef. It uses sarcasm as a form of humour to get its message across. **A** is incorrect. The text does describe aspects of the reef but this is not its purpose. **B** is incorrect. The text is not an explanation about climate change. **C** is incorrect because the text is not trying to sell holidays.

2 This is a **judgement** question. **D** is correct. You can judge that the text's main message is about the risks to the environment of the Great Barrier Reef. The likely author would be a group concerned about the environment. It is important to be able to identify the author of a text so that you can read the text with a critical mind and challenge assertions made in the text. **A** and **B** are incorrect. Although water sports and recreational fishing take place in the waters of the Great Barrier Reef these are not the main issues in the text. **C** is incorrect. A scientific research group could be responsible for the part of the text that presents factual content but not the persuasive or emotive content.

3 This is a **judgement** question. Connect information from across the text with your own knowledge and judgement to conclude that **A**, **B** and **D** are correct. **C** is incorrect. Readers can book a holiday to the Great Barrier Reef by calling 1300savetheGBR.

4 This is a **fact-finding** question. The answer is stated directly in the text. You read *SWIM with dugong and turtles before they starve to death because ... agricultural run-off and dredging spoil have destroyed their seagrass* (see lines 20–21). Your answer should state that turtles and dugongs eat seagrass and agricultural run-off kills sea grass and therefore causes turtles and dugongs to starve.

5 This is a **judgement** question. **A** and **D** are correct. You can judge that the exclamation *Urgent!* (see line 1) was chosen to gain the reader's attention and to focus on the writer's concern that action to protect the GBR is 'urgently' required. **B** is incorrect. The use of *Urgent!* does not work to make the information appear more believable. **C** is incorrect as the text is not an advertisement to convince people to take holidays to the reef.

6 This is a **language** question. You can tell this is a persuasive text because of the high modality statements (those that express the greatest degree of certainty) and the use of emotive words and phrases. High modality is represented by commands, modal adverbs such as 'definitely' and 'absolutely', and modal verbs such as 'must' and 'won't'. Examples of high modality statements in the text include *Visit before it's too late! Your last chance* (see lines 2–3) and *There's no time to delay!* ***You must book now!*** (see line 16). Emotive words and phrases in the text include *Visit before it's too late!* (see line 2), *SWIM with dugong and turtles before they starve to death* (see line 20) and *There's no time to delay!* (see line 16).

Bushfires (page 88)

1 C **2** See below **3** See below **4** See below
5 D **6** See below

Explanations

1 This is a **fact-finding** question. **C** is correct. The answer is stated directly in the text. You read *The most severe and largest bushfires in the world occur in south-eastern Australia* (see lines 10–11). **A** is incorrect as bushfires occur across forest rather than in trees although eucalypt fires are intense. **B** is incorrect as this is not a fact in the text. **D** is incorrect because it tells when bushfires are predicted to occur in the future rather than where the worst ones occur now.

2 This is a **synthesis** question. You read *The most severe and largest bushfires in the world occur in south-eastern Australia during summer and autumn. The north of Australia experiences bushfires during winter, which is the dry season there* (see lines 10–12) and *The south-east of mainland Australia will become hotter and drier in the future* (see lines 20–21). You synthesise this information to work out that bushfires need dry fuel. The south of Australia is driest in summer while the north of Australia is driest in winter.

3 This is a **language** question. You read *When bushfires are deliberately lit it is called arson* (see line 17). You can work out that an arsonist is a person who deliberately lights a fire.

4 This is a **language** question. Emotive words are words that are used to arouse the emotions of a reader or listener. Emotive words in paragraph one are *disasters, kill, destroy, threaten* and *devastating* (see lines 2–6). Each of these words carries emotional weight and gives the writer's position on the topic.

5 This is **a language** question. **D** is correct. High modality expresses certainty. **D** is the statement that expresses the most certainty. The modal verb *will* expresses certainty. **A** is incorrect because *is expected* doesn't mean 'definite'. **B** is incorrect because *could* doesn't mean 'will'. **C** is incorrect because *is likely* doesn't mean 'will definitely'.

6 This is a **judgement** question. You could judge these people to be careless, ignorant, foolish and/or irresponsible, or any synonyms for these labels. Your explanation needs to justify your opinions and give your reasons. For example, you could state that people in Australia are aware of bushfire danger. The media transmits fire warnings on hot, dry, windy days. Anyone who accidently causes a fire is plainly irresponsible and careless, or uneducated and ignorant. People who live in areas that have been devastated by bushfires would not accept any excuse for an accidentally lit bushfire.

Tribute (page 89)

1 C **2** A, C and D **3** D **4** C **5** See below **6** See below

Explanations

1 This is a **synthesis** question. **C** is correct. The texts are connected through their subject matter, Patyegarang. Text 1 introduces Patyegarang in relation to biographical notes about Lt William Dawes. Text 2 introduces her in relation to a dance performance about her. **A** is incorrect. Both texts are reports but the focus of Text 2 is not events in history. **B** is incorrect as only one First Australian, Patyegarang, is described in each text. **D** is incorrect because the focus of Text 2 is a contemporary dance group and not Indigenous Australians in early New South Wales.

2 This is a **judgement** question. **A, C** and **D** are correct. You can judge by the evidence in the text that Dawes respected First Nations people (**A**) and was interested to learn about their culture (**D**). **C** is a fact in the text so you can judge it to be true. **B** is incorrect. You read that his *outspoken defiance of Governor Phillip's punitive actions against First Nations Australians saw Dawes shipped back to England (see lines 14–16)*. You judge that this evidence in the text shows that Dawes and Phillip were in disagreement over Phillip's treatment of First Australians. Dawes did not influence Phillip. Phillip sent Dawes back to England so he could not speak out against him in regard to First Australians.

3 This is a **judgement** question. **D** is correct. You read *Patyegarang, who was largely responsible for teaching Dawes her language and about the ways and customs of her people (see lines 9–10)* and *Through sharing her language she* [Patyegarang] *is Dawes's guide to First Australian culture; an educator and a remarkable role model (see lines 23–24)*. You can judge by this evidence in the text that Patyegarang liked meeting new people, learning from them and teaching them about her culture. **A** is incorrect as this statement is about Bangarra rather than Patyegarang. **B** is incorrect as there is no evidence to suggest that she was a dancer at this time. **C** is incorrect because the evidence that she shared her knowledge with Dawes shows she was open to meeting people and sharing ideas.

4 This is a **synthesis** question. **C** is correct. To pay tribute means to praise, honour or show respect. The title *Tribute* relates to the work of Dawes, Patyegarang and Bangarra Dance. **A** and **D** are both partly correct. **B** is incorrect. The text is not persuasive. It gives information about Bangarra Dance and a 2014 performance. It praises the performance but the purpose of the text is not persuasion.

5 This is a **fact-finding** question. The answer is stated directly in the text. You read *Dawes is well regarded in history because of his work to learn and record the language of the First Nations peoples of Sydney (see lines 5–7).*

6 This is a **judgement** question. You read that *Dawes was the first European on record who attempted to defend First Australian rights (see line 14)*. You can judge from the evidence in the text that Dawes was in disagreement with the Governor of the colony over the treatment of First Australians. His views would likely have been at odds with most European settlers and the Army Corps. He spent a lot of time with Eora people and so you should judge that the majority of settlers would not have liked his behaviour.

Adventures of Huckleberry Finn (page 90)

1 C **2** A and C **3** C **4** B **5** See below **6** See below

Explanations

1 This is a **language** question. **C** is correct. You can tell by the way the word is used in the text that *scrouched (see line 3)* means a combination of 'scrunched' and 'crouched'. It means to get down low and make yourself look small so that you will not be seen. *Scrouched* is an example of a portmanteau word. A portmanteau word combines two (or more) words to make a new word. **A** is partly correct but keeping still is not implied in *scrouched*. **B** is incorrect as 'scooted' means hurried or scurried quickly. **D** is partly correct because 'ducked' is similar to 'crouched' but the implication of 'hid' is incorrect, as the narrator could not hide and could only make himself seem smaller and therefore less visible.

2 This is a **judgement** question. **A** and **C** are correct. You can judge that the author is representing the way the particular characters spoke at the time when the story is set. Authors do this to make their narratives more authentic. **B** is incorrect as the use of the vernacular is not evidence that the author was racist. You could equally judge that the author was an effective storyteller or that the author was highlighting racist attitudes at the time the story was written. **D** is incorrect. You cannot judge the story to be irrelevant to readers today based on the use of a racist label. Racism is still an issue around the world and well-written stories that encourage readers to reflect on values and attitudes will always be relevant. It is interesting to note that the author, Mark Twain, supported the abolition of slavery. He also supported women's suffrage. He died in 1910.

3 This is an **inferring** question. **C** is correct. You read *Well, I've noticed that thing plenty times since. If you are anywheres where it won't do for you to scratch, why you will itch all over in upwards of a thousand places* (see lines 9–11). The narrator starts to itch simply because he is focusing attention on not being able to scratch himself. **A** and **B** are incorrect because there is no evidence in the text to infer he is sitting on ants or has hives. **D** is incorrect because it tells where the narrator felt itchy rather than why he was itchy.

4 This is a **language** question. **B** is correct. You read *Pretty soon Jim says: "Say, who is you? Whar is you? Dog my cats ef I didn' hear sumf'n. Well, I know what I's gwyne to do: I's gwyne to set down here and listen tell I hears it agin."* (see lines 12–13) Translated, the text means: Pretty soon Jim says: "Who's there? Where are you? I'm sure I heard something. I know what I'm going to do. I am going to sit down here and listen until I hear it again." You can work out why Jim says *Dog my cats* by examining how the expression is used in the text. Jim uses it to express certainty that he has heard something. **A** and **D** are incorrect. The expression does not literally mean anything about cats and dogs. **C** is incorrect as it is low modality. Jim is certain: he uses high modality.

5 This is an **inferring** question. You read *Jim begun to breathe heavy; next he begun to snore* (see line 19). You can infer that Jim went to sleep. Once Jim was asleep the pressure not to move or scratch was lifted and the narrator was *pretty soon comfortable* (see lines 19–20). The narrator did not scratch to get comfortable. The narrator just relaxed and stopped focusing on not being able to scratch.

6 This is an **inferring** question. You read *We went tiptoeing along a path towards the end of the widow's garden* (see line 2). Then you read the rest of the text which tells of the narrator and his companion(s) hiding from Jim and most likely also from Miss Watson. You can infer that they are up to something sneaky, possibly thieving or spying, but certainly trespassing where they don't belong.

The further adventures of Toad (page 91)

1 D **2** A **3** C **4** A and D **5** See below **6** See below

Explanations

1 This is a **fact-finding** question. **D** is correct. The answer is stated directly in the text. You read that Toad was called from sleep *at an early hour; partly by the bright sunlight streaming in on him, partly by the exceeding coldness of his toes* (see lines 2–3). **A** is incorrect. The phrase *called at an early hour* (see line 2) rephrases the question and does not answer it. **B** is incorrect. Toad had a dream but it did not wake him. **C** is incorrect. The fact that the door faced east did not of itself wake him.

2 This is a **language** question. **A** is correct. You read that in Toad's dream *his bedclothes had got up, grumbling and protesting they couldn't stand the cold any longer, and had run downstairs to the kitchen fire to warm themselves; and he had followed, on bare feet, along miles and miles of icy stone-paved passages, arguing and beseeching them to be reasonable* (see lines 5–7). You can tell by the way the word *beseeching* is used in the text that it means 'begging' or 'pleading'. **B** is incorrect. You can tell that *beseeching* doesn't mean 'abusing'. Toad wants his bedclothes to come back so he won't be abusing them in this context. **C** is incorrect as Toad is following the bedclothes down long corridors so whispering would be useless. **D** is incorrect because Toad did not convince his bedclothes to come back to him.

3 This is a **fact-finding** question. **C** is correct. The answer is stated directly in the text. You read that it was *the exceeding coldness of his* [Toad's] *toes, which made him dream that … his bedclothes had got up … and had run downstairs to the kitchen fire to warm themselves* (see lines 3–6). The strange dream was Toad's mind attempting to explain the fact that he had cold toes. **A** is incorrect as this only happened in Toad's dream. **B** and **D** are true but not the reasons for the dream.

4 This is a **judgement** question. **A** and **D** are correct. You can judge that Toad is egotistical, spoilt and self-important because he thinks about his triumphal entrance to the world outside and how the world is *waiting eagerly for him … ready to serve him and play up to him, anxious to help him and to keep him company* (see lines 15–16). This is what he expects because you read this is *as it always had been* (see line 16). The fact that he wanted to make a *triumphal entrance* (see line 15) and that he *marched forth* (see line 18) also tells of his attitude. A triumphal march is a march by winning armies or conquerors to celebrate victory. This helps you judge that Toad is egotistical. **B** is incorrect. The fact that Toad had escaped his captors and been pursued by them is evidence that he is not cowardly. **C** is incorrect. The fact that Toad had been catching up on sleep is not evidence that he is lazy. He was looking forward to his walk in the sunshine so you cannot judge him to be lazy. He looked forward to greeting the waiting world so he is also not timid.

5 This is an **inferring** question. You read *had he not slept for some weeks on straw over stone flags, and almost forgotten the friendly feeling of thick blankets pulled well up round the chin* (see lines 8–9), and further that *with a leap of the heart,* [he] *remembered everything—his escape, his flight, his pursuit; remembered, first and best thing of all, that he was free!* (see lines 11–13). You can read between the lines to infer that Toad had been held captive somewhere where he had to sleep on a cold stone floor and look through a small barred window.

6 This is a **fact-finding** question. The answer is stated directly in the text. You read that Toad *marched forth into the comfortable morning sun, cold but confident, hungry but hopeful, all nervous terrors of yesterday dispelled by rest and sleep and frank and heartening sunshine* (see lines 18–20). Your answer should state that Toad had rested and slept well and he felt good in the sunshine. You might also suggest that he felt good about the day because his captivity was behind him and he was free to do as he wished.

Renewable energy (page 92)

1 B **2** A, C and D **3** A, B and D **4** A
5 C **6** See below

Explanations

1 This is a **fact-finding** question. **B** is correct. The answer is stated directly in the text. You read *I am really excited about the potential of wind energy* (see lines 16–17). **A**, **C** and **D** are statements made by Kath in the text but are incorrect because these facts are not what Kath says she is *really excited* about.

2 This is a **synthesis** question. **A**, **C** and **D** are correct. Read the whole text and you can conclude that the compere moves the program along by asking relevant questions (**A**) and keeping the interview at a pace that maintains viewer interest (**C**); and introducing and then thanking the guest for her time (**D**). **B** is incorrect. The compere does not give information. The compere needs to elicit information from the guest expert. If the compere thinks the information is not expressed in terms viewers will understand then the compere might paraphrase what the guest said or ask further questions for clarification.

3 This is a **fact-finding** question. **A**, **B** and **D** are correct. The answers are facts in the text. You read *Wind is a clean, safe, renewable resource* (see lines 13–14); *Wind power is environmentally sustainable* (see lines 42–43); and *Once they become operational wind farms produce negligible greenhouse gases* (see lines 35–37). **C** is incorrect as it is refuted by Kath's statement.

4 This is a **judgement** question. **A** is correct. Read that Kath Green is a *wind industry expert and government consultant* (see lines 8–9) and then read the facts across the whole text. You should judge that information given by a government consultant should be reliable and accurate. You should conclude that the text is only about wind energy. **B** is incorrect. You should judge that the evidence in the text includes sufficient technical and scientific information to support Kath's point of view. **C** is incorrect. There is no evidence to support a judgement that the text is biased against other renewable energy sources. **D** is incorrect. You can judge that Kath is excited about wind power (*Australia could lead the world*

in wind energy technology) (see lines 21–22) and uses high modality (*Wind energy does work*) (see line 45) but the text is not sensationalised or emotive.

5 This is a **judgement** question. **C** is correct. You should judge that a coalmining company executive would be the only person listed who is likely to disagree with ideas raised by Kath that suggest wind power is superior to coal power. This is because a coalmining company has a vested interest in the continued use of coal. **A**, **B** and **D** are incorrect as these people have vested interests in wind energy and would be likely to agree with Kath's viewpoint.

6 This is a **judgement** question. Your opinion can't be right or wrong as long as it is rationally supported by evidence in the text. For example, you might explain that the information in the text has made you more positive and accepting of wind power. You might say that you didn't realise before that wind energy was reliable or that you are excited by the prospect that Australia could be a world leader in wind energy technology. Alternatively, you might think that Kath's reference to Tocco da Casauria is not the best example of wind power use and that you would like more information about the success of wind-powered communities around the world.

Poo (page 93)

1 C **2** C **3** D **4** B **5** D **6** See below

Explanations

1 This is a **synthesis** question. C is correct. The text appears educational and informative but is designed to convince readers to purchase the product advertised. **A** and **B** are true about the text but incorrect answers. Advertisements often use humour to entertain their audience but their goal is to sell through being entertaining. Advertisements can also provide information about an issue or product in order to convince people to buy it. **D** is incorrect. This is not the purpose of the text.

2 This is a **synthesis** question. **C** is correct. You should recognise the thesis statement *Your poo can tell you a lot about your health* (see line 6). The information in the text builds on the thesis statement. **A**, **B** and **D** are incorrect answers even though they are facts in the text. They are supplementary ideas used to support the thesis.

3 This is a **fact-finding** question. **D** is correct. The answer is stated directly in the text. The high modality statement is a fact in the text. ***You can have healthy poo, too***! (see line 23). **A** is incorrect as there is no evidence in the text to support this. **B** is untrue and impossible. **C** is sometimes true. You read *It's a fact: vegetarians have less stinky poos! Especially if they avoid processed foods as well as animal foods* (see lines 20–22). You cannot draw the conclusion that vegetarians always have less stinky poo when in fact the smell is determined by total diet.

4 This is a **language** question. **B** is correct. The text is friendly and casual in the way it addresses the reader and describes the subject in a fun, humorous, light-hearted manner. The photo of an elephant and its poo is playful and humorous. The drawing of the person examining the contents of the toilet is light hearted and humorous. The text addresses the reader in a familiar way using *you* and *your* and giving instructions about a personal body function. **A**, **C** and **D** are incorrect. The text does not address the reader from a superior position (**A**). The text is not formal (**C**). **D** is incorrect. The text deals with a serious topic, but not in a serious way.

5 This is a **judgement** question. **D** is correct. You read the part of the text that tells about the capsules. You read *Eat lots of fruit and vegetables, whole-grain cereals and breads, and nuts and seeds, plus drink plenty of water and* ***TAKE ONE SUPER FOOD PLUS+ CAPSULE, DAILY*** (see lines 23–25). **A**, **B** and **C** are incorrect. The ad does not suggest that the capsules can replace a healthy diet. The ad recommends eating healthy food AND taking a capsule. The capsule is recommended by the advertisers as a supplement to a healthy diet. You should judge for yourself that the capsules are not necessary if you eat the healthy foods recommended.

6 This is a **judgement** question. This text is designed to gain your attention using illustrations and quick facts about a bodily function of every animal. The entertaining spiel keeps the reader's interest so the reader reads the whole text and gets to the bottom part, which is the sales pitch. A sales pitch is meant to persuade readers to buy the product. You could judge the text interesting, entertaining, informative and successful in gaining your attention. You could judge the ad unsuccessful in persuading you to buy the product because the ad actually makes clear that the product is unnecessary.

What Sophie was thinking (page 94)

1 C **2** D **3** C **4** C **5** See below
6 See below

Explanations

1 This is an **inferring** question. **C** is correct. You read *She'd rather be vegan* (see line 27) and *She didn't even eat cow* (see lines 4–5) so you can infer that Sophie eats little if any meat. This makes **A** incorrect. **B** is incorrect. You read *Sophie imagined herself chomping on a grasshopper, crunching into its spiky legs. Erk! Didn't seem particularly appealing to her. She'd rather be vegan* (see lines 26–27) than eat a grasshopper. You can infer that **D** is also incorrect because of Sophie's general attitude to eating what she thinks of as *weird things* (see line 10).

2 This is a **language** question. **D** is correct. The word *crazy* (see line 15) refers to a previous statement *there are over 1400 species of edible insects* (see lineS 14–15). None of the other options are correct based on the way language is used.

3 This is a **language** question. **C** is correct. You can work out the answer by examining the prefixes and suffixes in the words and relating these to similar words that you know the meanings of. You read *Entomophagy! … the practice of eating insects* (see line 23). You can work out that *entomo* is something to do with insects. The Greek word *entomon* means 'cut into sections or segmented'. It is used for insects because an insect's body is segmented. Combine *entomo* for insects and *ology* from *zoology* and you have *entomology*, the study of insects. **A** is incorrect. You can work out that *zoology* is the study of animals if you know words like biology and geology: *logy* is from the Greek *logia* meaning 'study or knowledge'. (*Zoo* is from the Greek word for animal.) **B** is incorrect. You read *Entomophagy! … the practice of eating insects* (see line 23). **D** is incorrect. *Fauna* refers to the animals of a particular region. *Entomofauna* refers to insects that live in a region.

4 This is a **language** question. **C** is correct. You read Sophie's statement and exclamation. Even though the word she uses is *crazy* she shakes her head in *wonderment* (see line 15). The tone is one of wonder, astonishment, interest and amazement. The idea of 1400 species of edible insects does not disgust her (**A**) or sicken her (**B**). Nor can you judge that she finds it weird because of the author's use of *wonderment* (**D**).

5 This is a **language** question. The answer is any four of the thinking verbs used in the text: *pondered, wondered, remembered, recalled, imagined* and *acknowledged*. Sophie is having a conversation with herself. Her thoughts are rambling and casual.

6 This is a **fact-finding** question. The answer is stated directly in the text. You read *Sophie was so hungry she could eat a horse. Not literally, of course. She imagined the sight that would make, then shrugged off the image* (see lines 3–4). Sophie has just imagined the sight of trying to eat a horse. She didn't really intend to eat a horse or want to eat a horse. *So hungry I could eat a horse* is an example of an idiom. It is an expression used when someone is extremely hungry. It is used figuratively and not literally. You could draw a cartoon version of Sophie and a horse in the situation Sophie imagined.

Tippy taps (page 95)

1 B **2** D **3** A, B and C **4** A **5** See below
6 See below

Explanations

1 This is a **fact-finding** question. **B** is correct. The answer is stated directly in the text. You read the first paragraph that stresses *the importance of hand washing for disease prevention* (see line 5). **A** and **C** are incorrect. These tell how to wash hands, not why. **D** is incorrect. It tells when to wash hands, not why.

2 This is a **synthesis** question. **D** is correct. Paragraph 3 explains how a tippy tap is constructed. You read *It consists of a recycled plastic container filled with water and attached to a frame. A rope links the water container to a foot lever. Soap is also attached by a rope. People use the foot lever to tip out water and wash their hands* (see lines 13–15). The tippy tap is technically not **A** or **C** . **B** is incorrect because people wash their own hands using the tippy tap. The tippy tap does not wash their hands for them.

3 This is a **judgement** question. **A, B** and **C** are correct. You can judge that all three are reasonable reasons people might have for not washing their hands after going to the toilet. **D** is incorrect as this is not a reason. It is a consequence of not washing your hands.

4 This is **a fact-finding** question. **A** is correct. The answer is stated directly in the text. The text says *our two Year 6 teachers … travelled to Papua New Guinea to see firsthand the result of last year's*

fundraising efforts (see lines 17–18). **B** and **C** are true in the text but not the main purpose of the teachers' travels. **D** is incorrect as the teachers did not visit PNG to fundraise there.

5 This is an **inferring** question. The foot lever allows people to access water without using their dirty hands to tip the container and get the water out. People would spread germs from their hands to the container if they touched it before washing their hands.

6 This is a **fact-finding** question. The answer is stated directly in the text. You read the evidence in the text that tippy taps are successful in preventing disease in rural PNG villages. You read *Community leaders say that there is less illness in the villages since introducing the tippy taps. Lives are being saved but also children don't miss school due to a preventable disease* (see lines 20–22).

Rabbit-Proof Fence (page 96)

1 C **2** B **3** B **4** D **5** B **6** See below

Explanations

1 This is a **synthesis** question. **C** is correct. The consensus of opinion is that what happened to the Stolen Generations was very sad. **A** is incorrect. Only Oliver expresses disbelief. **B** is true but not a consensus of opinion for the group. **D** is incorrect as only Ruby expresses shame.

2 This is a **synthesis** question. **B** is correct. Group members believed the film to be interesting and worth viewing. **A** and **C** are incorrect because the film is a story and therefore cannot be described as a factual film or documentary, even though the narrative is based on true events. **D** is incorrect as only Charlotte says she thought *the plot was suspenseful* (see lines 14–15).

3 This is a **language** question. **B** is correct. You can work out the meaning of *cinematography* from its use in the text. You read *Yeah, the acting was terrific and the cinematography was awesome—the vast Australian outback. I loved the landscape* (see lines 21–23). Also cinematography is made up of two Greek words, *kinema* which means 'movement' and *graphein* which means 'write or record', so you can work out that cinematography means the recording of movement.

4 This is a **judgement** question. **D** is correct. You can judge that authority, determination, family and belonging are themes of the film based on evidence in the discussion. **A** is incorrect because the film shows the outback but environmental issues are not mentioned as a theme of the story. **B** is incorrect because rabbits are not discussed as a theme of the film. **C** is incorrect because Australia today is not a theme of the film.

5 This is a **judgement** question. **B** is correct. You read the opinions in the text and judge that all express something positive about the film itself. Charlotte liked the plot and characters. Jack liked the acting and the cinematography. Ruby thinks the film did a great job of showing part of history. Oliver and Charlotte liked the symbolism of the fence. Oliver thought the soundtrack was amazing. You should conclude that overall the children enjoyed the film.

6 This is a **fact-finding** question. The answer is stated directly in the text. You read *Rabbits were introduced by white people. The fence was built to contain the rabbits* (see lines 43–45). You can infer that rabbits are an introduced species that became feral. At the time of the events described in the film, rabbits were breeding and spreading across Australia at a rapid rate, digging burrows and eating vegetation that was needed by native species and farm animals, so the government decided to build a fence in an attempt to contain the spread of rabbits.

TEXT OVERVIEW GRID

Page no.	Title	Type of text	Additional teaching points	Writing activity
		Fact-finding questions		
28	The law in Australia	Informative—report	Federal, state and council laws; technical terminology; factual writing	Choose a school rule or local council law. Write an argument that supports the law or recommends changes to the law.
32	Australia's highest military award	Informative—report	The Victoria Cross for Australia; bravery; the Commonwealth; factual writing	Choose a VC recipient to research and then write a biography. Or investigate other awards and honours and write a report. Or write about how you would feel if you or a family member received an award for something special.
33	Consumer glossary	Informative—glossary	Ethical consumerism; consumer terminology; definitions	Choose one of the glossary topics. Do further research and write a full report on the topic.
34	Asylum seekers	Informative—report	Refugees; immigration; technical terminology; factual writing	Write a text that presents a point of view about an aspect of immigration. Or imagine arriving in Australia as a refugee and write a first-person article to present a refugee's point of view about problems you face settling into your community and school.
35	The Last Whale	Informative—newspaper article	Whaling history; conservation; media texts	Research a historical event and write an article about the event for a newspaper of the time.
		Synthesis questions		
36	Jane Goodall: conservationist	Informative—biography	Conservation; the environment	Choose an environmental organisation. Research its origins and/or the people involved in establishing it. Write a report.
40	Burger Shack	Persuasive—advertising leaflet	Persuasive devices; emotive language; descriptive language	Write and record a radio advertisement for a place that sells food. Make sure to use emotive language and persuasive devices. Think about what customers will see, taste, hear, touch and smell in your establishment.
41	Citizenship	Informative—report	Immigration; rights and responsibilities of citizenship	Research one of the rights of citizenship. Write a persuasive text to present to the United Nations in support of this right.
42	Krill	Persuasive—radio interview	Conservation; the environment; the health food industry; point of view	Write an interview that presents the point of view of a guest speaker about a topic that interests you.
43	Suffrage	Informative—report	The history of women's suffrage	Choose one of the women involved in the suffrage movement in Australia. Research her work and write a biography or a timeline of the major events in her life.

Page no.	Title	Type of text	Additional teaching points	Writing activity
		Inferring questions		
44	Easter	Informative—personal email	Informal correspondence; Easter; religion; customs; point of view	Choose a festival or national day and write a text to present your opinion about the importance of the event. Or write a series of comments on a blog or a series of tweets about any national day.
48	Landmines	Informative—report	Landmines; humanitarian demining	Consider the consequences of landmines and write a poem that reflects on the effect of landmines on a community.
49	Palm oil	Persuasive—speech	Conservation; environmental issues; point of view	Choose an environmental issue that you feel strongly about and write a speech to present your point of view. Or imagine you are an animal threatened due to habitat loss and write a speech to present your point of view.
50	Giant slain, goose gone!	Imaginative—newspaper article	Parody; folktale; irony, interview quotes; point of view	Choose a fairytale or folktale and write a newspaper article about an event in the story. Write the article as a send-up or parody. Include interview quotes from the characters.
51	My grandparents	Informative—personal essay	Refugees; Vietnam; culture and heritage	Interview an elderly person you know about their experiences of life in Australia or overseas. Film or record the interview. Write a personal essay that shares your understanding of the person's history.
52	Clean Up Australia	Persuasive—speech	Environmental issues; volunteering; point of view; persuasive language	Create a poster or television advertisement to persuade people your age to volunteer for a particular task or community service.
53	Camping with Grandpa	Informative—recount	Family relationships; point of view	Write a personal recount of a family event. Or write a description of a family member.
54	Aliens attack Earth!	Imaginative—newspaper article	Sensationalism; emotive Language; point of view	Write a sensationalised newspaper article about an imaginary event or catastrophe. Or write a science-fiction narrative about aliens arriving on Earth.
55	Celebrity interview	Informative—interview	Point of view; racism; interview techniques	Write an imaginary interview with a celebrity that you are interested in. Create a set of interview questions and then write answers from the perspective of the person interviewed.
		Language questions		
56	White Fang	Imaginative—narrative	Narrative setting; mood; descriptive words and phrases	Find a photo of a remote or wild landscape and write a description of the landscape as a setting for an adventure narrative. Use emotive language and descriptive phrases to establish mood.
60	The man in a boy	Imaginative—poem	Self-acceptance; identity; relationships	Write a descriptive poem about a person you know, a story character or someone you imagine.

Page no.	Title	Type of text	Additional teaching points	Writing activity
		Language questions *(continued)*		
61	Enviro-holidays	Persuasive—advertisement	Environmental issues; eco-tourism; testimonials; persuasive devices	Investigate other eco-tourism options and choose one that interests you and write an advertisement for it. Or do some research and write an article about the increasing popularity and options available for eco-tourism.
62	Super 'S' Supermarkets	Persuasive—comic strip	Persuasive devices; send-up; parody; irony; point of view	Create a comic strip send-up to advertise a place or product of your own. Or choose a television ad that you really like or that you find totally annoying. Recreate it as a comic strip send-up.
63	My sister	Informative—personal reflection	Family relationships; siblings; thinking and feeling verbs; point of view	Reflect on your own family relationships. Write your thoughts and feelings as a diary-style text or as a poem. Or write a recount about something you said or did when you were younger that a parent or other adult thought was funny. You might like to draw the scene as a comic strip.
64	Uluru	Imaginative—poem	Uluru; the desert environment; native title; mood; descriptive language; metaphor	Find a photo of an iconic area of natural landscape. Use the photo as inspiration and write a descriptive poem that presents your feelings and personal views about the area.
65	Biosecurity is so important	Persuasive—Editorial/Letter to the Editor	Biosecurity; environmental issues; customs; persuasive devices; emotive language; modality	Write an Editorial on a topic of national interest or a topic relevant to your community. Then write a Letter to the Editor that either supports your Editorial or argues against it. Or write a Letter to the Editor about Biosecurity.
66	Lost	Imaginative—poem	Banjo Paterson's poetry; historical and situational context; point of view	Investigate and find a poem written by a well-known poet from Australia's past. Create a storyboard for the poem that shows how the poem could be depicted as a film.
67	Chief THINGS that are in the WORLD	Informative—encyclopedia entry	Historical context; definitions; terminology; factual writing	Write a modern-day encyclopedia entry for each subject listed in the historical encyclopedia. Write your reflections on the differences between the definitions then and now.
		Judgement questions		
68	Childminding	Persuasive—leaflet	Persuasive devices; references; visual elements; audience (tenor); modality	Write a leaflet offering your own services for childminding, carwashing, gardening, pet-walking or another activity. Include a written reference.
72	A coal seam gas debate	Persuasive—argument	Coal seam gas; environmental issues; point of view; modality; emotive language	Choose a topic of local concern or national interest, relevant to you. Write four texts that represent the points of view of people from different backgrounds about the topic.

Page no.	Title	Type of text	Additional teaching points	Writing activity
Judgement questions *(continued)*				
73	Disappointed resident	Persuasive—letter of complaint	Emotive language; point of view; animal welfare; audience (tenor); modality	Write a formal letter to your local council. Complain about a local issue or congratulate council for a job well done.
74	Fly like an eagle	Persuasive—advertisement	Target audience; mood/tone; persuasive devices; slogans; visual elements	Choose an item to advertise. Create a brand name, slogan and logo. Write an advertisement for your product that markets your product to a particular target audience. Then ask a friend for constructive criticism about your ad and its potential success with its target market.
75	Born lucky	Imaginative—poem	Developing countries; poverty; point of view	Research access to water, education or medicine in a developing country of your choice. Write a report to present your findings to an audience of your choice.
76	Octane Dance	Informative—web page	Persuasive devices; target audience; fitness and dance; visual elements/graphics; audience (tenor); modality	Choose a sport or physical activity that you enjoy. Create a script for a television advertisement to promote your activity. Ask friends or classmates to help you act out and film the ad. Then ask an audience to evaluate your ad.
77	Animal rights	Persuasive—discussion	Animal welfare; environmental issues; point of view	Write an argument text that presents your point of view on one or more of the topics discussed in this text.
78	Uncle Tom and Little Harry are sold	Imaginative—narrative	Extract from *Uncle Tom's Cabin* by Harriet Beecher Stowe, 1852; racism; slavery; values and attitudes; third-person narrator	Research Indigenous Rights, including Civil Rights and Land Rights in Australia. Choose a particular topic or person of interest to research. Write a report. Or find a novel that was published a long time ago. Find a passage in it that demonstrates the values and attitudes of people at the time. Share and discuss the text with an audience of your choice.
79	The bogeyman	Imaginative—narrative	Prejudice; first-person narrator; point of view; characterisation; plot	Write a first-person narrative that shows how a character learns about him- or herself and others, and how the character grows and develops as a result of events in the story.
Mixed questions				
80	Going going going gone	Imaginative—poem	Environmental issues; extinction; point of view; mood	Write a poem that presents your point of view about a current event or issue. For example, you could write a poem about a specific endangered animal.
81	World War II—the bombing of Australia	Informative—report	World War II; factual writing	Write a newspaper report from an Adelaide newspaper in February 1942 about events described in the text. You might need to do extra research. Or write a report or newspaper account about another aspect of Australia's history.
82	Bullying	Informative—conversation	Cyberbullying; point of view; empathy	Create a poster to promote online security or to advise people your age about cyberbullying.

Page no.	Title	Type of text	Additional teaching points	Writing activity
		Mixed questions *(continued)*		
83	Whale watching	Informative—recount	Humpback whales; technical terminology; emotive language; point of view; environmental issues	Write a review of something you have enjoyed—a class excursion, book or film. Use emotive language to present your point of view.
84	Plastic—it's a problem	Informative—report	Environmental issues; pollution; recycling; the ocean gyres	Research an aspect of recycling, such as glass, plastic, steel, aluminium, computer parts or mobile phone parts. Find out what happens to the materials. Write or draw an explanation to inform others about the process.
85	The magic seeds	Imaginative—narrative	Plot; folk tale: *Jack and the Beanstalk*; parody; send-up	Write a narrative based on the characters, events or setting in a folktale or fairytale. Give your version a twist to add humour. Or write a poem that tells the story of the fairytale.
86	The pacifist	Imaginative—narrative	Bullying; point of view; empathy; realism	Interview younger children and collate their points of view regarding bullying. Use the information to create an information leaflet to tell children how to deal with bullies.
87	Urgent! Great Barrier Reef Holiday Sale	Imaginative—advertisement	Persuasive devices; emotive language; sensationalism	Create a radio advertisement for an aspect of the environment in the form of an actual tourism ad or an advertisement to raise awareness of an environmental problem.
88	Bushfires	Informative—report	Climate change; technical terminology; factual reporting; descriptive language	Write a news article, narrative or poem that has bushfires as its subject matter. You might like to find some bushfire photos as inspiration for your writing.
89	Tribute	Informative—report	First Australian history; colonial Australia; contemporary Indigenous dance group	Choose a person from history that you think has made important contributions to Australia. Research the person and write a biography.
90	Adventures of Huckleberry Finn	Imaginative—narrative	*Adventures of Huckleberry Finn (Tom Sawyer's Comrade)* by Mark Twain, 1884; racism; context of culture; censorship	Write a play script. Create characters based on people that you know. Write their dialogue so that they sound authentic and true to life. Or choose two characters in history and write a conversation they might have had with each other.
91	The further adventures of Toad	Imaginative—narrative	*The Wind in the Willows* by Kenneth Grahame, 1908, Chapter 10; anthropomorphism	Write an anthropomorphic story. Use a first-person narrator to share your thoughts as the animal protagonist in your story. Plan the plot of your story and consider characterisation before you start.
92	Renewable energy	Informative—interview	Wind energy; interview techniques; technical terminology; explanation	Create the script for a television documentary that presents information about an aspect of renewable energy. Ensure that your documentary is informative, entertaining and interesting for viewers.

Page no.	Title	Type of text	Additional teaching points	Writing activity
		Mixed questions *(continued)*		
93	Poo	Persuasive—magazine advertisement	Persuasive devices; emotive language; writing in the second person; visual elements	Create a poster to promote an aspect of health or fitness. Use humour to get your message across.
94	What Sophie was thinking	Imaginative—personal reflection	Entomophagy; technical terminology; thinking and feeling verbs; point of view	Create a list of pros and cons for eating insects and then interview friends and family members to find out what they think about this subject. Write an informative text that summarises your findings.
95	Tippy taps	Informative—school newsletter	Hygiene; disease; developing countries	Write a school newsletter about something that is happening in your school or community. Or write a persuasive text to convince your school to raise money for a particular charity of your choice.
96	Rabbit-Proof Fence	Persuasive—film review	*Rabbit-Proof Fence*, 2002; point of view; Stolen Generations; plot; cinematography; characterisation; acting; setting; music	Write the script for a television movie review program. Have the presenters discuss a movie of your choice. Or write a review of a film for display in your school library or publication in an online newspaper.